MOLLIE'S SUBSTITUTE
HUSBAND

MOLLIE'S SUBSTITUTE HUSBAND

BY

MAX McCONN

1920

CONTENTS

vi CONTENTS

MOLLIE'S SUBSTITUTE
HUSBAND

MOLLIE'S SUBSTITUTE HUSBAND

CHAPTER I

"THE PROFESSOR" ON A SPREE

JOHN MERRIAM, Principal of the High School
at Riceville, Illinois—"Professor" Merriam, as
he was universally called by the citizens of Riceville—was wickedly, carnally, gloriously happy.
He was having an unwonted spree.

I fear the reader will be shocked. The principal
of a high school, he will say, has no right to a spree,
even an occasional one. The "Professor" has girl
students in his classes—mostly girls, indeed, and
usually the prettiest ones in town—and women
teachers under his supervision. Every seventh day
he teaches a young people's class in a Sunday
School. He makes addresses at meetings of the
Y. P. S. C. E., the Y. M. C. A., and other alpha-
betically designated societies that make for right-
eousness and decorum. He should at all times and
in all places be a model, an exemplar, to the bud-
ding young men and women of the community in
general and his school in particular.

In this reasoning the reader is in strict accord
with what the sentiment of all Riceville would have
been if it had known—if it could have known.

1

Nevertheless, it is the regrettable and shocking fact that John Merriam was sitting on that pleasant April evening in the Peacock Cabaret of the Hotel De Soto in the wicked city of Chicago. He was attired in evening clothes, a fact which in itself would have seemed both odd and reprehensible to Riceville, and he was alone at a tiny table with a yellow-silk-shaded lamp. He had just been guided to that table, and pending the arrival of a waiter, he was gazing eagerly, boyishly about him at such delights as the somewhat garish Peacock Cabaret displayed.

For John Merriam, though a " professor," was young. He was only twenty-eight. He was tall and blond and athletic, as young men who grow up on farms in the Middle West and then go to college have a way of being. And after his season of strenuous and highly virtuous labours at Riceville he was really hungry. keen, for something—well, just a little less virt ious.

A distinguished looking gentleman in a dinner jacket, conspicuously labeled with a number, somewhat haughtily and negligently approached, bearing a menu card.

About three paces away this gentleman, having glanced at young Merriam, fairly stopped and stared at him. An odd expression showed upon his face—an expression, one would almost have said, of intense animosity. Then, as he still stared, one might have decided that his look betokened perplexity. He winked his eyes several times and

once more scrutinised his waiting guest. At length
—perhaps ten seconds had passed—his face slowly,
wonderingly cleared, his usual air of vacant indifference returned, and he advanced and placed the
menu card in Merriam's hands. The latter, still
drinking in the sights and sounds of his unaccustomed environment, had noticed nothing.

Now it is always prudent to note a waiter's number when he first presents himself, for in case he
should decide to begin his summer vacation immediately after taking your order you may need to
mention his number to the head waiter. In this
case the number was 73.

The hauteur and negligence displayed were partly
habitual—professional, so to speak—but were inten-
sified perhaps by the reaction from the emotion,
whatever it was, which he had apparently just ex-
perienced—perhaps also by the look of alert and
genuine pleasure on Merriam's face. Such a look
did not wholly commend itself or him to a sophisticated metropolitan taste. What right had a patron
of the Peacock Cabaret to look really pleased? It
was hardly decent—and argued a small tip.

Inwardly Merriam, now aware of the waiter's
presence, reacted acutely to this clearly perceptible
disdain. Which shows how young and how rural
he was. We maturer, urban folk are never, of
course, in the least nonplused by those contemptu-
ous, blasé silences of waiters who possess the bearing and manner of a governor or a capitalist.

But John Merriam had been excellent in amateur

dramatics at college, and he now roused himself to a magnificent histrionic effort in the rôle of "man of the world."

He pushed the menu card aside without looking at it.

" A clam cocktail, please, and a stein of beer," he murmured, low enough to force the distinguished one to unbend slightly in order to catch the words.

" Yes, sir," said Waiter No. 73, with a tentative suggestion of respect in his tone. A customer who did not bother to look at the menu might be worth while after all.

" And then what? "

" I'll see how I feel then," said Merriam with a half yawn.

" Yes, sir," said Waiter No. 73, almost courteously, and departed at a pace slightly quickened over that of his approach, as a man strolling at complete leisure will instinctively increase the tempo of his step if he chances to recall a definite engagement on the day after to-morrow.

Merriam grinned delightedly. He had put it across—his little piece of acting. He had measurably imposed his rôle on his audience of one; at least he had shaken him.

And then—I shudder when I recall the views on nicotine of the Board of Education at Riceville—he drew from his pocket a package of cigarettes, and took a match from the table, and lit a cigarette, and sent a volume of smoke out through his nostrils—

proving, alas, that it was not his first indulgence,—
and, with a sigh that might almost be described as
ecstatic, turned his attention again to the scene
about him.

That scene was piquant to him—after the ugly
dining room of his boarding house at Riceville and
the barren assembly hall of the High School—to a
degree almost incredible to persons more habituated
to the Peacock Cabaret and similar resorts. Not
being quite so fresh from Riceville, nor yet the
advertising manager of the Hotel De Soto, I cannot,
I fear, paint the prospect as Merriam saw it. I
shall not be able to conceal some mental reserva-
tions as to its charms. The purple peacocks upon
the walls and ceiling, from which the restaurant
took its name, were certainly a trifle over-gorgeous,
just as the music which the orchestra intermittently
dispensed was too much syncopated. Again, the
scores of small tables, each with its silk-shaded
lamp, its slim glass vase for a single rosebud, its
water bottle bearing the arms of the Chevalier De
Soto, and its ash receptacle—all alike as shoe
boxes in a shoe shop are alike,—might to a tired
fancy suggest a certain monotony of pleasure, a
too-much-standardised, ready-made brand of bliss.
The small, skimped stage, with its undeniably banal
curtain, and the crowded dancing floor did not
really promise unlimited delights. Some perception of all this was apparent in the faces and bearing of many of the white-shirt-fronted men who sat
at the scores of tables and of the women who were

with them, however bird-of-paradise-like the rai-
ment of the latter might be.   Not a few indeed displayed an air of languor and ennui that might have
won approval even from Waiter No. 73.

But in speaking thus of the Peacock Cabaret I
am stepping outside my story, violating unity of
point of view—in short, committing a heinous literary crime.   For to Merriam at that moment the
screaming purple peacocks, the regiments of rosebuds, the musical comedy melodies, the gay attire
and bare shoulders of the women, and even the tired
look of his fellow-diners, which he interpreted as
sophistication rather than simple boredom, were
thrillingly symbolical of all the delights which the
great world held and which were absent from Riceville.   And when Waiter No. 73 leisurely returned,
to find him outwardly almost too near asleep to
keep his cigarette going, and deposited his clam
cocktail and the wicked stein before him, and at the
same moment the orchestra became more noisy than
ever, and all the lights except those upon the tables
went out, and the stage curtain rose upon a short-
skirted chorus, he was really in a sort of Omar
Khayyam paradise.   It was lucky that Waiter No.
73 had again departed to those unknown regions
where waiters spend the bulk of their time, for
Merriam could not have concealed the zest with
which he alternately ate and drank and surveyed
the moderately comely demoiselles upon the little
stage.

Having finished his cocktail and drunk some of

his beer and seen the curtain descend on the first "act" of the cabaret's dramatic entertainment, Merriam lit another cigarette, shifted his chair, and settled himself to await the probable future return of his servitor. His thoughts dwelt contentedly on the evening before him. For after his meal he would have a stroll with a cigar in the spring twilight (it was barely six-thirty then) through the noisy, brightly lighted streets of the Loop, which never failed to thrill him with a sense of a somehow wicked vastness, power, and riches in the great city of which they were the center. And then he was going to the "Follies." He fingered the small envelope in his pocket which held his ticket. And after the show he would have a supper in another cabaret.

Beyond that he did not let his fancy wander. For after that there was nothing for it but to catch the 2:00 A. M. train on the Illinois Central that would carry him back to Riceville for the remaining six weeks of the school year. He had come up to Chicago on this spring day—a Tuesday it was—to attend a convention of high-school principals and to engage a couple of new teachers for the next year, to replace two that were to be married in June. And he had faithfully done these things. And now he was giving himself just this one evening of amusement—two cabaret meals and a "show," sauced, so to speak, with a little tobacco and beer and the wearing of his evening clothes. Surely, whatever Riceville might have thought, he will not seem to most of us very derelict from the austere ideals of his profession.

The only real point against him—most of us might argue—lies in the fact that when you touch even the outermost fringes of the night life of a city, you are never quite certain what may come to you. For there are things happening all about you, under the conventional, monotonous surface — things amusing and things terrible—men and women playing with the fire of every known human passion,— and if the finger of some adventure reaches out for you you may not be able to resist its lure, perhaps even to escape its clutch.

CHAPTER II

I HAVE said that Merriam had shifted his chair a little as he lit his second cigarette. A moment later he was looking very hard at a certain pretty woman at a table half way across the room. His heart stopped. At least that is the phrase a novelist seems to be required to use to indicate the sudden pulse of amazement and pleasure and alarm which he certainly felt.

The young woman at whom he was staring had a name which is very important for this story and which I shall presently tell you, but in John Merriam's mind her name was " the prettiest girl," and her other name, which he seldom dared whisper to his heart, was " Mollie June." She was from Riceville—hence the alarm with which his pleasure was mixed,—and during his first four months of teaching, three years before, she had been in his senior class in the High School—the " prettiest girl " in the class and in the school and in the town—and in the State and the United States and the world, if you had asked John Merriam. Advanced algebra with Mollie June in the class had been the most golden of sciences—pleasure squared, delight cubed, and bliss to the nth power. I am not myself abso-

9

lutely convinced of Mollie June's proficiency in solving quadratic equations, yet the official records of the Riceville High School show that she received the highest mark in the class.

But she was the daughter of James P. Partridge, the owner of all Riceville; that is to say, of the coal mines outside the town, of the grain elevator, of the street car and electric light company, and of the First National Bank. Who was John Merriam, the son of a poor farmer in a southern county, who had worked his way through college and come out with nothing but a B. S. degree, a football reputation that was quite unnegotiable, and three hundred dollars of fraternity debts—an enormous sum,—to mix anything warmer or livelier than a^2-b^2 in his thoughts of a class to which Mollie June Partridge deigned to belong? Even if Mollie June herself did come up to his desk in the assembly room two or three times a week for help in her algebra and spend most of the time asking him about college instead, and join his Young People's Class, which she had previously refused to attend, and allow him to " see her home " from church sociables, and compel that docile magnate, John P. Partridge, her father, to invite the new " professor " to dinner twice during the half year? As well almost might a humble tutor in the castle of a feudal lord have raised his eyes to the baron's daughter.

Almost, but not quite. After all this is a free republic. Even a poor pedagogue is a citizen with a vote and a potential candidate for the presidency—which at least two poor pedagogues have attained. So John Merriam permitted himself to be very happy during those four months and was not in the least hopeless. Only he saw that he must bide his time.

But early in January Mollie June left school, and in a few days it came out that she had left to be married—married to Senator Norman!

Senator Norman was the famous " boy senator " from Illinois—at the time of his election the youngest man who had ever sat in the upper house of Congress. The ruddiness of his cheeks, the abundance of his wavy blond hair, and the athletic jauntiness of his carriage won votes whenever he stumped the State. They went far to counteract malicious insinuations as to the means by which he was rolling up a fortune and his solidity with " interests " which the proletariat viewed with suspicion.

And now, having been a widower for eighteen months—his first wife was older than he and had brought him money,—he had stayed for a week-end during the Christmas holidays with James P. Partridge, who was a cousin of the Senator's first wife and his political lieutenant for a certain group of counties, and had seen Mollie June and wanted her and asked for her and got her, as George Norman always asked for and got whatever he wanted.

All this was, of course, in John Merriam's mind as he gazed across a dozen tables in the Peacock Cabaret at the unchanged profile of the prettiest girl—that is to say, Mrs. Senator Norman. And with it came an acute revival of the desolation of that January and February at Riceville, when he had perceived with the Hebrew sage that "in much learning"—or in little, for that matter—"is much weariness," and that algebra should have been buried with the medieval Arabians who invented it—when even the State championship in basket ball, won by the Riceville Five under his coaching, was only a trouble and a bore.

There is no doubt he stared rudely. At least it would have been rudely if his eyes had held the look which eyes that stare at pretty women commonly hold. But such a look as stood in Merriam's eyes can hardly be rude, however intent and prolonged it may be.

He was merely entranced in the literal sense of that word. Her girlish white shoulders—he had never seen her shoulders before—in Riceville women no more have shoulders than they have legs—the soft brown hair over her ears—even the mode of the day, which called for close net effects and tight knobs, could not conceal its fine softness—the colour in her cheeks, which unquestionably shamed all the neighbouring rosebuds—the quite inexplicable deliciousness of those particular small curves described by the lines of her nose and chin and throat as he saw them in half profile—were more than he could draw his eyes away from for an unconscionable number of seconds. Of her charmingly simple and unquestionably very expensive frock as a separate fact, and of the thin, pale, and elderly, but gorgeously arrayed woman who was her companion, he had no clear perception, but undoubtedly they both contributed, along with the lights and colours and music of the Peacock Cabaret, to the deplorable confusion of his mind.

Out of that confusion there presently arose certain clear images and tones and words, which made up his memory of the last time he had seen and spoken with the present Mrs. Senator Norman.

It was at and after a miscellaneous kind of young people's entertainment which occurred at the Methodist Church on the evening of that bitter day on which the news of her engagement to Senator Norman had run like a prairie fire through the streets and homes of Riceville, fiercely incinerating all other topics of conversation, and consuming also the joy in life, the ambition, the very youth, it seemed to him, of John Merriam. He would not have gone to that entertainment if he could have escaped. But there were to be charades, and he had arranged and coached most of them and was to be in several. He "simply had to go," as Ricevillians might have said.

She was there with her mother. When had she ever come just with her mother, that is to say, without a male escort, before? That fact alone was symbolical of the closing of the gates of matrimony upon her. Naturally, in his pain he followed his primitive and childish instincts and avoided her.

But he was aware—he was almost sure—of her

eyes continually following him throughout the evening, and during " refreshments " she deliberately came up to him and said that her mother was obliged to leave early, and would he see her home? Well, of course, if she asked him, he had to. I am afraid that the tone if not the words of his reply said as much, and Mollie June had turned away with quick tears in her eyes. Yet I question whether she was really hurt by his rudeness. For why should he be rude to-night when he had never been so before unless he—to use the most expressive of Americanisms—" cared "?

For the rest of the evening, as a result of those tears, which he had seen, it was his eyes that followed her, while hers avoided him. But he did not speak with her again until " seeing-home " time arrived.

Mollie June lingered till the very end of everything. Perhaps the little girl in her—for she was barely eighteen—clung to this last shred of the familiar, homely social life of her girlhood before she should be plunged into the frightful brilliance of real " society " in terrific places known as Chicago and Washington—as a senator's wife!

But at last they were walking together towards her home.

" Take my arm, please," said Mollie June.

The boys in Riceville always take the girls' arms at night, though never in the daytime. John ought to have taken her arm before. He took it.

" Have you heard that I am going to be mar-

ried?" asked Mollie June—as if she did not know
that everybody in the county knew it by that
time.

"Yes," said John, his tone as succinct as his
monosyllable.

But girls learn early to deal with the conversational difficulties and recalcitrances of males under stress of emotion.

"It means leaving school and Riceville and—
everything," said Mollie June.

John could not fail to catch the note of pitiful-
ness in her sentence. If the prospective marriage
had been with any one less dazzling than George
Norman, he might have reacted more properly. As
it was, he replied with a stilted impersonality
which might have been caught from the bright
stars shining through the bare branches under
which they walked.

"You will have a very rich and brilliant life,"
he said.

"I suppose so," said Mollie June.

They walked on, he still obediently clutching her
arm, in silence; conversation not accompaniable
with laughter is so difficult an art for youth.

Presently Mollie June tried again.

"Aren't you sorry I'm leaving the school—Mr.
Merriam?"

"I'm very sorry indeed," responded "Professor"
Merriam. "You ought to have stayed to graduate."

"I don't care about graduating," said Mollie
June.

Again their footsteps echoed in the cold January silence.

Then Mollie June made a third attempt:

"You look ever so much like Mr. Norman."

"I know it," said Merriam.   "We're related."

"Oh, *are you?*"

"On my mother's side. We're second cousins. But the two branches of the family have nothing to do with each other now."

"He has the same hair and the same shape of head and the same way of sitting and moving," Mollie June declared with enthusiasm, "and almost the same eyes and voice.   Only his are ——"

"Older!" said John Merriam rudely.

"Yes," said Mollie June.

Distances are not great in Riceville. For this reason the ceremony of "seeing home" is usually performed by a circuitous route, sometimes involving the entire circumference of the "nice" part of the town.   But on this occasion John and Mollie June had gone directly, as though their object had been to arrive.   They reached her home—a matter of two blocks from the church—before another word had been said.

There Mollie June carefully extricated her arm from his mechanical grasp and confronted him.

He looked at her face, peeping out of the fur collar of her coat in the starlight, and for one instant into her eyes.

She was saying: "I am very grateful to you, Mr.

Merriam, for all the help you have given me—in—algebra."

He ought to have kissed her. She wanted him to. He half divined as much—afterwards.

But the awkward, callow, Anglo-Saxon, rural, pedagogical cub in him replied, "I am glad if I have been able to help you in anything."

That, I judge, was too much for Mollie June. She held out her little gloved hand.

"Good-bye, Mr. Merriam!"

He took her hand. And now appears the advantage of a college education, including amateur dramatics and courses in English poetry and romantic fiction. He did what no other swain in Riceville could have done. He raised her hand to his lips and kissed it! At least he kissed the glove which tightly enclosed the hand.

"Good-bye, Mollie June!" he said, using that name for the first time.

Then he dropped her hand, somewhat suddenly, I fear, turned abruptly, and walked rapidly away.

As to what Mollie June said or thought or felt, how should I know? There was nothing for her to do but to go into the house, and that is what she did.

CHAPTER III

JOHN MERRIAM raised his eyes from the table-cloth on which they had rested while these images from the distant past—two and one-half years ago—moved across the screen of his memory. To his now mature perceptions the stupidity and gaucherie of his own part in that scene—save for the redeeming kissing of the glove—were clearly apparent, and were for the moment almost as painful to him as the fact that Mollie June was another man's wife.

He glanced around, avoiding only the table at which Mrs. Senator Norman sat. The glory was gone from the Peacock Cabaret. The garishness of the peacocks, the tin-panniness of the music, the futility of beer and cigarettes and evening clothes, were desolatingly revealed to him. He put his cigarette aside, to smoke itself up unregarded on the ash tray.

It had been his duty to " forget," and it is neither more nor less than justice to say that after a' fashion he had succeeded in doing so. His winter and spring, three years ago, had been miserable; but he had undeniably enjoyed his summer vacation, and had found interest in his work again in the fall.

18

To be sure, the edge was gone from his ambition. He had stuck ploddingly at teaching, too indifferent to try to better himself. Still he had not been actively unhappy. But now ——

He was diverted by the return of Waiter No. 73. No need of play-acting now to conceal any unsophisticated delight in his surroundings. But he must pull himself together. He must not exhibit to the world, as incarnated in Waiter No. 73, a depression as boyish as his previous pleasure. He must still be the stoical, tranquil man of the world, who knows women and tears them from his heart when need be. It was the same rôle—with a difference!

"What next, sir?"

Merriam glanced hastily at the menu card and ordered a steak with French fried potatoes and a lettuce-and-tomato salad. He was not up to an attack on any unfamiliar viands.

As he gave his order he was aware of a party of three persons, seated a little to his left—the opposite direction from the fateful spot inhabited by Mollie June,—who seemed to be taking particular note of him. And as he lit another cigarette after the waiter had left him he noticed them again. Unquestionably they were furtively regarding him. Now and then they exchanged remarks of which he was sure he was the subject.

The three persons included a square-jawed man of about forty-five, a pale, benevolent-looking priest and a very beautiful woman. The woman

had not only shoulders and arms but also a great
deal of bosom and back, all dazzlingly, powderedly
fair and ideally plump. She had black hair and
eyes—brilliantly, even aggressively, black. Her
gown was a lavender silk net with spangles. Her
age—well, she was certainly older than Mollie June
and certainly within, safely within, "the age at
which women cease to be interesting to men," whatever that age may be.

Our youthful man of the world was a little embarrassed at first by the scrutiny of this gorgeous
trio. He glanced quickly down at his own attire,
as a girl might have done. But there could be
nothing wrong with his evening clothes. (A man
is so safe in that respect.) They were only five
years old, having been acquired, in a heroic burst of
extravagance, during his senior year in college.
He wanted to put his hand up to his white bow to
make sure it was not askew, but restrained himself.

Presently Merriam began to enjoy the attention
he was receiving. If one must play a part, it is
pleasant to have an audience. It helped him to keep
his eyes off Mollie June. He began to give attention to the smoking of his cigarette. He handled
it with nonchalant grace. He exhaled smoke
through his nostrils. He recalled an envied ac-
complishment of his college days and carefully blew
a couple of tolerably perfect smoke rings. And he
wished that Mollie June would turn and see him
in his evening clothes.

Presently the clerical gentleman, after an earnest

colloquy with the square-jawed one, rose and came across to Merriam's table, while the other two now openly watched.

The priest rested two white hands on the edge of the table and bent over him with a friendly smile.

"Will you pardon a frank question from a stranger?" he asked.

"I guess a question won't hurt me," said Merriam.

At this simple reply the cleric straightened up quickly as if startled and looked at Merriam closely and curiously. Then he said:

"Are you by any chance related to Senator Norman?"

"Yes, I am," said Merriam.

"May I ask what the relationship is?"

Merriam told him.

"Thank you," said the priest. "The resemblance is really remarkable. And we saw you looking at Mrs. Norman. Do you know her?"

"Yes. I knew her before—before she—was married."

"I see. Thank you so much."

The inquisitive priest returned to his friends, who appeared to listen intently to his report.

At the same time Waiter No. 73 arrived with Merriam's steak and salad.

He ate self-consciously, feeling himself still under observation from the other table. But when he was half way through his salad his attention was effectually distracted from those watchers. For Mollie June and her companion had risen to go.

Merriam put down his fork and looked at her. She was really beautiful to any eyes—so fresh and young and alive amid the tawdry ennui of her surroundings, a human girl among the labouring ghosts of a *danse macabre*. To Merriam she was— what you will—radiant, divine. He wished he had not lost a moment from looking at her since he first saw her.

A waiter had brought a fur cloak and now held it for her. As she adjusted it about her shoulders she glanced around and saw Merriam.

For a moment she looked straight at him. Merriam would have sworn that her colour heightened ever so little and then paled. She smiled a mechanical little smile, bowed slightly, spoke to her companion, and threaded her way quickly among tables to an exit.

" I beg your pardon! "

Merriam started and looked up—to find the black-eyed, white-bosomed woman from the other table standing beside him. He was conscious of a faint fragrance, which a more sophisticated person would have recognised as that of an extremely expensive perfume, widely advertised under the name of a famous opera singer.

He rose mechanically, dropping his napkin.

" No, no," she smiled. " Won't you sit down— and let me sit down a moment, too? "

She took the chair opposite him.

"My name is Alicia Wayward," she said. There was a kind of deliberate sweetness in her tone.

John Merriam got back somehow into his chair and looked at her, but did not reply. His eyes saw the face of Mollie June, peeping out of her furs, as on that last night at Riceville, her changing colour, her mechanical smile, and the hurrying away without giving him a chance to go to her for a single word.

"Won't you tell me your name?" said Alicia, with the barest suggestion in her voice of sharpness in the midst of sweet.

"John Merriam."

"And you are a second cousin of Senator Norman?"

"Yes."

"I am an old friend of Senator Norman's," said Alicia. "We are all friends of his." She nodded towards the other table. "And we should very much like to have a little private talk with you about a very important matter.—How do you do, Simpson?"

Merriam looked up again. Waiter No. 73 was standing over them. But he was a transformed being. The ramrod had somehow been extracted from his spine, and his stern features were transfigured in an expression of happy and ingratiating servility.

"Very well, Miss Alicia," he said.

"Simpson used to be my father's butler," ex-

plained Miss Wayward. " We've never had so good
a butler since."

" Thank you, Miss Alicia," said Simpson fer-
vently.

" Send me the head waiter," said Miss Wayward.

" Yes, Miss Alicia," and Simpson departed almost with alacrity.

" You are just ready for your dessert, I see," said
Alicia. " I am going to ask the head waiter to
change us both to one of the private rooms and give
us Simpson to wait on us. Then I can present you
to my friends, and we can have the private talk I
spoke of. You don't mind, do you? "

Merriam thought of the " Follies." But the idea
of the " Follies " bored him after seeing Mollie
June. And one cannot refuse a lady. He re-
captured some fraction of his manners.

" I shall be pleased," he said.

" Thank you," said Alicia, with augmented
sweetness.

CHAPTER IV

AN UNSCRUPULOUS REFORMER

THE head waiter arrived. Could they be removed to a private dining-room? Most certainly they could. Yes, Simpson should serve them. Obviously anything that Miss Alicia Wayward desired could be done, must be done, and it was done.

They ordered ices and *café noir*.

"And a liqueur? " suggested Alicia.

Merriam assented.

" What should you prefer? "

Now Merriam knew the name of just one liqueur. He made prompt use of that solitary scrap of information.

" Benedictine, perhaps," he suggested, as who should say, " Out of all the world's vintages my mature choice among liqueurs is Benedictine."

" Good," smiled Alicia. (I am afraid she was not effectually deceived.)

Merriam was introduced first to Father Murray.

" He isn't a real Father," said Alicia. " He's not a Romanist. Only a paltry Anglican. But he's so very, very High Church that a layman can hardly tell the difference."

Father Murray was deprecatory but unruffled. A Christian priest must forgive all things.

"This is Mr. Philip Rockwell of the Reform League," said Alicia. "His fame has doubtless reached you. 'One-Thing-at-a-Time Rockwell.'"

His fame had not reached Merriam, but the latter bowed and shook hands as though it had, instinctively meeting the stare in the other man's eyes with an unblinking steadiness of his own.

After the introductions Merriam glanced about him with perhaps insufficiently concealed curiosity. He had never been in a private dining-room before, and this adventure was beginning to interest him. It was better than spending his evening—his one evening—in sad thoughts of Mollie June.

The room was just large enough to afford comfortable space for a table for four persons, with a small sideboard to serve from. It was really rather pretty. Subdued purple hangings at the door and windows and a frieze of small peacocks above the plate rail indicated its affiliation, so to speak, with the Peacock Cabaret. There were attractive French prints in garland frames on the walls. The table was charmingly laid, with a bowl of yellow roses in the center, and the ices were already served. On the sideboard the coffee in a silver pot was bubbling over an alcohol flame, and there was a long bottle which Merriam correctly interpreted as the container of his choice among liqueurs.

"This is much cosier, isn't it?" said Alicia.

She took the head of the table.

"Father Murray shall sit opposite me," she said, "to see that I behave. You, Mr. Merriman, shall

sit on my right, as the guest of honour. That leaves
this place for you, Philip. Reformers must be content with what they can get."

Merriam mustered the gallantry to hold Alicia's
chair for her, and was warmed by the approving
smile with which she thanked him. He had not
especially liked Alicia at first, but she grew upon
him.

They consumed ices, and Alicia conversed, in the
sprightly fashion she affected, with Merriam. The
other two men hardly participated at all.

In the course of that conversation Alicia art-
lessly, tactfully, but efficiently pumped Merriam.
By the time Simpson was pouring the sweet-
scented wine into thimble-like glasses she—and her
companions—were in possession of all the substantial facts of his brief biography and had
guessed the secret of his heart. They knew of his
boyhood on the farm, of his father's death, and his
mother's a few years later, of his college days, with
something of their athletic, dramatic, and fraternity incidents, of his teaching at Riceville, of the
Riceville football and basket-ball teams, of the occasion for this trip to Chicago—and of Mollie June.

At length the sherbet glasses were removed and
some of the coffees, including Merriam's, refilled,
and they all lit cigarettes. Merriam was pleasantly startled when Alicia too took a cigarette. He
had read, of course, of women smoking, but he had
never seen it, or expected to see it with his own
eyes, except on the stage. It was more shocking

to his secret soul than any amount of bosom and back.

"You need not wait, Simpson," said Alicia. "We'll ring if we need you again."

When the waiter had withdrawn Philip Rockwell took the center of the stage. He tilted back in his chair and abruptly began to talk. Part of the time he looked straight ahead of him as if addressing an audience, but now and again he turned his head and aimed his discourse straight at Merriam. He made only a pretence of smoking.

"Mr. Merriam," he said, "by a curious chance— a freak of nature, as it were—you, who have thus far taken no part in the politics of the State and Nation, are in a position to render a great service this very night to the cause of Reform and incidentally to Senator and Mrs. Norman."

"How so?" said Merriam. He was rather on his guard against Mr. Philip Rockwell.

"It is a long story, perhaps," said that gentleman. "I gathered when we were introduced that you had heard of me. But I was not sure how much you have heard. I am at the present time the President of the Reform League of this city and its guiding and moving spirit."

"And endowed with the superb modesty so characteristic of reformers," interjected Alicia.

The reformer paid no attention to this frivolous parenthesis.

"Miss Wayward," he continued, "alluded earlier to my sobriquet—' One-Thing-at-a-Time Rockwell.'

The epithet was first applied to me derisively by opposition newspapers. But it is a true description. Indeed it was derived from my frequent use of the phrase in my own speeches. I believe that to be successful, practically successful, Reform must center its efforts on one thing at a time—not waste its energies, its munitions, so to speak, by bombarding the whole entrenched line of evil and privilege at once, but concentrate its fire on one exposed position after another—take that one position—accomplish finally one definite thing—and then go on to some other one definite thing. Do you get me?"

Merriam signified that he comprehended.

Father Murray was more enthusiastic. "It is a truly splendid idea," he volunteered. "Since we have adopted it, under the leadership of Mr. Rockwell, the Reform League has really begun to do things. *To do things!*" he repeated, with an almost mysterious emphasis.

"At the present time," Rockwell resumed, "the one thing which the Reform League is undertaking to *do* is to secure decent traction conditions in this city—adequate service. We have so far succeeded that we have forced an unfriendly city council to pass the new Traction Ordinance. You are familiar with the new Ordinance, Mr. Merriam?"

"Yes," said Merriam. By which we must suppose he meant that he had read headlines about it in the Chicago papers.

"Those rascals," continued Rockwell, "never

would have passed it—the men who own them would never have permitted them to pass it, no matter how unmistakable the demand of the people might be,—if they had not counted on one thing."

Merriam perceived that an interrogation was demanded of him and took his cue.

"What is that?" he asked.

"They are counting," said Rockwell impressively, "they are counting on Mayor Black. They have believed the whole time that he can be depended on to veto it. And they are right! The scoundrels usually are. The Mayor, as every one knows, is a mere puppet. He will do as he is told. Only, the League has made such a stir, the people are so tremendously aroused, that he is frightened. And so, before acting, before writing the veto, which he has sense enough to see is likely to mean political suicide, he is coming here to-night to see Senator Norman, to get his instructions. That's what it amounts to. Norman holds the State machine in the hollow of his hand. If Norman tells him to veto, Black will veto. It may be bad for him with the voters if he does it, but it would be certain political death for a man like him to cross Norman. *And Norman will say, 'Veto!'*"

"I see," said Merriam.

Which was hardly true; he did not as yet see an inch ahead of his nose into this thing, but he thought it sounded well.

"Where do I come in, though?" he added, belying his assumption of sagacity.

"That's my very next point," said Rockwell.

His chair came down on all fours. He squared it to the table, laid his neglected cigarette aside, put his arms on the cloth, and looked very straight at Merriam.

"Are you aware, Mr. Merriam, that you bear a most striking physical resemblance to Senator Norman?"

"I have been told so," said Merriam. "My mother often spoke of it. And—Mrs. Norman mentioned it to me before she was married. I have seen his pictures, of course, in the papers. I have never seen him in person." (This was true, for John Merriam had, quite inexcusably, stayed away from Mollie June's wedding.)

"He has never seen you, then?"

"He probably doesn't know of my existence."

"So much the better," said Rockwell. "The only difficulty then is Mrs. Norman. And she can be eliminated."

This facile elimination of Mollie June did not make an irresistible appeal to Merriam, but he held his tongue.

Alicia Wayward saw the reformer's mistake.

"Mr. Rockwell means," she threw in, "that Mrs. Norman can be shielded from the difficulties of the situation."

"Exactly," said Rockwell quickly. "Mr. Merriam," he continued, "if you have never seen the Senator with your own eyes, you can have no realisation of the closeness of your resemblance to him.

Hair, eyes, nose, mouth, size, carriage, manner, movement—it is truly wonderful. And it is the same with your voice. Father Murray here says he fairly jumped when you first spoke to him out in the Cabaret when he went over to question you."

"He also says," interrupted Alicia, as if mischievously, "that it is Providential."

"Please do not be irreverent, Miss Alicia," said the priest. "It does surely seem Providential—on this night of all nights. It surely seems so."

"Well," said Merriam, a trifle bluntly perhaps, "I don't know what you mean by that. If my cousin and I look so much alike as you say, no doubt it's quite remarkable. Still such things happen often enough in families. What of it?"

"I have explained," said Rockwell, with an air of much patience, "that Mayor Black is coming here, to this hotel, to-night, to see Senator Norman about the Ordinance, and that Norman will order him to veto it. We thought we had Norman fixed, but he has gone over to the magnates—as he always does in the end! Black will do as he is bid, and it will be a death blow. We can never pass it over his veto. It means the total ruin of five years of work, involving the expenditure of tens of thousands of dollars. And the cause of Reform in this city will be dead for years to come. The League will never survive, if we fail at this last ditch. It will collapse."

"In short," said Alicia sweetly, "Mr. Rockwell himself will collapse."

Rockwell took no heed of her.

"Half an hour ago," he said, "I was sitting yonder in the Cabaret, dining with Miss Wayward and Father Murray. I was eating turtle soup and olives "—he laughed theatrically,—" but I was a desperate man. I had no hope, no interest left in life. Then I looked up and saw you. At first I mistook you for Senator Norman—even I, who have known the old hypocrite for a dozen years. I stared at you, wondering whether I should go over and make one last personal appeal to you—to him. And then I realised that you could not be he. For I knew positively that he was dining in his room. I looked closer. I saw that you were really a younger man —not that massaged, laced old roué. I stared on in my amazement, till Miss Wayward and Father Murray looked too, and Miss Wayward said, ' Why, there's Senator Norman now.' ' By God! ' said I, ' perhaps it is ! ' Do you see, Mr. Merriam? "

"No," said Merriam, "I don't."

"Ah, but you will, you must," said Rockwell. "Listen!" He looked at his watch. "It is now twenty minutes past seven. Norman is dining in his room. There is a man with him, a Mr. Crockett —one of the dozen men who own Chicago. He is as much interested in the Ordinance as I am—on the other side. He is giving Norman *his* instructions, for the Senator is Crockett's puppet, of course, as much as the Mayor is Norman's. Crockett will leave promptly at a quarter to eight. Mayor Black is due at eight."

"How do you know these things?" interrupted Merriam.

"It is my business to know things," said Rockwell. "The fact is," he added, "I planned to burst in on Norman and Black at their conference and threaten them in the name of the Reform League. It would have done no good, but I owed that much ·to the League."

"And to yourself," said Alicia softly.

"And to myself, yes!" said Rockwell, infinitesimally pricked at last. But he hurried on:

"At ten minutes to eight, Mr. Merriam, I will telephone Norman. I will pretend to be old Schubert, the Mayor's private secretary. He has a dry, clipped voice that is easy to imitate. I will say that the Mayor is sick at his house. I will imply that he is drunk. He often is. I will say he is not too sick to veto the Ordinance before the Council meets at nine, but that he insists on seeing Senator Norman before he does it and asks that Norman come out to his house. I will say that I am sending a car for him. Norman will curse, but he will go. He is under orders, too, you see. At five minutes to eight we will send up word that Mayor Black's car is waiting for Senator Norman. There will be a car waiting. The driver will be Simpson."

"I can fix it with the hotel people to get him off," said Alicia in response to a look from Merriam. "He was a chauffeur once for a while.—And he will do anything I ask him to," she added.

"Norman will go down and get into that car.

He will be driven, not to the Mayor's house, of
course, but to—a certain flat, where he will be detained for several hours—very possibly all night."

" By force? " asked Merriam, rather sternly.

" Only by force of the affections," said Rockwell
suavely. " The flat belongs, for the time being, to
a certain young woman, a manicurist by profession,
who is undoubtedly very pretty and in whom Norman—takes an interest. I happen to know that he
pays the rent of the flat."

Rockwell paused, but Merriam made no reply.
He blushed, subcutaneously at any rate, for Alicia
and Father Murray. The latter indeed affected in-
attention to this portion of Mr. Rockwell's discourse. But Alicia Wayward made no pretence of
either misunderstanding or horror.

In Merriam's mind a slight embarrassment
quickly gave place to anger. That George Norman
after three years—how much sooner who could tell?
—should leave Mollie June for a—his mind paused
before a word too ancient and too frank for profes-
sorial sensibilities.

Rockwell quickly resumed:

". As soon as Norman has gone I will take you to
his room. We will put his famous crimson smoking jacket on you and establish you in his big armchair with a cigar and some whiskey and soda beside you. When Black comes he will find Senator
Norman—you. All you will have to do is to be curt
and sulky, damn him a bit, and tell him to sign the
Ordinance. He'll never suspect you. As a matter

of fact, he doesn't know the Senator well—never spoke with him privately above three times in his life. We'll have only side lights on. He won't stay. He'll be mightily relieved about the Ordinance and in a hurry to get away. Then you yourself can get away and catch your train for—for ——"

"Riceville," supplied Alicia.

"That will be a real adventure for you, young man, and you will have saved the cause of Reform in the city of Chicago!"

John Merriam smiled, frostily.

"The reasons, then, Mr. Rockwell, why I should fraudulently impersonate a Senator of the United States, who happens to be my cousin, and in his name act in an important matter directly contrary to his own wishes are for the fun of the adventure and to save your Reform League from a setback. Is that correct?"

"Philip," said Alicia quickly, "you and Father Murray go for a walk. I want to have a little talk with Mr. Merriam alone. Come back in twenty minutes."

The implication of her last phrase was distinctly flattering to Merriam if he had understood it. Alicia Wayward would not have asked for more than ten minutes with most men.

Rockwell smiled with lowered eyelids—a smile which it was certainly a mistake for him to permit himself, for it could not and did not fail to put Merriam on his guard—against Alicia.

"Come, Murray," said Rockwell rising, "I should like a breath of real air, shouldn't you? And when Miss Wayward commands ——" He waved his hand grandly. "Au revoir!"

And he and the priest hastily departed.

CHAPTER V

ALICIA AND THE MOTIVES OF MEN

"TAKE another cigarette, won't you, Mr. Merriam?" said Alicia, as the curtain at the door fell behind Rockwell and Father Murray.

"Thank you," said Merriam.

He was excited, of course. All the stimulations of his evening, including more coffee than he was used to and an unaccustomed taste of wine and mystery and intrigue, could not fail to tell on the blood of youth. But he felt extraordinarily calm, and he was not in the least afraid of Alicia. He had not fully made up his mind about the proposed adventure, but Alicia knew several things about the wantings of men.

"Let me light it for you," she pursued.

She struck a match, which somehow she already had out of its box, put out a white hand and arm, took the cigarette from his fingers, put it to her own lips and lighted it, and handed it back to him.

"Thank you," said Merriam again, just a little confused. Hesitatingly, with an undeniable trace of thrill, he put the cigarette to his own lips. Poor boy! It was an uneven contest!

Alicia deftly moved her chair to the corner of the

table, bringing it not very close but much closer to Merriam's. Close enough for him to catch the faint, unfamiliar perfume. She put out her hand again and drew one of the yellow roses from their bowl. She rested both arms on the table and played with the rose, drawing it through her fingers and up and down one white, rounded forearm.

"Mr. Merriam," she said, "perhaps you have wondered why I am in this thing."

As a matter of fact he had neglected to be curious on that point, but now he was.

"Yes," he said.

"Mr. Rockwell converted me. Oh, I can see you don't like him. You think he is hard and unscrupulous and self-seeking. Well, he is. All men are—at least, almost all men are"—she glanced at Merriam. "But he is a genuine reformer for all that. He is heart and soul for what he calls the People. He works tremendously for them all his time. And he is shrewd and fearless."

Now it is probable that Alicia's little character sketch presented a very just picture of Philip Rockwell. But it did not appeal to Merriam as true, much less as likable. He was too young. He still wanted his heroes all heroic and his villains naught but black and red with almost visible horns and tail.

He did not reply. He could not, however, remove his eyes from the felicitous meanderings of the yellow rose.

"Well," sighed Alicia, "I was going to tell you

how Mr. Rockwell converted me. You see, my
father—but you don't know who my father is, do
you? The newspapers always refer to him as 'the
billionaire brewer.' They like the alliteration, I
suppose. He's very busy now converting all his
plants for the manufacture of near-beer." (She
laughed as if that were a good joke.) "His youngest sister, my Aunt Geraldine, was Senator Norman's first wife. So I know George Norman well.
I was quite a favourite of his when he used to come
to our house before poor Aunt Jerry died. So
Philip wanted me to 'use my influence' with Mr.
Norman about his precious Ordinance. I wasn't
much interested at first. I hadn't ridden in a
street car, of course, in years."

"Hadn't you?" said Merriam, quite at a loss.

"No. When I go out I take either the limousine
or the electric. So I really didn't know much about
conditions, except, of course, from the cartoons
about strap-hangers in the newspapers. Philip
saw that that was why I was unsympathetic. So
he dared me to go for a street-car ride with him.
Of course I wouldn't take a dare.

"It was about five o'clock in the afternoon. We
took the limousine down to Wabash and Madison.
There Philip made me get out on the street corner.
It was horrid weather—a cold, blowy spring rain.
But Philip was hard as a rock. He told the chauf-
feur to drive to the corner of Cottage Grove and
Thirty-Ninth Street and wait for us. And *we*
waited for a car. It was terrible. We stood out in

the street under the Elevated—by one of the posts,
you know—for a little protection from the train.
We hadn't any umbrella. The wird tore at my
skirts and my hair. The trains going by overhead
nearly burst your ears with noise. And automo-
biles and great motor trucks crashed past within a
few inches of us and splashed mud and nearly
stifled us with gasoline smells. And a crowd of
other people got around us and knocked into us and
walked on our feet and stuck umbrellas in our eyes.
For a long time no car at all came. Then three or
four came together, but they were all jammed full
to the steps, so that we couldn't get on.

" I was ready to give up. I told Philip so.

" ' Let's go into Mandel's,' I begged, ' and you can
call a taxi.'

" ' No you don't,' he said. ' Here, we can get on
this one.'

" Another car had stopped about twenty feet
from us. We joined a kind of football rush for the
rear end. I tripped on my skirt when I tried to
climb the steps, but Philip caught me by the arm
and dragged me on, as though I had been a sack of
flour.

" Then for a long time we couldn't get inside but
had to stand on the platform wedged like olives in
a bottle. It was so dark and cold and noisy, and
everybody was so wet and crushed and smelly. A
man beside me smelled so strong of tobacco and
whiskey and of—not having had a bath for a long
time, that I was nearly ill. And I thought a poor

little shop girl on the other side of me was going to faint.

"After a long time some people got out at the other end of the car—at Twelfth Street, Philip says,—and some of us squeezed inside into the crowded aisle. Inside it was warm—hot, in fact,— but still smellier. Philip got me a strap, and I hung on to it. I don't care for strap-hanger jokes any more. It's terribly tiring, and it pulls your waist all out of shape.

" 'Bet you won't get a seat,' grinned Philip.

"Of course I was bound then that I would. I looked about. Some of the men who were seated were reading papers the way they are in the cartoons. Others just sat and stared in front of them. I didn't blame them much. They looked tired, too. But I had to get a seat to spite Philip. The young man in the one before which I was standing, or hanging, looked rather nice. I made up my mind to get his seat. I had to look down inside his newspaper and crowd against his legs. At last, after looking up at me three or four times, he got up with a jerk as if he had just noticed me and took off his hat, and I smiled at him and at Philip and sat down. But he kept staring at me so that I wished I had let him alone.

"I made the poor little shop girl sit on my lap. Nobody gave her a seat. I suppose she wouldn't work for it the way I did. She was a pretty little thing, too. Just a tiny bit like Mollie June Norman. Not so pretty, of course, but the same type.

"Then there was nothing to do but wait till we got to Thirty-Ninth Street. Ages and ages. They ought to have been able to go to the South Pole and back.

"When we did get there I put the little girl in my seat—she was going to Eighty-First Street, poor little thing,—and Philip and I got out and went home in the limousine, and he told me all about how the Ordinance would better things, and I promised to help him if I could."

"And you did?" said Merriam. He was touched—whether by Alicia's own sufferings in the course of her remarkable exploration or by those of the little shop girl who looked like Mollie June, does not, perhaps, matter. He now quite fully liked Alicia. He saw that, in spite of her extreme décolleté and her cigarettes, she had a generous heart.

"I tried to," replied Alicia. "I saw George Norman, and I did my best—my very best. But he wouldn't promise anything. He only laughed and tried to kiss me."

"Tried to kiss you!" echoed Merriam, naïvely aghast.

"Yes," said Alicia, with her eyes demurely on the rose between her fingers.

And John Merriam, looking at her, grasped clearly the possibility that a "boy senator" with whom Alicia had done her very best might try to kiss her.

"So that is one reason why I am in it to the

death," Alicia went on, " because George Norman—
wouldn't listen to me. And I don't want Philip to
fail."

She laid one hand quickly over one of Merriam's
hands, startling him so that he nearly drew his
away. " I love him," she said, and her eyes shone
effulgently into Merriam's. " He hasn't much
money, and he *is* hard and—and conceited, but he is
courageous. He dares anything. He dared to
take me on that street-car ride. He would dare to
burst in on the Senator and Mayor Black to-night.
He dares think up this plan. A woman loves a
Man."

There is no doubt that Alicia pronounced " man "
with a capital letter, and she looked challengingly
at Merriam.

" We are to be married next month," she added.

" Oh ! " gasped Merriam, his eyes staring in spite
of himself at her hand that lay on his.

The hand flew away as quickly as it had alighted,
but he still felt its soft coolness on his fingers as she
said :

" Of course all this is why *I* am in it, not why you
should be. You can't do it just to please me. But
you really ought to think of all those poor people,
like the little shop girl—all the tired men and
women—millions of them, Philip says—who have
to endure that torture every night after long days
of hard work. It's truly awful, and it might all be
so much better if we only got the Ordinance. You
could get it for them in one little half hour ! "

She looked hopefully at Merriam. He was in fact hesitant. To have the fun of the thing, to gratify this strange, attractive Alicia, and to render an important service to the population of a great city—it was tempting.

"There's another thing," Alicia hurried on. "You knew Mollie June Norman. She was one of your students. I think you ought to do it for her sake."

"Why so?" Merriam's question came swift and sharp.

"Because if Senator Norman kills the Ordinance it will be his ruin. It will cost him Chicago's vote in the next election, and he can't win on the Down-State vote alone."

"I thought Rockwell said the League would collapse."

Possibly Alicia had forgotten this. But she only shrugged her shoulders.

"It may or it mayn't. But either way the people are aroused. Philip swears they will beat Norman if he betrays them now. He is sure they can and will. And if the 'boy senator' were unseated and had to retire to private life it would be terrible for Mollie June. He's bad enough to live with as it is."

At this point Merriam was visited by a sudden and splendid idea. Since he did not disclose it to Alicia, I feel in honour bound to conceal it for the present from the reader.

Alicia detected its presence in his eyes and judiciously kept silent.

It took about ten seconds for that idea to grow from nothingness into full flower. For perhaps five seconds longer Merriam inwardly contemplated its unique beauty. Then he said:

" I'll do it! "

CHAPTER VI

STAGE-SETTING

ALICIA gave him no time for reconsideration or after-thoughts.

"Good!" she cried, "I was sure you would."

She was on her feet in an instant, and as he got to his she held out her hand. Merriam took it—to shake hands on their bargain was his thought. But Alicia never exactly shook hands. She touched or pressed or squeezed according to circumstances. On this occasion it was a warm, clinging squeeze. Her other hand patted Merriam's shoulder.

"I was sure you would," she repeated. "No Man"—again the capital letter was unmistakable —"could have resisted—the—the opportunity."

The curtain at the door was lifted, and Philip Rockwell's voice said: "May I come in? The twenty minutes are up."

They were. Just up. Alicia had done her part in exactly the fraction of an hour she had given herself. No vaudeville act could have been more precisely timed.

"Yes. Come in, dear," said Alicia. "Mr. Merriam will do it. We were just shaking hands on it."

Rockwell crossed the room in a rush and caught

47

Merriam's hand as Alicia relinquished it. He pumped vigorously. In his eyes shone the unmistakable light of that genuine enthusiasm which Alicia had described to her skeptical auditor.

"You're the right sort," he cried. "You are doing a great thing, Mr. Merriam. You will never regret it. But I can't thank you now," he added, dropping Merriam's hand in mid-air, so to speak. "It's ten minutes of eight. That money-bag, Crockett, came out of the elevator just before I came back. I have a car at the Ladies' Entrance."

"With Simpson?" asked Alicia.

"Yes. I had to get things ready. The time was so short. I fixed the head waiter. Simpson seemed ready enough. Has some old grudge against Norman, I think."

"Yes," said Alicia, "he has. I'm a little afraid— I wish I could have seen him. Never mind. It can't be helped. Where's Father Murray?"

"Watching to buttonhole the Mayor if he should come too soon."

He looked critically for a moment at Merriam, seemed satisfied, and crossed to the telephone on the sideboard.

"I'll ring up the curtain," he said.

He laughed boyishly in his excitement and new hope. He seemed very different now from the hard-eyed, middle-aged fellow of an hour ago. Merriam saw how Alicia might admire him.

"Give me Room Three-Two-Three," he said into the telephone, his eyes smiling at them.

A moment later a harsh, dry old man's voice was saying:

"Is this Senator Norman?—This is Mr. Schubert, private secretary to Mayor Black. The Mayor is sick.—I can't help it, sir. He's sick all right. He's out here at his house.—Yes, he can veto the Ordinance all right if it's necessary. But he won't do it without seeing you first. He wants you to come out. He's sent a car for you. It ought to be down there at the Ladies' Entrance by now.—No, it won't do any good to call him up. I'm here at his house now. He's in bed. And he won't veto unless he sees you. Really, sir, if you'll pardon me, you'd better come.—Thank you, sir!"

Rockwell clicked the receiver triumphantly into its hook.

"That's done," he said. "Alicia, dear, go up to the lobby on the women's side and watch the hallway leading to the Ladies' Entrance. Norman should pass out that way within five minutes. Follow him far enough to make sure that Simpson gets him. And then let us know. Meanwhile I'll coach Mr. Merriam a little."

"Right," said Alicia.

She moved to the door. The eyes of both men followed her. When Alicia moved the eyes of men did follow. And she knew it. At the doorway she turned and blew a kiss, which might be said to fall with gracious impartiality between her lover and the younger man. It was a pretty exit.

"She's a splendid girl," said Rockwell, his eyes

lingering on the curtain that had cut her off from them.

"Yes," said Merriam.

Rockwell, still by the sideboard, reached for the long bottle.

"Have another glass of this?"

"I don't mind," said Merriam. The fact is, a bit of stage fright had come in for him when Alicia went out.

"There's not much I can tell you," Rockwell said, as he poured out the yellow fluid. "You'll have to depend mostly on the inspiration of the moment. You look the part all right. Your voice is all right, too. Act as grumpy as you like. Damn him about a bit.—You can swear?" he asked hastily. A sudden horrible doubt of pedagogical capabilities had crossed his mind.

Now Merriam was not a profane man, but some of his fraternity brethren had been. Also he remembered the vituperative exploits of his football coach between halves when the game was going badly.

"Swear?" he cried, as harshly as possible. "Of course I can swear, you damn fool!"

For three seconds Rockwell was startled. Then he laughed.

"Fine!" he cried. "You'll do it! All there is to it, really, is to tell him to sign the Ordinance and to get out. He may ask about Crockett. If he wants to know why he's changed his mind, tell him it's none of his damn business. If he refers

to a Madame Couteau, you must look pleased.
She's the pretty little manicurist whom Norman
will be on his way to visit. Black knows of that
affair, and he knows Norman likes to talk about it.
So he may drag it in with the idea of getting on
your blind side. You can tell him to shut up, of
course, but you must act gratified."

"Yes," said Merriam in a noncommittal tone.

But Rockwell did not notice. He was sipping
the Benedictine, with his mind on his problem.

"That's all I can think of," he said in a moment.
"I'll be in the next room—the bedroom of the suite,
you know,—and if you should get into deep water,
I'll burst in, just as I meant to on the real Senator,
and pull you out. We ought to get it over in fifteen
minutes at the outside and get you off. There's
just the least chance in the world, of course, that
Senator Norman might get away from Simpson and
come back. And there's Mrs. Norman."

"Where will she be? " asked Merriam as he took
a rather large sip of his cordial.

"She's in the lobby now with Miss Norman—the
Senator's sister, you know,—listening to the orchestra." (Merriam vaguely recalled the elderly woman
whom he had seen with Mollie June in the Cabaret.) "The Senator was going to take them to the
theater after he had finished with Black."

"What will they do when he doesn't show up? "
Merriam inquired; but to all appearances he was
chiefly interested at the moment in the best of
liqueurs.

"Probably go without him. She's used to George Norman's broken engagements by now."

"I see," said Merriam without expression.

"Alicia and Murray will keep an eye on them, of course," Rockwell added.

And then both men jumped. It was only the telephone, but conspiracy makes neurasthenics of us all.

Rockwell answered it.

"Yes. — Good. — That's all right. — Oh! — Yes, we'll go at once."

He turned excitedly to Merriam.

"It's Alicia. Norman has come down and got into Simpson's car. Mrs. Norman is still in the lobby. And the Mayor has come in. Murray's got him, but he won't be able to hold him long. We must go right up to the room. Come—Senator!"

Merriam followed out of the private dining-room and down the corridor at a great pace into a main hallway and to an elevator.

Several people looked hard at Merriam. One important-looking elderly man stopped and held out his hand:

"How are you, Senator?"

But Rockwell crowded rudely between them.

"Excuse me, Colonel, but we *must* catch this car.—Very urgent!" he called as the door clicked.

And Merriam had the presence of mind to add, "Look you up later!"

" Good ——" Rockwell began as they stopped at the main floor, but he paused on the first word with his mouth open.

A very large man, large every way, in evening clothes, with a fine head of white hair and an air of conscious distinction, was stepping into the car. He saw Merriam and Rockwell. Then instantly he appeared not to have observed them, hesitated, backed gracefully out of the little group that was entering the elevator, and was gone.

The car smoothly ascended.

" Three! " said Rockwell to the elevator man. Then to Merriam he whispered, " That was the Mayor! He's got away from Murray."

" Ask for your key," whispered Rockwell, as they stepped out.

For five protracted steps Merriam's mind struggled frantically after the room number. He had just grasped it (3–2–3!) when he perceived that his perturbation had been unnecessary.

For the floor clerk—a pretty blonde of about thirty—was looking at him with her sunniest smile.

" Your key, Senator? "

" Yes, please," he managed to say.

As she handed him the key her fingers lightly touched his for a second, and she said in a low tone, " The violets are lovely."

He saw that she was wearing a large bunch of those expensively modest flowers at her waist and understood that his cousin's extra-marital interests might not be limited to Madame Couteau.

He lingered just a moment and replied in a tone as low as her own, "They look lovely where they are now."

But an appalling difficulty loomed over him even as he murmured. For he did not know whether Room 323 lay to the right or the left, and if he should start in the wrong direction ——

But Rockwell knew and was already moving to the left. Merriam followed. In his relief he smiled brightly back at the floor clerk.

At the corner where the hall turned Rockwell stopped, and Merriam, coming up with him, read " 323 " on the door before them. Both men looked up at the transom. It was dark.

" In! " said Rockwell.

Merriam inserted the key, turned it, and cautiously opened the door a couple of inches, becoming, as he did so, thrillingly conscious of the burglarious quality of their enterprise.

No light or sound came from within.

For only three or four seconds Rockwell listened. Then he pushed the door wide, stepped past Merriam, and felt for the switch.

" You haven't invited me in, Senator," he said as the room went alight, " but I'm a forward sort of fellow.—Come inside, and close the door," he added.

Merriam pushed the door shut behind him and stared about. The apartment was probably the most gorgeous he had ever seen. The walls were a soft cream colour, the woodwork white, the carpet and hangings and lampshades rose. Most of the furniture was mahogany, some of it upholstered in rose-coloured tapestry. On a table half way down one side of the room stood a bowl of red roses. In the wall opposite Merriam, between the windows, was a fireplace of white marble, containing a gas log, with a large mirror above the mantel in a frame of white and gold. Before this fireplace stood a huge upholstered easy chair, with a pink-shaded floor lamp on one side of it and a small mahogany tabaret on the other.

While Merriam was endeavouring to appreciate this magnificence, Rockwell quickly crossed the sitting room and passed through a door at one side. After a moment he returned, crossed the room again, and disappeared through a second door. Reëmerging, he announced triumphantly, " No one in the bedrooms! "

But Merriam's eyes rested, fascinated, on a garment which Rockwell had brought back with him from the second bedroom—a luxurious smoking jacket of a most lurid crimson colour, which clashed outrageously with the rose and pinks of the senatorial sitting room.

Rockwell grinned at the look on Merriam's face.

" A historic garment, sir," he declared. " The Boy Senator's crimson smoking jacket is a household word with most of the six million souls of this commonwealth of Illinois. Off with your tails, sir, and into it! "

"Hurry!" he cried, as Merriam hesitated. "The Mayor will be here any minute."

"Why didn't he come up in the elevator with us?" Merriam asked while changing.

"All because of me, sir," replied Rockwell, in excellent spirits. "The Mayor abhors me and all my works so sincerely that I feel I have not lived in vain.—Now, then, sit in that big chair before the fireplace. Here, light this cigar. I'll start the gas log going and bring in the tray with the siphon and glasses and rye that I saw in the other room.— Ah!"

The telephone had rung, and Merriam had leapt out of his chair.

"Answer it," said Rockwell.

Merriam stepped to the telephone, which was on the wall, laid down his cigar, gripped his nerve hard, and put the receiver to his ear:

"Hello!"

A deep voice, boomingly suave, replied:

"Senator Norman?"

"Yes."

"This is Mr. Black. Have you got rid of Rockwell yet?"

"No, not yet."

"Well, can't you throw him out? I am due at the Council meeting at nine, of course. And I don't care to discuss—matters—with you in his presence, naturally. When shall I come up?"

Now the Mayor's rather long speech had given Merriam time to think. He recalled his great idea,

and a new inspiration, as to ways and means, came
to him.

"Eight-thirty," he replied curtly.

"But, good God!" cried the Mayor, "that gives
us so little time. Can't you ——"

"I said eight-thirty, damn you!"

And Merriam hung up and turned to face Rockwell at his elbow.

"But why eight-thirty?" demanded the latter as
soon as he understood that it had been the Mayor.
"Man alive, we ought to be gone by then! What
are we to do with the next twenty minutes? You
must have lost your head. Call him again. Call
the desk and have him paged and told to come
right up."

Without a word Merriam turned to the telephone
again and asked for the desk.

But a moment later he gave Philip Rockwell one
of the major surprises of the latter's life. For what
he said was:

"Please page Mrs. George Norman, with the message that Senator Norman would like to see her
right away in their rooms. Repeat that, please.—
That's right. Thank you!"

"What in hell!" cried Rockwell, belatedly released by the click of the receiver from a paralysis
of astonishment.

Merriam picked up his cigar, walked back to the
easy chair, and seated himself comfortably. He
was excited now to the point of a quite theatrical
composure.

"Nothing in hell," he said. "Quite the contrary, in fact. I want to have a few minutes' conversation with Mrs. Norman. That's all."

"See here!" said Rockwell. "What funny business is this? I won't have——"

"Won't you? All right. Just as you say. If you don't like the way I'm playing my part, I'll drop it and walk right out of that door. I have a ticket for the theater to-night. I can still be in time."

The other man stared and gulped. It was hard for him to realise that this young cub was master of the situation, and not he, Rockwell.

"But this is serious!" he cried. "The Ordinance! The Reform League! The whole city of Chicago! You can't risk these for——"

He stopped. Then:

"Do you realise, you young fool, that if we're caught in this room, it will mean jail for both of us?"

But Merriam in his present mood was incapable of realising anything of the sort. In his mind's eye he saw Mollie June stepping into the elevator and saying in a voice of heavenly sweetness to the happy elevator man, "Three, please!"

An outer crust of his consciousness made pert reply to Rockwell:

"That would be bad for the Reform League, wouldn't it?" and added, "But you're willing to risk it for the Ordinance?"

"Yes, I am," began Rockwell, "but——"

"Would you risk it for Alicia?" Merriam interrupted.

"What has Alicia got to do with it?"

But he understood, and knew that argument was useless, and stared in helpless anger and alarm while the younger man carefully, grandly blew a beautifully perfect smoke ring into the air.

It was the youngster who spoke, still theatrically calm:

"You'd better go into the bedroom. She'll be here in a moment. Shut the door, please. And keep away from it!"

It was one of the secrets of Philip Rockwell's success in politics that, masterful as he was, he knew when to yield. He took a step towards one of the bedrooms.

"Make it short," he pleaded.

"Eight-thirty!" said Merriam.

A gentle knocking sounded at the door.

Merriam was on his feet without volition of his own, while Rockwell, almost as instinctively, slipped into the bedroom.

Then the younger man recovered himself, sat down, his feet to the gas log and his back to the door, and called, "Come in!"

CHAPTER VII

BOY AND GIRL

THE door was opened and closed. John Merriam's straining ears could catch no definite sound of footsteps or skirts, and he did not dare to look around. Yet by some sixth sense, it seemed, he was aware of Mollie June's progress half way across the room and aware that she had stopped, some feet away from him.

"What is it—George?" she asked.

It was only too clear that Mollie June's lord and master was not in the habit of sending for her.

"Where is—Miss Norman?"

Merriam was conscious that Senator Norman probably did not refer to his sister in that fashion, but he did not know her given name.

"Aunt Mary? I left her in the lobby. Did you want her too?"

There was a note of eagerness in the question.

"No!"

Silence. Mollie June stood waiting in the center of the room. The significance of her failure to approach her husband was unmistakable.

Then he said: "Would you very much mind if you should miss the theater to-night?"

"Why—no. Is there anything the matter, George?"

"Not for me," said Merriam, and he rose and faced her.

"I was afraid——" She stopped, looked hard. "George, you look—oh!"

She passed her hand across her eyes. It was a stage gesture, but when stage situations occur in real life the conventional "business" of the boards is often justified.

She looked again.

"Mr. Merriam!"

John Merriam stepped quickly forward. It occurred to him that she might faint. He had read many novels.

But Mollie June did nothing of the sort.

"Mr. Merriam!" she cried again. "How do you come here? Where is—Mr. Norman? How did you get in *that?*"

She pointed to the famous smoking jacket. Her bewilderment was increasing. She looked nervously about, as if suspecting that Merriam, for the sake of the crimson garment, had murdered her husband and concealed his body.

Merriam had stopped. Almost he might have wished that she had fainted. It would have been delicious to carry her in his arms and place her in the Senator's easy chair and bring water and when her eyes opened wonderingly upon him softly whisper her name. As it was he could only say formally:

"Let me take your cloak—Mrs. Norman—won't you? And sit down."

Mechanically she let him take the opera cloak from her shoulders, and when he caught hold of the senatorial chair and swung it around and pushed it towards her she sat tremblingly erect on the edge of it. Her eyes dwelt upon his face as if fascinated.

"Isn't it funny you look so *much* alike? I never realised it—so much. But—where is *he?* Why ——? "

Merriam caught up a small chair, placed it in front of hers, and sat down.

"Listen, Mollie June," he said pleadingly, using unconsciously the name that ran in his thoughts.

His plan, as it had taken shape while he talked with Mayor Black on the telephone, was to tell her in advance of Rockwell's plot and to carry it through only with her approval or consent—for was not his first loyalty to her? His original idea, and his real motive, of course, had been only to see her. And now that he had her there he found he hated to waste time on explanations. But there was nothing for it. She could not be at ease or clear in her mind until she understood. So, rapidly and candidly, he related how at the instance of Mr. Rockwell the Senator had been decoyed away, while he was there to impersonate him with Mayor Black, so that the latter should sign instead of vetoing the Traction Ordinance. Then he waited for he knew not what—amazement, fright, anger, dissuasion.

But Mollie June did not seem much interested in

traction ordinances. Presumably Senator Norman
had not cared to educate his young wife about political matters.

"Why did you send for *me?*" she asked.

Her question was almost too direct for him. He
could not say, to ask her approval of the plan
against her husband.

"I had to see you," was all he could reply.

"Why?"

But she knew the real reason. The turning of
her eyes away from him confessed it.

It was his chance to say, "Because I love you."
An older man might have said it. But the young
are timid and conventional—not bold and reckless,
as is alleged. He remembered that she was another
man's wife and only spoke her name:

"Mollie June!"

Perhaps that did as well. In fact it was, in the
reticent dialect of youth, the same thing.

She looked at him a moment, then quickly away
again.

"You never called me that but once before—to-
night," she said.

At first he found no answer. His mind scarcely
sought one. He was absorbed in merely looking at
her. She was indeed girlishly perfect as she sat
there, almost primly upright, in her white frock,
her slender figure framed in the rose-coloured tapestry of the big chair's back and arms, which gave
an effect as of a blush to her cheeks and to the white
shoulders which he had never seen before except

across the spaces of the Peacock Cabaret. To the eyes of middle age she would have been, perhaps, merely "charming." In his she shone with the divine radiance of Aphrodite. And his were right, of course.

He was almost trembling when at length he said:

"That was on—that last night."

"Yes," said Aphrodite, who is always chary of speech.

Suddenly he saw that her averted face was wistful, sad.

"Are you happy, Mollie June?" he cried.

Though she turned only partly to him he saw that her eyes were more a woman's eyes than he had known them and were full of tears.

"Not—very," she said.

He sat dumbly on his chair, full of pain for her, yet not altogether saddened that she should not be entirely happy with another man.

But now her face was fully towards him, and her eyes had become dry and looked past him.

"Oh, Mr. Merriam—you don't know! I can't tell you ——"

He was filled with horror—almost boyishly terrified—by such dim visions as a man may have of what her lot might be.

"If I could only help you!" he cried, as earnestly as all the other separated lovers in the world have said those very words.

The eyes that looked beyond him came back to his face. The Mollie June whom he had known had

had her girlish poise, and this more tragic Mollie June did not lose her self-control for long.

"You *have* helped me—Mr. Merriam. Oh, I am glad you brought me here! When I saw you in—the Cabaret, I just ran away from you. I couldn't even let you speak to me. Afterwards I waited up-stairs in the lobby. I thought—I might see you there. But you didn't come. Then I thought George had sent for me!"

She stopped as if that was a climax.

Merriam leaned forward. He wanted to put his hand over one of hers that lay on the arm of her chair, but did not dare to. His tongue, however, was released at last.

"If ever I can help you in any way, Mollie June, you must let me know. I would do anything for you. I will always be ready."

He paused abruptly, though only for a second. A dark thought had crossed his mind: after all the "Boy Senator" was an old man (from the stand-point of twenty-eight), and leading a life unhealthy for old men. He hurried on:

"I will wait for you always. Perhaps some day ——"

Did she comprehend his meaning? He could not tell, and he did not know whether to hope she did or did not. But stress of conflicting emotions made him venturesome. He did put his hand over hers.

Hers did not move.

His fingers slipped under hers, ready to raise her hand.

"That last night in Riceville, Mollie June, I kissed your—glove. To-night I want to kiss your hand—to make me yours—if you should need me."

She did not draw her hand away, but she said:

"You oughtn't to—now—Mr. Merriam."

The formal name by which she had continually addressed him pricked.

"Won't you call me ' John,' Mollie June, just for this quarter of an hour before the Mayor comes? "

" Oh, the Mayor! " she cried in alarmed remembrance.

" Call me ' John,' dear—for fifteen minutes! "

In his voice and eyes were both entreaty and command, and Mollie June could not resist them.

" John! " she whispered.

And he raised her hand and bent quickly forward, and his lips pressed her fingers. A bare second. Yet it was in his mind a solemn, a sacramental kiss. He straightened up triumphant, happy. Youth asks so little.

"Now you know you have a right to me! " he cried. " To send for me. To use me any way, any time! "

There came a loud knocking at the door.

Mollie June started half way out of the chair and then sank back. Merriam, on his feet and part way across the floor, stopped confused. He perceived that he ought to get Mollie June out of the room.

The knocking resounded again. And immediately the door was tried and opened, and a man stepped in. It was the large man with the white hair who had started to enter the elevator—Mayor Black.

CHAPTER VIII

PASSAGES WITH MAYOR BLACK

THE Mayor of the great city of Chicago was hurriedly apologetic:

"I beg your pardon, Senator. You said eight-thirty, you know, and it's that now. I came up and knocked. Evidently you did not hear. A man I met in the lobby told me that you had left the hotel in a taxi half an hour ago. He said he saw you go. So I tried the door and when it opened stepped in, just to make sure. I am sorry to have intruded."

Apparently, however, he did not intend to withdraw.

Mollie June crouched frightened in her chair, but Merriam was rapidly pulling himself together.

"It is I who should apologise for keeping you waiting, Mayor Black," he said. "I will ask Mrs. Norman to excuse us. Will you step into the next room for a few minutes, Mollie June? We shall not be long."

He went back to her chair and held out his hand.

She took it and rose. Her spirit, too, was reasserting itself. She faced the Mayor with a smile:

"Good evening, Mr. Black."

"Good evening, Mrs. Norman." He bowed gallantly. "I am very sorry ——"

"Oh," she cried lightly, one would have said happily, "business is business, I know." Then to Merriam: "You won't be long?"

"Only a minute—dear."

(Perhaps we can hardly blame him for profiting by the license his rôle gave him to address her so.)

He moved to the door opposite to that through which Rockwell had slipped away fifteen minutes earlier and opened it for her. She passed through into the darkness of the other room. He felt for the switch and pushed it.

As the light went on she turned and smiled at him:

"Thank you."

For an instant it seemed to him—perhaps to both of them—that she was really his wife, who was leaving him for a few minutes only, whom he would soon rejoin.

Then he turned to face Mayor Black.

"I need stay only a minute, Senator," the Mayor was saying. "If I had known you were engaged with Mrs. Norman, I shouldn't have bothered you. It wasn't really necessary. I met Mr. Crockett downstairs while I was waiting. He told me the answer. But since I had the engagement with you I came up. If I may, I'll write the veto right here, and then I can go on to the Council meeting."

As he spoke he drew a thick roll of paper from his overcoat pocket, unfolded it, opened it at the last sheet, and laid it on a small writing table.

"I shan't give any reasons," he added, sitting down and picking up a pen. "Least said, soonest mended—eh, Senator?"

"But you're not to veto! You're to sign!" cried Merriam.

Perhaps if he had more fully grasped the significance of the other's statement about Mr. Crockett he would have been less abrupt; but that mighty financier was only a dim name to his mind.

"What?" said Black, turning in his chair.

The Mayor's tone gave Merriam some realisation of the seriousness of the new situation. But he could only stand to his guns.

"You're to *sign!* I don't care what Crockett said. I don't care a damn what he said," he corrected himself. "You do what I say, damn you!"

"But how is this?" exclaimed the Mayor. "Crockett said you fully agreed that the best interests ——"

He stopped, looking intently at Merriam.

In the excitement of the dialogue which had followed Merriam's sending for Mollie June Rockwell had neglected the precaution he had had in mind of having only side lights on. Rockwell had planned, also, that Merriam should sit facing the gas log with his back to the room and look at the Mayor as little as possible. Now the boy stood where the full glare of the chandelier shone on his face. Perhaps, too, the emotions of a youthful love scene, such as he had just passed through, were not the best preparation in the world for counterfeiting the slightly

worn cheeks and slightly tired eyes of an elderly if
well-preserved politician.

"Who in hell are you?" gasped the Mayor.

Merriam was certainly startled. Perhaps he
showed it just a little. But he stood up bravely.

"You know damn well who I am. And you do
as I say or get out of Chicago politics. I'll attend
to Crockett," he added. "That's my affair."

"Is that so? Well, I guess it's my affair who
makes a monkey of me! I——"

Again the Mayor stopped abruptly and stared.
Then suddenly he rose.

"I was told the Senator had left the hotel. I
think I was correctly informed. What sort of a
trick is this? Who *are* you?"

"Damn you——" Merriam began, with realistic
sincerity, but with the vaguest ideas as to what
more substantial statement should follow.

At this moment, however, Rockwell opened his
door and stepped into the room.

"Aha!" cried the Mayor. No stage villain could
have said it better. "Mr. Rockwell! Of the Reform League, I believe!" He bowed sardonically.
"'One-Thing-at-a-Time Rockwell!' Well, one
thing at a time like this"—he pointed at Merriam
—"ought to be enough for a reformer!"

"Good evening, Mayor Black," said Rockwell.
"I believe you were about to sign the Ordinance."

"I was *not*. In spite of the *Senator* here. I
don't get a chance to defy Senator Norman every
day. I rather enjoy it!—And let me tell you,"

he added, " if you and your friends in that damned League make any more trouble for me or Senator Norman or the Ordinance or anything else after this—if you don't shut up and lie low and keep pretty damn quiet, we'll show you up, my boy. This would make a pretty little story for the newspapers—and for the State's Attorney, too! We might call it ' The Ethics of Reform!' Oh, we have you where we want you now, Mr. Reformer! As for this young impostor here, we'll have to look him up a bit. A very promising young gentleman!"

The Mayor evidently enjoyed the center of the stage. He towered tall and imposing and righteous, and looked triumphantly from Rockwell to Merriam and back again.

"I really think you'd better sign it," said Rockwell. He spoke rather low.

"What do you mean?" cried the Mayor.

Then he thought he saw.

"Oh, it's strong-arm work next, is it?"

There was a note of alarm mingled with his irony, and the magnificence of his pose weakened a little. Rockwell was a determined-looking fellow, and there was Merriam to help him, and the Mayor was not really a very brave man. But he went on talking to save his face:

"You certainly are a jewel of a reformer, Rockwell!"

Then he saw a point and quickly recovered his full grandeur.

"I don't quite see how you're going to manage, though. Of course, if it were a case of *preventing* me from signing, you might do it—the two of you! But signing's rather different, isn't it? You can lead a horse to water —— Of course, you can club me or hold a revolver to my head. But, you see, I know you wouldn't dare to fire a revolver here in this room. So just how will you force my fingers to form the letters? Or perhaps you will try forgery? Is forgery the next act, Mr. Reformer?"

Rockwell smiled. He was in no hurry to reply. Merriam still stood, as he had throughout this unforeseen dialogue, a rigid spectator.

Then, in the moment's silence, very inopportunely, a clock, somewhere outside, struck the hour —a quarter to nine.

Rockwell tried to drown it, saying, "I'm hardly so versatile as that."

But the Mayor had heard and understood.

"Oh, that's it!" he cried.

"Yes, that's it!" said Rockwell, and the center of the stage automatically shifted to him. "If that Ordinance is not returned to the Council with your veto by nine o'clock to-night, it becomes a law whether you sign it or not! You're a bit slow, Mr. Mayor, but you've got it at last!"

The Mayor did not answer. He shifted slightly on his feet. His hand shot out. He grabbed the Ordinance from the writing table and rushed for the door.

"Catch him!" shouted Rockwell. "Hold him!"

Merriam had been a football player. As if released from a spring he darted after the Mayor. From habit he tackled low. They went down with something of a crash, knocking over an ash stand as they fell, and the Mayor gave a groan. If he had ever known how to fall properly, he had forgotten. Merriam hoped there were no bones broken.

But Rockwell was wasting no thoughts on commiseration. He was kneeling over the fallen ruler of the city with his hands clapped over his mouth— to prevent further groans or other outcry.

"Get the paper!" he said.

Merriam scrambled forward and tried to pull the Ordinance from the hand at the end of the outstretched arm. It was held tight. He was afraid of tearing it.

"Twist his arm," said Rockwell.

A very little twist sufficed. The Mayor gave up. Merriam rose to his feet with the document.

"Will you be quiet?" Rockwell demanded in the Mayor's ear, and released his mouth enough to enable him to answer.

"Yes," said the Mayor feebly. "Let me up."

"All right. That's better. If you make any rumpus we'll down you again, you know, and tie you up and gag you.—Give me the paper," he added to Merriam, "and help him up, will you?"

He stood watching while the younger man assisted the Mayor in the ponderous job of getting on his feet.

"I hope you aren't hurt, sir," said Merriam.

The Mayor looked sourly at him. "Thanks!" He felt of his arms and passed his hands up and down over his ribs. "I guess I'm all right—except my clothes."

In fact his white shirt front was crumpled and his broadcloth coat and trousers were dusty with cigar ash from the fallen stand. Merriam was in little better condition. They were not dressed for football practice. Rockwell only was still immaculate.

"I'll get a brush," said Merriam. No longer a Senator, he felt very boyish and anxious to be useful.

As he spoke he turned to the room—the fall had occurred near the door into the hall—and stopped nonplused. For in her bedroom door stood Mollie June, her eyes full at once of eagerness and of apprehension.

How much she had heard I do not pretend to know. Perhaps some of Merriam's unprofessorial profanity, possibly the Mayor's triumphant irony, certainly Rockwell's shout, "Catch him!" and the fall. Doubtless the silence after that thud had been too much for her self-control.

The Mayor's rueful gaze travelling past Merriam also rested on Mollie June. A light came into his eyes. He drew himself up.

"Come in, Mrs. Norman," he said. "Your *husband*"—with a significant emphasis on the word—"has been giving a demonstration of his athletic prowess. He is indeed the Boy Senator and a suit-

able mate for a woman as young and pretty as yourself."

He paid no attention to Merriam's angry and
threatening glance but turned to Rockwell.

"Mr. Rockwell," he said, "I think you'd better
give me that Ordinance after all."

Rockwell spoke in a low tone to Merriam:
"Get her out!"

The Mayor had no objection to that.   The older
men watched while Merriam walked rapidly across
the room to Mollie June.

"You'd better go into the other room again,
dear," he said.

But Mollie June's eyes were bright and her
colour high and her white shoulders very straight.

"No!" she said.

"You really will oblige us greatly, Mrs. Norman," said the Mayor, "if you will withdraw for a
moment longer."

"No!" said Mollie June.   "This is my room.   I
have a right to be here.   And I don't like scuffling."

She cast a disdainful glance at their crumpled
shirts and dusty trousers.   And, womanlike, she
sought a diversion.

"What a mess you are in!" she cried.   "Mr.—
George,—get the whisk broom from the bedroom
there!"

It was an almost haughty command.   And Merriam rejoiced to obey this new mistress of the situation.   He darted into the bedroom.

The two older men looked at each other.   Rock-

well was content: time was passing. When the
Mayor started to speak he forestalled him.

"She's really right," he said. "You can't leave
like this. And some one mignt come in."

Merriam was back with the whisk broom.

"Come under the light," ordered Mollie June,
addressing the Mayor.

That dignitary reluctantly advanced.

"Turn around. Now, George, brush him."

Merriam sought diligently to remove the ashes
from the Mayor's garments. It required vigorous
work, for the dust was rubbed deeply into the cloth.
Mollie June superintended closely. The Mayor had
to turn about several times and raise an arm and
then the other arm. He could not make much
progress in the regaining of his dignity; and he, no
less than Rockwell, was conscious of the fleeing moments. But, glancing again and again at Mollie
June, girlishly imperious and intent, he could not
as yet muster his brutality for what he saw the next
move in his game must be. Rockwell waited se-
renely in the background, the Ordinance in his
hand.

At last the Mayor's broadcloth was fairly pre-
sentable. Nothing could be done, of course, with
his shirt front.

"Now, George," said Mollie June, "it's your
turn. Give me the broom."

"No, no!"

"*Give me the broom!*" She took it from his
hand. "Turn around!"

And with her own hands and in the manner of wifely solicitude she began to dust his collar and lapels.

This was not unpleasant for Merriam, but it prompted the Mayor to take his cue. As he watched his eyes hardened, and in a moment he said:

" You take good care of your *husband,* don't you, Mrs. Norman? "

" I try to," said Mollie June rather pertly, dusting away. Evidently she had not heard enough to know that Merriam had been found out.

" It must be pleasant," said the Mayor, " to have such a nice *young* husband."

Mollie June stopped her work and looked at him in sudden alarm.

" What do you mean? " she said.

Rockwell stepped forward and caught her arm:

" Let me lead you into the next room, Mrs. Norman. You must let us talk with the Mayor."

" No! " she cried, snatching her arm away, and turning eyes of angry innocence on Mayor Black. " What do you mean? "

" I mean," he said, with smiling suavity—he was not to be daunted now, and, short of violence, there was no way of stopping him,—" that you are a young woman. This gentleman—whose name I do not have the honour of knowing—is also young, and rather handsome. The Senator, of course, is getting old. I find you two alone in your husband's rooms, your husband having been tricked away. You can hardly expect me to believe that *you* mis-

took him for your husband. You display no dislike
for his person. I draw my own conclusions. Every
one in Chicago will draw the same conclusions if
this interesting situation, quite worthy of Boccac-
cio, should become known. That's why I think "—
he turned suddenly to Rockwell—" that you'd better give me the Ordinance after all."

Mollie June's cheeks were blazing. Merriam's
also; he could not look at her. But Rockwell
pulled his watch from his pocket.

"It is now two minutes past nine," he said.
"The Ordinance has become law. You can have it
now, Mr. Mayor." He held out the document.

The Mayor snatched it.

"It's not legal!" he cried. "And it won't stand.
I can prove that I was prevented by foul means—
by foul means," he repeated, "from exercising my
charter right of veto. I'll take out an injunction,
and I'll fight it to the Supreme Court. And in the
process all Chicago—the whole United States—
shall be entertained with the piquant story of these
young people "—he waved a hand towards Merriam
and Mollie June,—" aided and abetted by Mr. Reformer Rockwell. I'll ruin them, and you and your
League, whatever else comes of it. Oh, you're a
clever lot, you—you reformers!"

He paused out of breath. Then, dramatically,
for he was always self-conscious and inclined to
pose:

"Madame and gentlemen!"—but the effectiveness of his bow was somewhat marred by the sorry

state of his shirt front—" I wish you a very good evening! "

But Rockwell was before him with his back to the hall door.

" You've forgotten your hat, Mayor," he said.

(In fact, his tall hat still stood on the writing table where he had set it down before he spread out the Ordinance there to write his veto.)

" Damn my hat! Let me go! "

" Presently, presently. I still think you'd better sign the Ordinance."

" Do you mean to knock me down again? "

" I'd like nothing better, you—cad! " cried Merriam, who had stood bursting with outrage a minute longer than he could endure.

The Mayor almost jumped at the savage sincerity of this threat in his rear. Rockwell smiled at the startled look on his face, but he spoke quietly:

" No violence. I hope to convince you that it would be to your best interests to sign it. Since it has become a law anyway."

" Never! " cried the Mayor. " Do you think I would be a traitor to—to—my party? And I mean to get even with this gang, whatever else I do! "

But the next instant he jumped indeed. A new voice spoke—a woman's.

" Mayor Black," it said, " you're a fool! "

CHAPTER IX

AUNT MARY

ALL four of the actors in the little scene turned, and Mollie June uttered an exclamation: "Aunt Mary!"

In the doorway from which Rockwell had emerged a few minutes earlier stood the thin, pale, elderly woman whom Merriam had seen with Mollie June in the Peacock Cabaret. She wore a black evening gown, rather too heavily overlaid with jet, was tall and very erect, and had streaked gray hair, a Roman nose, and a firm mouth. The effect as she stood there, framed in the door, was decidedly striking—sibylline.

Mollie June ran to her.

"Oh, Aunt Mary!" she cried.

Merriam was afraid that Mollie June would burst into tears. Very possibly she would have liked to do so, but Aunt Mary gave her no opportunity.

"Lock the door, Mr. Rockwell," she said, putting an arm about Mollie June's waist. Her tone and manner were vigorous and dominant.

"Good evening, Mr. Black," she continued, while Rockwell hastened to obey her. And to Merriam: "Good evening, Mr.—Wilson. Now I think we had better all sit down and talk it over."

81

"I can't," said the Mayor. "I'm late for the Council meeting already. I've been shamefully tricked, Miss Norman."

"I think you have," returned Aunt Mary, releasing Mollie June and advancing a step or two into the room. "But that's the very reason why you need to consider your position at once. You're in a mess. So are we. Perhaps we can help each other out. The Council can wait. 'Phone them that you've been detained. They can go ahead, I suppose. Really, Mr. Black, I see a point or two in this business that I think will interest you."

Mayor Black met Mary Norman's direct, purposeful gaze. He was impressed by her air of command and intelligence. He recalled gossip to the effect that it was really she who ran George Norman's campaigns, that she even wrote some of his speeches.

"Very well," he said, "I'll stay ten minutes. Never mind 'phoning."

"Good," said Aunt Mary. "There are seats for all of us, I believe. Take that one, Mayor."

She indicated the large armchair with the rose-coloured tapestry in which Mollie June had been ensconced half an hour before, and laid her own hand on the back of the smaller one close by in which Merriam had sat.

Then she turned to Mollie June:

"Do you wish to leave us, dear, or to stay?"

"I'll stay!" said Mollie June. Her colour was still high, and the glance she threw in the Mayor's direction was distinctly hostile, but she had recovered her self-control. We shall be able to forgive young Merriam a throb of admiration at her spirit.

"Very well," said Aunt Mary. "Sit over there, then. Mr.—Wilson," she added, to Merriam, "on that table yonder you will find a humidor. Pass the cigars, please. And pick up that ash stand and set it here by the Mayor."

She and the Mayor and Mollie June sat down. Rockwell remained standing. Merriam, though somewhat confused at having turned from Norman into Wilson, hastened to do as he was bid. He picked up the ash stand, straightening the box of matches into place, and brought it and set it by the Mayor's chair. Then he got the humidor, opened its heavy lid, and passed the gold-banded perfectos therein to the Mayor and to Rockwell.

"Are you leaving me out, young man?" demanded Aunt Mary, who had watched him in appraising silence.

Merriam turned to her with the humidor, hesitating.

"There don't seem to be any cigarettes," he said. "I have some in my pocket."

But Aunt Mary leaned forward and took from the humidor a package of "little cigars" that had been slipped in at one end of the box of perfectos.

"No cigarettes for me," she said. "I smoke when I'm with men so as to be one of them. A cigarette leaves me a woman. A cigar, even one of these little ones, makes a man of me. Give me a match, please."

With what seemed to himself amazing self-control, Merriam took a match from the ash stand, struck it, and would have held the light for her. But Aunt Mary took it from him and, looking all the while amazingly like his own mother, deliberately and efficiently ignited the "little cigar."

Then she looked up quizzically at Merriam, blew out the match, handed it to him, and said, "Sit down, Mr. Wilson."

Having seated himself, Merriam found Aunt Mary looking intently at the Mayor, who was smoking and returning her gaze.

But Rockwell broke in:

"How much do you know, Miss Norman? And how do you know it?"

"As to how I know it," said Aunt Mary, "that's my own business for the present. Not because there need be any secret about it, but because we haven't time for explanations." She puffed at her little cigar. "As to how much I know, I believe I understand the whole affair—except how Mrs. Norman came into it." She looked at Rockwell.

That gentleman did not reply. Merriam broke the silence:

"I sent for her."

He said it very well—not defiantly, but as a plain, necessary statement of fact.

Aunt Mary turned in her chair to look at him.

"Ah!" she said.

He felt that he was colouring under her gaze.
Perhaps that colour answered her obvious next
question as to why he had done so. She did not ask
that question, but turned back to the Mayor:

"I overheard a little of your conversation from
the doorway before I spoke. Mr. Rockwell was
saying he thought that, as things stand now, it
would be best for you to sign the Ordinance. I
think so too."

The Mayor would have interrupted, but she
waved her little cigar at him.

"You can, of course," she continued, "explain
that you were tricked. But how much would that
help you with Mr. Crockett or any of his cronies
and allies? They would only think the worse of
you and throw you over the more quickly. A man
of your age and standing cannot afford to be
tricked. If he is, he had better conceal the fact.
And how about the people of Chicago, before whom
you come up for reëlection in the fall? Will their
sympathies be with you or with the persons who
tricked you into giving them the Ordinance they
wanted? The American people love a clever trick.
And a trick is clever if it succeeds. As for the
illegality, they won't care a picayune for that. You
said you would fight it in the courts. Well, you
might. But it would be a long fight. You yourself mentioned the Supreme Court. And in the
meantime it is a law and goes into effect at once.
Unless, of course, you take out an injunction. And
if you do that, you will make yourself so unpopular

that you can never even be nominated again. Let us suppose it goes into effect. Then by the time your fight was won, if you won it, the new conditions would be established, and nobody would dare try to unscramble the eggs. The Council would simply have to pass it over again, and you—or your successor, rather, for you would be out by then—would promptly sign it. No, my friend, there is no road for you in that direction. You would lose out both ways—with the bosses, who would have no more use for a man who had allowed himself to be fooled at a critical juncture, and with the people. Your only chance—unless you wish to retire quickly and ignominiously to private life—is to cut loose from the bosses and throw in your lot with the people—sign the Ordinance, claim the credit, join forces with Rockwell here, defy Crockett, and come out as the people's champion! "

The Mayor was not smoking. He was looking hard at Aunt Mary, as one man looks at another. (Her little cigar had effected that.) There was aroused interest in his eyes.

" Wouldn't you rather like to go into politics as your own boss for a change? " Aunt Mary asked. " Rather than as one miserable little cog in a big, dirty machine? "

The Mayor flushed a little and took refuge behind a puff of smoke.

" Perhaps I would," he said. Then, suddenly: " How about Senator Norman? Do I defy him too? "

"Not at all," said Aunt Mary. " He also will go over to the people."

" Can you answer for him? "

" I think I can. He will be forced to do so in the same way you are. He too has been victimised."

She leaned forward and deposited her small cigar, of which she had really smoked very little, in the ash tray. Sitting erect, she folded her hands in her lap and became forthwith a woman again—a sedate, almost prim, elderly woman.

" That," she explained simply, " is the source of my interest in this matter. I like you, Mayor Black, because you have some of the courtliness of the old school in your manner. I should be sorry to see you in misfortune. But I care much more, naturally, for my brother, George Norman, and more still for the name of Norman "—from her tone she might have referred to the Deity,—" which has been an honourable name in this country for eight generations, and which George, with his spoils politics and his dissipations, is compromising. I have long wanted him to break with his present associates, to live straight, and to become a real leader, as the Normans were in New York State in the early years of the last century. I have tried again and again to get him to do so. Over and over he has promised me he would. But he is weak. He has never done it. Now he will have to do it! "

All the members of the little group looked with some admiration, I fancy, at Aunt Mary, sitting straight, an incarnation of aristocratic, elderly

femininity, in her chair.   Where a moment or two
before she had been an unsexed modern, she looked
now like an old family portrait.

Rockwell broke the momentary silence:

"Miss Norman has presented, so much better
than I could have done, the argument which I tried
to suggest to Mr. Black."

It was probably unfortunate that Rockwell had
recalled attention to himself.   The Mayor glanced
at him with animosity, and at the silent Merriam, and over at Mollie June, listening eagerly
in the background.   Then at Aunt Mary again.
He leaned back, pulling at his cigar, thinking
hard.

In the silence a slight noise became audible from
the bedroom behind Aunt Mary—a word or two of
whispering and then a sound as if some one tip-
toeing had stumbled a little.

The Mayor jumped to his feet.

"Who's there?" he cried, pointing.

For an instant Aunt Mary was out of countenance.   But only for an instant.   Then, without
rising or turning her head, she called:

"Come in, Alicia."

A moment's silence.   Then a laugh, of a pre-
meditated sweetness which Merriam remembered,
and Alicia Wayward stood in the doorway.

The Mayor and Merriam rose.   Mollie June, too,
jumped up.   Only Aunt Mary remained calmly
seated.

After a second's pause in the effective framing of

the door, Alicia advanced with an air of eager
pleasure and held out her hand to the Mayor.

" Good evening, Mr. Black."

The Mayor was a very susceptible male where
women like Alicia were concerned. He took her
hand.

" Good evening, Miss Wayward." But, still holding the hand, he looked steadily at her and asked,
" Who else is in there? "

" Who else? " repeated Alicia, raising her pretty
dark eyebrows.

" Or were you whispering to yourself? " pursued
the Mayor.

Alicia laughed and drew her hand away. " It's
only Father Murray." Then, raising her voice a
little: " You'll have to come in, Father Murray, to
save my reputation. This is really all of us," she
added, as the priest rather sheepishly presented
himself. " You can search the room if you
like."

She smiled at him in the manner which novelists
commonly describe as roguish.

The Mayor smiled back at her, but he turned to
the latest arrival.

" Were you in this plot, too, Father Murray? "

" Indeed he was," Alicia answered for him. " He
didn't quite approve of it at first. But we quite
easily converted him. So, you see, it can't be so
black as it first seemed to you, Mr. Mayor. And
really," she hurried on, " you ought to do as Miss
Norman suggests. It's a splendid chance for you.

To really be a—a Man, you know! And I can help."

"How can you help?" asked the Mayor.

"I am quite sure," said Alicia, "that I can get my father to subscribe quite a lot of money—a hundred thousand dollars, say—to your campaign fund—yours and Senator Norman's and the Reform League's."

"Is Mr. Wayward so keen on reform? I should think he had had nearly enough of it. They've practically put him out of business, these reformers."

"He's rather keen on me, you know," said Alicia. "And he likes Mollie June and Miss Norman and George Norman and ——"

"Father Murray, I suppose," interrupted the Mayor, "and anybody else you can think of. You mean you can get it out of him." But his appreciative smile made a compliment of the accusation.

Alicia only raised her eyebrows again.

Aunt Mary rose and took the reins of business into her own hands once more.

"I should be willing to subscribe something, too, out of my own income," she said. "And the League can raise plenty of money. You won't lack for funds. Here's my proposition, Mr. Black. You lie low and keep still till noon to-morrow. Don't go to the Council meeting at all. Keep the Ordinance in your own possession. Refuse to see any one. See what the papers say in the morning. And

wait for a message from George Norman. If by
noon to-morrow he telephones you that he will go
with you, will you go over to the League, sign the
Ordinance, break with Crockett and the rest of
them, and appeal to the people on your own? "

The Mayor looked from Aunt Mary to Alicia's
appealing and admiring eyes and back at Aunt
Mary. He avoided Rockwell and Merriam and
Mollie June.

" That's fair enough," he said. " I'll do that."
Then: " You know where Norman is, do you? "

" Yes," said Aunt Mary. It was plain, however,
that she did not intend to communicate the information.

"And what becomes of this young gentleman? "
The Mayor looked at Merriam.

" He will disappear where he came from."

" Well, well," said the Mayor genially, " it has
been a very stimulating evening. Rather like a
play. You have certainly put me in a box. But
I'll admit I'm interested in your suggestion, Miss
Norman. I'll think it over carefully. Now I believe I'll call a taxi."

" Let me," said Rockwell, and he stepped to the
telephone.

The Mayor addressed himself to Merriam:

" Will you bring me my hat, Mr.—Wilson? "

Merriam was near the writing table on which the
hat stood. He picked it up and brought it.

" The resemblance is marvellously close," said
the Mayor, studying his face. "And you did your

part very well, young man. But let me advise you to keep away from the neighbourhood of Senator Norman. You might get into serious trouble."

Merriam did not reply or smile but handed him the hat.

"There's a taxi ready," said Rockwell, turning from the telephone into which he had been speaking.

"Thank you," said the Mayor. He looked at Mollie June, who stood some distance from him:

"I hope you will forgive me, Mrs. Norman, for my—rudeness earlier this evening. I am afraid I was too angry then to know what I was saying."

Like Merriam, Mollie June did not answer or smile. Possibly she was imitating his demeanour. But she bowed slightly.

"Really," interjected Alicia, "Mollie June had never seen Mr.—Mr. Wilson since before she was married until five minutes before you came in."

"Quite so. Of course," said the Mayor. He held out his hand to Aunt Mary. "You are a wonderful woman, Miss Norman."

"George shall telephone before noon," she replied, shaking hands like a man.

"Till then at least you can depend on me."

He turned to Alicia.

Alicia kept his hand a long minute. "We have always liked you, Mr. Black—we women," she said. "In your new rôle we shall admire you so much!"

"I would do much to win your admiration," returned the Mayor, somewhat guardedly gallant.

"Good night, Father Murray. Good night, Rockwell—you precious reformer! Good night, Mr. Wilson. That's only a stage name, isn't it? Well, good night, all!"

The suave politician bowed himself out.

CHAPTER X

A SENATOR MISSING

THE members of the group that remained looked at one another. Alicia dropped into a chair.

"Whew!" she said.

Father Murray crossed quickly from the doorway, where he had stood silent ever since his shamefaced entrance, to Aunt Mary's side.

"Wonderful, Miss Norman!" he cried.

Aunt Mary smiled at him—her first smile in that scene. "Thank you, Arthur," she said.

But she added instantly to Rockwell:

"See if George is *there*. Telephone. He must be by now. Then you and Arthur must take a taxi and go after him and bring him back here. The number is Harrison 3731."

Rockwell turned back to the telephone.

Merriam walked over to Mollie June and put his hands on the back of the chair in which she had been sitting prior to the entrance of Alicia.

"Hadn't you better sit down?" he said.

"Yes, if you'll move it up a little." She wanted to be closer to the rest of the group.

He pushed the chair forward, and she sat and smiled up at him:

94

" Thank you! "

A woman's eyes are never so appealingly beautiful as in a quick upward glance. Merriam fell suddenly more deeply in love with her than he had ever been. And he was for the moment very happy. There was something between them, something very slight, as tenuous and as innocent as youth itself, but existent and precious.

Rockwell turned from the telephone.

" He's not *there*," he said, " and he's not been there."

(There was a tacit conspiracy among them, on account of Mollie June, not to refer more definitely to George's destination.)

" Not! " exclaimed Aunt Mary. Like the men, she was still standing. She looked at Alicia. " The driver was instructed to go directly there? "

" Yes," said Alicia. Then she added in a low tone:

" The driver was Simpson."

" Simpson! " Aunt Mary echoed. " That's dangerous. Why didn't you tell me that before? "

The reader will have guessed the explanation of Aunt Mary's presence, and Alicia's and Father Murray's, and I insert it here only to gratify his sense of acumen: that Alicia and Murray, " keeping an eye on " Mollie June and Aunt Mary in accordance with Rockwell's plan, in the hotel lobby, had witnessed the former's unexpected departure in response to Merriam's summons, and had joined Miss Norman to find out what had happened; and that Aunt Mary, who was more than a match for both of them, especially in their alarm over Mollie June's being dragged into the affair, had obtained first an inkling and presently the whole story of the plot, and had insisted on coming upstairs, and had entered through the bedroom.

Alicia did not reply to Aunt Mary's question. Indeed she hardly had time to do so, for Aunt Mary followed it quickly with another of a more practical character:

"What time is it?"

Merriam was the most prompt in producing his watch.   "Ten o'clock," he said.

"And it was barely eight when George left the hotel. How long should it have taken to get there?"

"Less than half an hour," said Rockwell.

"Are you sure he's not there?   They might have lied to you."

"They might.   But I didn't think so."

"Mr. Rockwell and I can go and see," volunteered Father Murray, who seemed very eager to be helpful.

While Aunt Mary was considering this suggestion, Merriam had an idea.

"My voice is very like Senator Norman's?" he asked.

"Yes, it is," said Aunt Mary.

"Then let me telephone."

"Good!" cried Rockwell.   "From the bedroom." This was, of course, to spare Mollie June.

"Very well," said Aunt Mary.

The two men stepped into George Norman's bed-room—the one into which Mollie June had earlier retreated. As they did so, Aunt Mary's eyes fol-lowed Merriam with the appraising look which they had held whenever she regarded him through-out the evening.

Rockwell shut the door.

"Harrison 3731," he said. "Say, 'This is George Norman,' and ask for 'Jennie.'"

The telephone was on the night table. Merriam sat down on the edge of the bed and raised the in-strument. He realised that he had not the slight-est idea what to expect. Rockwell sat beside him, close enough to hear what should come through the receiver.

In a moment Merriam had the connection. A not unmusical voice said: "Who is it, please?"

"This is George Norman. Is Jennie there?"

"Why, Georgie, boy! Don't you know me? You always do. And you ought to!" A tender little laugh followed, which thrilled Merriam in spite of himself.

"I didn't at first," he answered and stopped at a loss.

Rockwell put his mouth close to Merriam's ear and formed a tunnel from the one orifice to the other with his hands. "Can I see you to-night, dearie?" he prompted.

"Can I see you to-night, dearie?" Merriam obediently repeated.

"Oh, can you come? Goodie! But"—the unmistakably loving voice was lowered—"you must be careful, Georgie."

"Careful?" Merriam queried cautiously.

"Yes. Some one thinks you're here already."

"Who?"

"I don't know. Some man. He wouldn't tell me who he was. He called up just a minute ago. He was awfully sure you were here. He wouldn't believe me when I said you weren't. Is it dangerous?" There was a touching note of anxiety in Jennie's voice.

"I guess not."

"Can you come anyway?" eagerly.

"I'm not sure. Don't wait for me long. I'll come within an hour if I can get away."

"You'll telephone again?"

"Yes—if I can."

"Georgie, boy!" There followed a little sound of lips moved in a certain way—unmistakably a kiss.

John Merriam played up with an effectiveness that surprised himself very much.

"Dearie!" he whispered tenderly into the telephone, "good night!"—and abruptly hung up.

"You don't need much prompting!" exclaimed Rockwell, rising. "Well, she didn't lie to me."

"No," Merriam assented confusedly. Whatever else he had anticipated from Norman's mistress, the disreputable manicurist, it had not been that note of sincere affection or that he himself would be for an instant carried off his feet. As he automatically followed Rockwell, who made for the sitting room, he was unwillingly conscious of a new charity for George Norman.

"He's not there," Rockwell reported. "And he hasn't been."

"Sure?" Aunt Mary looked at Merriam.

Our hero nodded. He could not speak. And he dared not look at Mollie June, of whose bright eyes fixed on his face he was nevertheless acutely aware.

In a moment, however, it was of Aunt Mary's gaze that he was sensible. She seemed to read him through. He thought, ridiculously, that that momentary telephonic tenderness could not be hid from her.

But when she spoke her question both relieved and startled him.

"At what hour in the morning does your train go?"

"It goes to-night. At 2:00 A. M."

"If George is back here by then, it does," said Aunt Mary. "If not, you stay."

"But I *must* go to-night," cried Merriam, suddenly awakened to realities and feeling as though the curtain had descended abruptly on some mad combination of melodrama and farce. "I must meet my classes in the morning!"

Aunt Mary, who must have sat down while the two men were telephoning, rose and walked up to Merriam.

"Mr. Merriam," she said, "you more than any

one else are responsible for the present situation—
because of your sending for Mrs. Norman. I don't
ask why you did that, but you did it. If you hadn't
stepped outside your part that way, I verily believe, when I look at you, that the trick could have
been played as Mr. Rockwell planned it. The
Mayor would not have seen Crockett downstairs.
I don't believe he would have recognised you. He
would have signed the Ordinance and gone away
committed and ignorant of the deception. Now
he's only half committed, and he has recognised
you as an impostor. If he doesn't hear from
George Norman by noon to-morrow as I promised,
if he turns against us and tells his story, he can
ruin us—all." (She said " all," but she glanced at
Mollie June.) "And now we don't know where
George is. As soon as we find him, you can go.
But Mayor Black *must* get a message from Senator Norman before noon to-morrow—from the true
one or the false one! Do you see? Until we find
George you must stay."

"Yes, by Jove!" cried Rockwell. "You can't
back out now. You can telegraph to—where
is it? "

"Riceville," said Alicia, who was leaning excitedly forward in her chair. "Oh, you will! "

Merriam looked at Alicia. The same combination of appeal and admiration in her eyes which he
had seen her work a few minutes before on the
Mayor did not move him.

His eyes travelled to the face of Mollie June.

She was not leaning forward, but sat erect on the edge of her chair. There was a flush of excitement—was it eagerness?—on her cheeks. Unwillingly he compared her with the warm seductiveness of the voice on the telephone. She was not like that,—though perhaps she could be. But she was radiantly bright and pure, a girl, a woman, to be worshipped—and protected from all evil. He remembered how he had wished to help her. He had said he would be always ready. Now was his chance. And he desired passionately to expiate his involuntary infidelity of feeling and tone over the telephone. He rose superior to the cares, the duties, of a "professor," even before she spoke.

"Oh, please—Mr. Merriam," she said.

Merriam smiled at her, but looked back at Aunt Mary.

"You think it very necessary?" he asked—not because he had not decided but to avoid any shadow of compromising Mollie June by seeming to yield directly to her.

"I do," said Aunt Mary.

"Then of course I'll stay," said Merriam.

CHAPTER XI

CONFESSIONS OF WAITER NO. 73

FROM a sleep which had been heavy but was becoming restless and dreamful, Merriam was awakened about seven o'clock the next morning by a knocking at his door. He leaned over and pulled the little chain of the night lamp, and as the light glowed asked, " Who is it? "

" Rockwell," came the answer.

By a rather athletic bit of stretching Merriam was able to turn the key in his lock without getting out of bed. " Come in," he called.

Rockwell entered, closed the door behind him, and stood looking down at Merriam, who had lain back on his pillow.

" Slept well? " he asked.

" Like a football player," laughed Merriam, somehow ashamed of this fact.

" Feeling fit? "

" Certainly. Always feel fit."

For a moment longer Rockwell looked, with perhaps a touch of an older man's envy of the unconscionable imperturbability of youthful health. Then he said:

" Well, I have news."

Merriam waited.

"About half an hour ago I called up 'Jennie' again. When I said I was a friend of Norman's, she admitted he was there. By asking a good many questions I learned that he turned up about two o'clock this morning and that he was very drunk. I judge he's having a touch of D. T. 'Jennie' was evidently rather disgusted at his arriving so late and in that condition—after your affectionate tone earlier in the evening, you know."

Merriam evaded this thrust with a question:

"Where can he have been in the meantime?"

"That is a point on which we shall have to seek information from our friend Simpson. Since telephoning I have seen Miss Norman, and we have agreed to order breakfast for all of us in Senator Norman's rooms with Simpson to serve us. He goes on duty again at seven o'clock, and I have asked that he be sent here as soon as he reports to take a breakfast order."

"Why here?"

"Well, he will be more likely to talk freely to you and me alone than to you and me and Miss Norman—to say nothing of Mrs. Norman. And, if he has played some trick on us, he might refuse to go to Senator Norman's suite, but this room will mean nothing to him. Of course, he may not show up at all this morning. Ah, there he is, I hope!"

A vigorous knock had sounded at the door. It proved, however, to be only a porter with Merriam's suit case and hand bag, for which the industrious

Rockwell had also sent so early that morning to the more modest hotel at which Merriam had been registered.

"Now I can dress," said Merriam. "I was afraid I should have to turn waiter myself, having only evening clothes to put on."

"Yes, get into your things," said Rockwell, "and let me think some more. This conspiracy business takes a lot more thinking than mere Reform!"

Merriam hurried through a bath—a tubful of hot water early in the morning was so unwonted a luxury to a citizen of Riceville that he could not bring himself to forego it even on this occasion—and began to dress carefully, realising with pleasant excitement that he was to have breakfast with Mollie June.

He had no more than got into his trousers when another knock came at the door.

Rockwell motioned to Merriam to step into the bathroom and himself went to the door. "Come in," he said and opened it, keeping behind it.

Sure enough, Simpson stepped into the room with his napkin and order pad.

Rockwell promptly closed the door behind him, locked it, and stood with his back against it. He also pushed the switch for the center chandelier—for only the dim night lamp had been on.

In the sudden light Simpson whirled with a startled and most unprofessional agility to face Rockwell.

"Good morning, Simpson."

The waiter fairly moistened his lips before he could answer.

"Good morning, Mr. Rockwell."

The man's face was certainly haggard. His eyes even were a trifle bloodshot. It was clear he had had a strange night. But after a moment of hostile confrontation the professional impassivity of a waiter—which is perhaps the ultimate perfection of *sang froid*—descended about him like a cloak and mask.

"I was sent to this room—Mr. Wilson's room, I understood—to take a breakfast order."

"Right, Simpson!" cried Merriam cheerily, emerging from the bathroom in his shirt sleeves.

For a moment the human gleamed again through the eyes of the functionary.

"Are you Mr. Wilson?" he asked. His manner was perfect servility, but there was mockery and malice in the tone.

"Yes, Simpson," said Merriam. "This morning I am Mr. Wilson. I have read of an English duke. who puts on a new pair of trousers each morning. But I go him one better. I put on an entire new personality each morning."

"Very good, sir," was the ironical, stage-butler reply to this sally. "The grapefruit is very good this morning. Will you have some?"

Merriam glanced at Rockwell.

"Very likely we'll have some," said the latter, "but we want something else first."

"Before the grapefruit?" inquired Simpson.

"Yes, before the grapefruit," said Rockwell, a trifle sharply. "And what we propose to have before the grapefruit is a bit of talk with you, Mr. Simpson—about last night. Do you care to sit down?" He pointed to a chair.

Simpson was undoubtedly agitated, but he controlled himself excellently. He even lifted his eyebrows:

"I hope I know my place, sir."

He raised his pad and wrote on it.

"Grapefruit," he said with insolent suavity. "For two? And then what? We have some excellent ham."

"Damn your ham!" cried Rockwell. He snatched the man's pad and threw it on the floor. "Sit down in that chair and drop this damned pose! We're going to talk to you man to man."

But Simpson only stooped and picked up his pad.

"Mr. Rockwell," he said, "I know my place. It is a very humble one. It is to take orders—for meals, to be served in this hotel. So long as that is what you want I am yours to command. But"— the American citizen stood up in him; no European waiter could have said it—"outside of that I am my own master as much as you are. When you call me 'Mr. Simpson' and tell me to sit down, I don't have to do it. And I don't have to talk of my personal affairs unless I choose, any more than any one else!"

For an instant he glared at Rockwell as one angry man at another, his equal. Then he quietly

became the waiter again. He lifted his pad and
poised his pencil:

"Shall we say some ham?"

Rockwell looked at him a moment longer. Then
he laughed: "Ham let it be!"

"Yes, sir," said Simpson, deferentially writing.
"And some baked potatoes, perhaps? And coffee?"

"Yes," said Rockwell, "and the telephone book.
Hand me the telephone book, please."

Simpson hesitated, but this was clearly within
the line of his duties.

"Yes, sir," he said, and stepped towards the
stand on which the book lay.

"Wait!" said Rockwell. "Perhaps it isn't
necessary. I think you can tell me the number I
want."

He paused a moment to let this sink in. Then:

"Miss Alicia Wayward's number. I see I shall
have to bring her here. You see," he explained
pleasantly, "I have locked the door. There are
two of us against you."

He indicated Merriam, who still stood in the
bathroom door, following the progress of the interview with excited interest.

"We are going to keep you here, not by any
authority that we as guests of this hotel may have
over you—as you have very well pointed out, we
have none in such a matter,—but by simple force,
till Miss Wayward can come down. We shall see
whether she can make you talk."

To Merriam's astonishment the waiter, with a

sound somewhere between a sigh and a groan, sank into the chair which he had thus far so pertinaciously refused to take. For a moment he stared at the floor. Then he raised his eyes to Rockwell:

"What do you want to know?"

"That's better," said Rockwell, leaving the door and preparing to sit down opposite Simpson. "Will you have a cigar?"

Simpson shook his head and repeated his question.

"What do you want?"

Rockwell dropped into his chair and glancing at Merriam pointed to another seat. Merriam was too much excited to care to sit down, but he came forward and leaned on the back of the chair.

"We want to know about last night, of course," said Rockwell. "At five minutes to eight Senator Norman got into the taxi which you were driving. At about two o'clock this morning he tumbled into Madame Couteau's, delirious with drink. We want the whole story of what happened between eight and two."

Simpson sat on the edge of his chair, his hands on his knees. His order pad was under one hand, and its flexure showed that he was exerting intense pressure. His napkin dangled loosely half off his arm. He was looking at the floor again.

He remained in this position for a number of seconds, the other two men intently regarding him. Then he straightened up, pushed himself farther back in his chair, and looked at Rockwell.

"You shall have it," he said.

For a moment he stared. Then:

"I hate Senator Norman—enough to kill him."

The reader will observe that I use no exclamation points in punctuating Simpson's sentence. There were none in his delivery of it. But it was the more startling on that account.

"Do you know why?" he unexpectedly demanded.

"No," said Rockwell.

"Five years ago I was butler to Mr. Wayward. The—the—girl you call Madame Couteau was the parlour maid there. Her real name is Jennie Higgins. I was in love with her, and she had promised to marry me. I had a little money saved up. At that time Senator Norman's first wife was still alive, who was Mr. Wayward's sister, you know, Miss Wayward's aunt. Senator Norman came often to the house. He took a fancy to Jennie and turned her head. The fact that she was in his own brother-in-law's house made no difference to him. She—went off with him—on a lake cruise, in his yacht. When they came back he set her up in that flat and got her work as a manicurist. Ever since he has been her paramour!"

The odd, old-fashioned word, which Simpson must have gleaned from some novel, came out queerly. But it served to express his bitterness as no ordinary word could have done.

"That's all. A parlour maid ruined. A butler cheated of his wife. It's nothing, of course."

He was looking down again. Neither Rockwell nor Merriam ventured to speak. When he raised his eyes there was a gleam in them.

"Last night I had him in my power." (One sensed novels again.) "In my taxi, not knowing who I was. I was minded to kill him. You had told me to drive him directly to—to Jennie's. Not much! I drove as fast as I dared out Michigan Avenue. For a long time he suspected nothing. He thought he was on his way to the Mayor's, and that was the right direction. But when I turned into Washington Park he got scared. He called through the tube to know where in hell I was going. I answered, 'This is Simpson. You can try jumping, if you like—into hell!' I put the machine up to forty miles an hour. He opened the door once, but I guess he didn't dare try it. He shut it again. Of course, it was pure luck I didn't get stopped for speeding. But I got through Washington Park and across the Midway and out into a lonely place at the south end of Jackson Park. Then I stopped and got down and opened the door and ordered him out."

The man stopped. When he spoke again there was more contempt than hatred in his voice.

"The coward. He went down on his knees on the wet road and cried and begged me not to hurt him. He said he was sorry, and he didn't know I cared so much, and he would make it all right yet. He would give me a lot of money and set me up in a business, and I could marry Jennie after all,

and wouldn't I forgive him and go back to town
and have a drink? The worm! I could have spit
on him. *Senator* Norman!

"He saved his life all right," he added reflectively. "If he had showed fight I would have
strangled him and thrown his body in the Lake."
Simpson shuddered a little. "But you couldn't
strangle a crying baby. I kicked him once or
twice. But what more could I do? He kept
begging me not to hurt him but to go back to town
and have a drink. That gave me an idea. I jerked
him up and pitched him into the car and drove back
to a saloon. We sat at a table and drank, and he
kept offering me money and saying I should marry
Jennie. As if I would take his leavings! He
drank a lot. I only took one or two to steady my
nerves—poured out the rest. But he drank four or
five cocktails. Then we went on in the taxi to another saloon and did it again. And then to another. And about midnight we ended up at a cheap
dance hall on the West Side, and I turned him
loose among the roughnecks and the women there.

"He was pretty drunk—told everybody who he
was and showed his money,—and in a few minutes
a lot of the girls were around him to get the money
away from him. Most of the men they were with
didn't mind—egged them on. Pretty soon he had
a dozen couples in the bar with him and was paying
for drinks all around. But one big foreigner, who
was with the prettiest girl in the room, was ugly.
When Norman, after buying a second round of

drinks, tried to kiss his girl, he roared out at him and knocked him down. But Norman only stumbled up again with his lip bleeding and begged his pardon and handed the girl a fifty-dollar bill and bought drinks again. And then he got his arm about another girl and took her out to dance. It was an' hour before I found him again. He was sitting on the stairs, with his collar off, crazy drunk—seeing things—and all cleaned out as to money.

"I thought then he was about ripe for what I wanted. I carried him downstairs and put him in the taxi and drove to—Madame Couteau's! There I carried him up to her flat and propped him against the door and knocked and then waited part way down the stairs. When the door was opened he fell in, and I ran downstairs and took my taxi home."

Evidently Simpson had finished his tale. And it had done him good to tell it. He was much less agitated than when he began. He looked steadily rather than angrily at Rockwell.

"That's the story you wanted," he said. "Of course now you can get me fired and blacklisted. It's little I'll care."

Rockwell had let his cigar go out while Simpson talked. Now he lit it again with a good deal of deliberation. He was evidently thinking. Even Merriam perceived the point that was uppermost in his mind, namely, that with Norman still at Jennie's they had need of Simpson's silence and would be likely to need his help again. They must try to conciliate him and win his loyal support.

"I see no reason why I should do anything like that," Rockwell began, referring to Simpson's defiant suggestion. "I can hardly pronounce your conduct virtuous. But it was very natural—very excusable. It's lucky you did no worse!"'

(Merriam had a sudden vision of the horrid predicament they would have been in if Norman had actually been murdered in Jackson Park at the very time when he was impersonating him at the hotel.)

"Still," continued Rockwell, "I think you made a mistake."

"A mistake!" echoed Simpson.

"Yes.—Do you still love—Miss Higgins?"

"What's that to you?"

"Evidently you do. Why didn't you take his offer—his money, and marry her? It would have been the sensible thing to do and the kind thing to her. You might be happy after all. Of course, if you're too stern a moralist!"

The man's face worked queerly. "It's not that. But she wouldn't have a waiter now. And he wouldn't have done it—let her alone."

"Well, perhaps not, as things stood. But he will now. Have you seen the morning papers?"

"The papers? No, sir."

"If you'll read them you'll find that Senator Norman has broken with all his old life and turned

over a new leaf entirely, which he can't turn back.
You have helped him do it, in fact!"

"What's the idea?" growled Simpson suspiciously.

"Listen, Mr. Simpson."

Rapidly Rockwell sketched the principal events
which had taken place at the hotel while the waiter
was driving his enemy about Chicago: Merriam's
impersonation, the Mayor's failure to veto the Ordinance in time, and the necessity which both the
Mayor and Norman were now under of breaking
with the "interests" and coming out as the candidates of the Reform League.

"In that rôle," he concluded, "George Norman
will have to lead a strictly virtuous life. It will
be the business of his friends and backers—my
business, for example—to see that he does so. I
will personally undertake to see that you get the
money he promised you. All you will have to do
is to make it up with Jennie. You may not be able
or willing to do that right away. But in a few
months —— There's no reason why you shouldn't
be set up in a nice little business of your own—a
delicatessen or caterer's, or a taxicab firm, or
whatever you would like—in some other city, with
Jennie for your wife. Will you think it over?"

Simpson looked at Rockwell and then at Merriam.

"You certainly are as like as two plates," he
said irrelevantly to the latter.

"Won't you think it over?" returned Merriam,

as persuasively as if he had been reasoning with some irate patron of the Riceville High School.

"Yes," said Simpson after a bit, "I'll think it over."

"In the meantime," said Rockwell, "you must keep still about all this, of course. And we may need your help again—for taxi driving and so forth."

"What if I choose to blow the whole thing?"

"In that case you will do more than any one else could to help Norman to the thing he will most want—a reconciliation with Crockett and the rest of the gang. And he will go on in his old ways—Jennie included."

Rockwell let Simpson digest that for a moment, and then said:

"Well, think it over as you have promised. And now we really do want breakfast."

Simpson got to his feet. He straightened the napkin on his arm and mechanically enunciated his servile formula:

"Yes, sir."

"And, Simpson!"

"Yes, sir?"

"I will talk with you again this afternoon. Till then, at least, keep your mouth shut and think. Think sensibly."

"Very good, sir."

Waiter No. 73 bowed gravely and left the bedroom.

CHAPTER XII

GRAPEFRUIT AND TELEGRAMS

WHEN the door closed behind Simpson, Rockwell and Merriam naturally looked at each other.

"Poor fellow!" said Merriam.

In spite of himself his mind was visited by a tantalising recollection of Jennie's voice as it had come to him over the telephone. With no more evidence than that he was inclined to think that Simpson was right in saying that she would not have a waiter now. But it was impossible to speak of this to Rockwell.

The latter had apparently dismissed the incident and was looking at his watch.

"It's nearly eight o'clock," he said. "Put the rest of your things on and go down to Norman's rooms on the next floor. You're to have breakfast there with Miss Norman and Mrs. Norman. You'd better go down the stairs rather than in the elevator; you will be less likely to meet some one who will take you for the Senator. I am going to hunt up Dr. Hobart, the house physician here, and take him with me to this Madame Couteau's, or Jennie's, to see Norman. We must get him on his feet at once. A hotel physician will be the very man for that."

116

" I must shave," said Merriam.

" Oh, never mind that. Time is precious."

Merriam thought of the train which he now planned to take. It left at nine-fifteen and would get him to Riceville a little after noon. He remembered, too, that he must telegraph to his assistant principal that he would miss the morning session. And he thought of the coming breakfast hour with Mollie June. Certainly time *was* precious to him. Nevertheless he said decidedly:

" I'm going to shave all the same."

Rockwell looked at him with a comprehending smile. "All right, my boy," said the older man. " Doubtless it's very necessary. Hurry up and try not to cut yourself. I'll run along with the doctor."

He moved to the door, stopped with his hand on the knob to say, " I shall probably drop in at the rooms before you're through breakfast," and was gone.

Merriam sighed a certain relief and went into the bathroom to shave.

A few minutes later, following Rockwell's injunction, he descended to the floor below by the stairs rather than the elevator. He forgot even to look at the pretty floor clerk on Floor Three, who last night was wearing his—Norman's—violets.

When he knocked at the door labeled 323 it was the voice he most desired to hear that said, " Come in."

He opened the door. The rose-and-white room was bright with morning sunshine, and half way

down its length Mollie June, in a blue satin breakfast coat, with a lacy boudoir cap covering her hair,
was standing before the little table which held the
bowl of roses.

"Good morning, Mr.—John," she said.

He half perceived that her voice sounded tired
and a little sad. But the daintiness of breakfast
coats and boudoir caps was as strange in Merriam's
world as white shoulders were. His eyes drank it
in delightfully. In his pleasure her note of sadness escaped him. He answered almost gaily:

"Good morning—Mollie June!"

His tone probably betrayed his mood, and I dare
say Mollie June guessed the reason for his happiness. But she ignored both mood and reason. She
had turned back to the roses.

"Come and help me," she said. "These flowers
must have fresh water."

Merriam pushed the door shut behind him and
advanced rapidly. I am almost afraid he might
have taken her in his arms. But Mollie June was
already half way across the room with the roses, to
lay them on a newspaper which she had previously
spread on the seat of a straight-backed chair. So
all that Merriam got his hands on was the bowl.

"Empty it in there," said Mollie June, indicating the bathroom between the sitting room and
Norman's empty bedroom, "and fill it with cold
water."

Thankful that no reply was immediately demanded, Merriam did as he was bid.

When he reëntered the sitting room with the fresh water, Mollie June stooped over the chair, gathered up the roses, and came towards him.

" Set it back in the same place," she said.

Merriam did so, and she came up to him—that is to say, to the bowl—and inserted the stems all together, and with her pink fingers wet from the cool water deftly arranged the blossoms. Then, drying her finger tips on a very small handkerchief, she turned and raised her eyes to him gravely. He saw at last that she was pale—that she had been wakeful. Perhaps she had been crying. In sudden concern he stood dumb.

" Did you sleep well? " she asked.

He mustered his forces to reply.

" I am afraid I did," he said, ashamed.

She looked at him forgivingly.

" Of course you must have been dreadfully tired," she said. " I hardly slept at all," she added. " I am terribly worried about George. We didn't even know where he was until—a little while ago." Evidently Rockwell had already reported some part, at least, of Simpson's disclosure.

For a moment they stood silent, tacitly avoiding reference to George Norman's ascertained whereabouts.

Then Mollie June raised her eyes again.

" I'm worried, too, about—what we did last night. We mustn't do—so, again."

She met his eyes, very serious.

" No! " Merriam assented.

"I can't call you 'Mr. Merriam,' though," she cried. "And I mustn't call you 'John.' I've decided to call you 'Mr. John'!"

"Thank you," said Merriam gravely. He was deeply touched by the unconscious confession.

Mollie June turned away. "I must tell Aunt Mary you are here."

Just then there came a knocking at the hall door.

For an instant the boy and girl stared at each other as though in guilty alarm. Merriam started to go to the door. But Mollie June had recovered her wits.

"No," she said. "You must be careful about being seen. Sit there." She pointed to the armchair which still faced the gas log between the windows at the end of the room farthest from the hall. "I'll see who it is."

It proved to be no one more dangerous than Simpson, who with an assistant was prepared to set up a table in the sitting room and serve the grapefruit.

And even while Mollie June was bidding him come in, Aunt Mary entered from the bedroom. With her was Miss Alicia Wayward, apparently much excited, with her hands full of newspapers.

Merriam stood up, and Alicia, catching sight of him, dropped on the floor the paper she held in her right hand and advanced with an air of eagerness.

"Oh, Mr.——," she began. Then, as Merriam took her hand, she stopped short in her sentence, laughed, and said, "Who are you this morning?"

Merriam, whom Alicia always stimulated to play
up, bowed over her hand as elegantly as he could
and replied:

"Senator Norman, I believe—at your service.
Good morning, Miss Norman," he added, politely,
to the older woman.

Aunt Mary merely nodded, rather grimly, and
turned away as if to inspect Simpson's preparation
of the breakfast table. Merriam wondered how
much of Simpson's confession Rockwell had found
time to report to her.

But Alicia gave him little time for speculation.

"Well, Senator," she rejoined, withdrawing her
hand (you were always conscious when Alicia gave
her hand and when she withdrew it), "you and the
Mayor have made quite a noise in the world this
morning. See!"

She displayed the newspaper which she still held
in her left hand. It was one of the leading Chicago
dailies, which invariably prints one bold black
headline across the top of the entire front page.
The topic may be a world war or a dog fight, but
the headline is always there in the same size and
startling blackness of type. This morning it read:

Mayor Black Signs Ordinance

And one of the columns below carried the further
head:

The Mayor and Senator Norman
Reported to Have Broken
With Traction Interests

"Oh!" exclaimed Mollie June, who had approached and read these captions. She looked at Merriam with wide-open eyes. I surmise that the newspaper headlines gave her, as indeed they gave to Merriam himself, the first actual realisation of the public interest attaching to what they had really felt to be a little private drama of their own.

Aunt Mary had joined them.

"Mr. Black has definitely signed it, you see," she said, with a touch of triumph in her tone.

It appeared that the Mayor had not gone to the Council meeting at all, and the paper did not fail to point out that the Ordinance had become law without his signature, under the provisions of the City Charter, at nine o'clock; but late in the evening, shortly before the Council adjourned, the document had arrived by a messenger, with the Mayor's signature attached.

Reporters had immediately set out in relentless pursuit and had routed the Mayor out of bed at his house between twelve and one o'clock and obtained a brief interview; the substance of which was that the public interest of the city demanded the improved conditions which the new law would insure, and that he was proud to complete with his approval the public-spirited action of the Councilmen in passing it.

The rest was mere rumour and speculation, interlarded with many prudent "it is said's," but it seemed that some if not all of it must have been inspired by the Mayor. "It was said" that an im-

portant representative of the Traction interests had
seen Senator Norman in his rooms at the Hotel
De Soto early in the evening and pleaded with him
the cause of the interested bondholders and stock-
holders, whose investments would be imperilled by
the changes involved, but that he had stood firm on
the ground of the public welfare. " It was said,"
too, that later Mayor Black had had a long conference with the Senator—well, it *had* been rather
long,—and that they had agreed that the interests
of the plain people of Chicago must at all costs
decide the issue. " It was said," finally, that both
Senator Norman and Mayor Black would probably
join forces with the Reform League, whose program
they had finally so powerfully supported, in demanding and obtaining other needed improvements
in municipal conditions.

From all of which it seemed to be clear that the
Mayor, having taken an hour or so to think over
the situation in which he found himself, had become convinced of the soundness of Aunt Mary's
logic and had decided, without waiting for any
further communication from the Norman camp, to
claim the credit for the Ordinance and appeal for
popular support thereon, taking care, however, to
involve Senator Norman's name so that the real
Norman should be compelled to join forces with
him in his new departure.

By the time the column of news and comment
and a brief and cautious editorial on the occurrence
had been read out by Alicia and one or two other

papers glanced at, Simpson had set up and laid his table and had his first course served. He respectfully approached and inquired if they were ready for breakfast.

"Certainly!" said Aunt Mary.

Merriam looked at his watch. It was half past eight.

"I ought to send my telegram to Riceville first," he said, "to let them know I shall be there on the noon train."

"After the grapefruit," said Aunt Mary, with a decided note in her voice which led Merriam to look at her inquiringly.

But he desired to exhibit the coolness of a man of the world, to whom telegrams were customary incidents of daily living and who habitually ran close to the wind in the matter of trains. So he acquiesced with a bookish "As you please," and moved with the others to the table.

Simpson had decorated the center of the board with one of the hotel's slim glass vases holding a couple of pink carnations. Mollie June regarded this ornament with disfavour.

"Let's have the roses instead, Mr. John," she said.

And Merriam, to the scandal of Simpson, himself removed the carnations and set the bowl of roses in their place.

They said little over the grapefruit. Alicia added a few humorous comments on points in the newspaper article, but Aunt Mary was divided be-

tween an anxious absent-mindedness and a curious
questioning scrutiny of Merriam, and Merriam was
distracted between a suppressed worry over his
telegram and approaching train time and the delight of stolen glances at—Mrs. Senator Norman.
As for Mrs. Senator Norman, she devoted herself
chiefly to the fruit. Once or twice, in looking up,
she almost unavoidably intercepted one of Merriam's guilty glances. When this happened, she
met his eyes frankly but with a gravity that was
pathetically, forgivingly rebuking.

Presently Simpson was removing the fruit rinds
and placing finger bowls. Merriam looked quickly
at his watch again and spoke to the waiter:

"Bring me a telegraph form, please."

Aunt Mary's absent-mindedness instantly van-
ished.

"What message are you going to send?" she
asked in a restrained voice.

"Missed night train. Will arrive at noon."

"No!" said Aunt Mary. "Mr. Merriam," she
pursued quickly, "until George is brought back
here you must stay. After all this in the papers
this morning there will be scores of people to see
him to-day. He is known to be a late riser and
never sees any one before ten or they would have
been here before this. In a very few minutes they
will begin to come. We will put off most of them,
of course. But there are likely to be some whom
we can't put off. We can't tell where George is,
and we can't say we don't know where he is, and

there will be one or two to whom we can't say we won't tell where he is. We must have you in reserve. You shall go to bed in George's room, ill with—with—lumbago. Dr. Hobart will attend you. When absolutely necessary we can show a man into the room, and you can say a few words. I will tell you what to say in each case. You can have your head half way under the covers, and can make your voice weak and husky. You will be safe enough from detection. Then by this evening at the latest we shall bring George back, and you can go down to Riceville on the night train. You will only have missed one day, and you will have saved us from a most serious dilemma."

There was an appeal in the elderly woman's voice to which Merriam was not insensible, though the pull of habitual regularity at his school was strong in him.

It is to be feared that Alicia spoiled Aunt Mary's effect. Across the table from Merriam, she was partly hidden from him by the flowers. But she leaned forward, bringing her face almost beside the roses, and spoke in her most honeyed tones:

" Oh, do, Mr. Merriam! How can you resist it? " she added. " If I were a man and had the chance to be Mollie June's husband even for a day ——" She stopped with her archest smile.

Mollie June, with possibly the slightest augmentation of colour, brought forward a practical argument.

" Since you will miss the morning anyway, it

won't much matter if you miss the whole day.
You haven't but one class in the afternoon, have
you? "

" Only senior algebra," said Merriam.

" Miss Eldon can take that."

" I suppose she could," said Merriam, who was
realising that on this particular day advanced
algebra would be to him the most distasteful of all
branches of human learning.

" Then you'll stay and help us—Mr. John! "

The reader will perceive that this simple appeal
was really much superior to any which the too
sophisticated and calculating Alicia could contrive.
A touch of wistfulness came into Mollie June's face
with the word " help." His high promise of the
night before was irresistibly recalled. And " Mr.
John " reminded him of the delightfulness of fresh
water for roses and of the unconscious confession
which her compromise name for him had implied.

Alicia discreetly retired behind the roses, and
Aunt Mary waited with lips somewhat grimly
pursed.

Then, while Merriam hesitated, with his eyes
on Mollie June's face—we must suppose that
he was weighing her very practical argument,—the
telephone rang.

Simpson, with telegraph blanks in his hand, answered it, and reported that Mr. Rockwell wished
to speak to Senator Norman.

" This is—Norman," said Merriam cautiously
into the telephone.

"Ah!" said Rockwell's voice. "Well, you'll be pleased to learn that you are quieter. You aren't seeing things any more." (I'm not sure of that, thought Merriam.) "But you, he has a severe cold—fever and a cough—touch of bronchitis, probably. Hobart says he can't possibly be moved till to-night. Anyway, I don't see how we could get him into the hotel till then. You must stay, Merriam."

"All right," said Merriam, surprising his interlocutor by his ready acquiescence, "I'll stay."

"Good! I'll be down at the hotel in half an hour." Rockwell rang off.

Merriam turned to face the three women.

When Aunt Mary heard the news about George, she held out her hand to Simpson for the telegraph forms and wrote.

In a moment she read:

"'Ill with a touch of bronchitis. Hope to be back to-morrow. John Merriam.' Will that do?"

"I suppose so," he assented.

His words were almost drowned by a loud knock at the door.

"Our day has begun," said Aunt Mary, rising with admirable composure. She handed the telegram to Simpson. "Send it at once. Into the bedroom, Mr. Merriam. Get into bed as soon as you can. You have bronchitis, you know,—not lumbago."

But before Merriam could obey the door was suddenly opened.

CHAPTER XIII

A CHANGE OF MANAGEMENT

THE man who thus burst into Senator Norman's sitting room at nine o'clock in the morning without waiting for an invitation was an unpleasant but important personage—none other than J. J. Thompson (one never thought of calling him " Mr."), Norman's private political manager in all matters that involved handling the people's vote.

He was a short, stoutish, belligerent type, about forty-five, with thin, untidy hair, a thin, untidy moustache, and, somewhere between the moustache and the hair, a pair of small blue eyes, which seemed incapable of any other expressions than aggressiveness and anger. Senator Norman—the real Norman—had long found him nearly as disagreeable as the reader will find him, but so useful in many political contingencies that he had never been able to bring himself to dispense with him.

Having popped explosively into the room, Thompson stopped short at sight of the three women. For the first instant or two he did not notice Merriam, who had quietly slipped into the great armchair that faced the gas log, with his back almost squarely to the room.

"Good morning, Mr. Thompson," said Aunt Mary. "We were just having breakfast."

Alicia and Mollie June still sat at the table, and Simpson stood a little at one side. Thompson knew who the two girls were, and they knew who he was, but he had never been presented in Norman's family except to Miss Norman—a fact which he resented keenly,—so they did not speak. Alicia sat back in her chair and stared insolently, while Mollie June leaned forward and rearranged a rose in the bowl.

"I'm sorry to break in this way," Thompson said—even he was slightly abashed,—"but I've got to speak to the Senator."

"Come back a little later, Mr. Thompson," ventured Merriam in a hoarse whisper.

The "Mr." was a false note, and its effect was to anger Thompson.

"No!" he cried, the pugnacious gleam that was never far below the surface of his little eyes appearing in them. "I've got to speak to you now! I've got a right to!"

He advanced. He would have passed the table so as to approach Merriam. But there was only a narrow space on either side of it, and in one of those avenues stood Simpson behind Alicia, while Aunt Mary had quietly moved into the other, standing with her hand on the back of the chair in which Merriam had been sitting. So Thompson found himself barricaded, as it were, and stopped short and shouted across the table and over the head of Mollie June.

" What in—what's the meaning of all this—this stuff in the papers? "

Thompson's difficulty in expressing himself under the handicap of the interdiction against profanity imposed by the presence of the women was a trifle ludicrous. But his tone and manner were almost as bad as an oath would have been.

Alicia's eyebrows rose. She rose herself.

" Perhaps we had better withdraw," she said.

If Merriam, who had never seen her in any other than a gracious and seductive mood, could have turned his head to look, he would have marvelled at her freezing disdain. Mollie June imitated her in rising and in a more youthful hauteur. Without waiting for any reply Alicia turned and walked into the bedroom, and Mollie June followed.

But feminine disdain, however magnificent, had little effect on Thompson. He was obviously relieved. He looked at Aunt Mary, plainly desiring that she should go too.

" No, I think I'll remain, Mr. Thompson," she said pleasantly.

Then he looked at Simpson, and the latter cast an inquiring glance at Aunt Mary.

" You may stay, please, Simpson," said she. " We shall be finishing our breakfast presently."

Before Thompson could digest this snub Alicia

reëntered from the bedroom. She carried a white knitted wool scarf, with which she went to Merriam.

"Don't you feel chilly, George?" she asked. "You can't be too careful with that throat."

She knelt down by his chair, put the scarf over his head, brought it down past his cheeks, tied it loosely under his chin, and threw the ends back over his shoulders.

"Now, lean back. Isn't that better? Mr. Norman has a severe cold," she said in the general direction of Thompson. "The doctor is afraid of bronchitis," she added, as she rose and drew the shades. "That light is getting too bright for your eyes."

She flashed a glance at Aunt Mary and returned to the bedroom.

Merriam had been feeling that it was only a matter of minutes before Thompson—whoever Thompson might be—would somehow force his way to his side and look down into his face and, probably, perceive the imposture as Mayor Black had done. But now, with the welcome aid of the scarf, he had the bravado to turn partly in his chair and say throatily:

"What do you want?"

Thompson had remained a gaping spectator of the tying up of Merriam's head, but this question enabled him to recover his natural aggressiveness. With one defiant glance at Aunt Mary, he started forward and pushed his way past Simpson, who could have stopped him only by an actual physical offensive.

"What do I want?" he repeated sarcastically, as he stood looking down on the senatorial head bundled in the scarf. "I want to know what the hell you've gone and done—you and Black—without letting anybody know you were going to! What about Crockett? Didn't you promise him at eight o'clock last night that you would tell Black to veto? And then this!"

Thompson had drawn a folded newspaper from his coat pocket. He struck it with his other hand.

"Is that the way to treat your friends who've stuck by you? What about the election next week? What about the state machine? What about your campaign fund? Have you gone nutty? Did you really do it, or is the Mayor lying? That's what I want to know!"

"What business is it of yours?" asked the victim of this torrent of questions as he stared from between the folds of his woolen scarf at the unlighted gas log.

Merriam really was asking for information, but the politician could not know this. It seemed to him the last insult—and repudiation. He fell back a step dramatically.

"So that's it!" he cried. "After I've managed two campaigns for you! I've done your dirty work for ten years! And now, over night, what business is it of mine? You throw me over! And all your friends. The men who sent you to the Senate of

the United States and kept you there. And what
for? To join that fool Black! And the Reform
League, I suppose. Philip Rockwell and his gang
of preachers and short-haired women and long-
haired mollycoddles! You'll appeal to the dear
People! Bah!"

Thompson had by this time apparently forgotten
entirely the presence of Aunt Mary and Simpson.
He snatched a cigar from his waistcoat pocket and
bit the end off it, produced a match from somewhere, and lighted it, emitting volumes of smoke.
He thumped with his newspaper on the arm of Merriam's chair and in an impressively lowered tone
continued:

"Listen to me. It won't do, Senator. You can't
get away with it. Not you. Reform and the people
and pure politics and all that. If you'd started in
on that line twenty years ago,—may be! I don't
say it couldn't be made to pay. But not by you, at
this time of day. It's too late. You've tied up
with the other gang. They know you. They know
too much about you. They won't let you do it.
It's no use trying. Of course, if you're tired of your
job—if you're hankering to quit—if you want to go
down in a grand smash,—all right! But if you
want to stay in the United States Senate, there's
just one way you can do it, and that's to play the
old game in the old way with the old crowd.
Savez?"

All this was a trifle hard on young Merriam.
Thompson had told who he was, so that the boy

realised the critical character of the interview.
But there was so much else he needed to know.
How had the real Norman been in the habit of
treating this man? How would he probably have
acted in such a situation as they were pretending?
The only thing he could do was to say as little as
possible. Now that it was necessary to make some
response, what he said was:

"We'll see about that."

Thompson was rather encouraged than otherwise
by this remark. He had not, of course, expected
any immediate acquiescence.

"You'll see all right if you keep on," he retorted
with elephantine irony. "But for God's sake, Senator, try to *see* things in time. It's not too late
yet. Turn the Mayor down. You aren't committed openly. He is, but you aren't. Let him go
smash alone. He was always a fool! You can
swear to Crockett that you told Black to veto. It
don't matter whether he believes you or not. He'll
take you back. This Ordinance business don't
matter. They'll fix that some way. There are
bigger things than that coming, and they know
how useful you can be. You can't keep on with this
other."

"Can't I?" asked Merriam, not unskillfully fish-
ing for further revelations.

"Listen to me, Senator. Didn't you accept fifty
thousand dollars of common stock in the United
Traction Companies? Are you going to give that
back? Will Crockett *let* you give it back? Not he!

Have you forgotten how we cornered the vote in
Kankakee County when you ran six years ago?
Crockett knows about that. The whole crowd know
it. And what about that nice little honorarium
you received for your vote in the Senate on the last
amendment to the Interstate Commerce Act? If
you've forgotten it, the men who put it up haven't!
Do you think they'll let you go off like this? As
long as you play the game and keep your good looks
and can make your popular speeches they'll keep
you in the Senate, and the good things will come
your way. They'll get you a Cabinet job if you
want it. Just say the word. But if you throw
them over, they'll turn on you. These little things
I've been reminding you of will leak out. Man
alive, you're liable to end in the pen!"

"Perhaps," said Merriam, "but I shouldn't go
alone. A man named Thompson would go with
me, eh? And maybe even Mr. Crockett. And
others I might name." (Merriam wished he *could*
name them.)

"That for your threats!" he finished grandly
and snapped his fingers, thanking heaven for the
rôle of villain he had enacted in a certain college
melodrama, in connection with which he had, by
diligent practice, acquired the not common art of
snapping one's fingers effectively.

Thompson, who had unwontedly removed his
cigar from his mouth at Merriam's speech, now
backed away from the huddled figure.

"You think you'd do that!" he said, in a voice in

which cynical scorn contended with something a
little like fright.

"Not unless I am forced to," said Merriam.
"But I have chosen a new course, and I mean to
follow it."

But Thompson, standing solidly in the spot to
which he had retreated, as if he had "dug in" there,
restored his cigar to the accustomed corner of his
face and narrowed his little eyes till they were
hideously smaller than usual.

"It's unfortunate, Senator," he said, with a kind
of exaggerated suavity, "that this reform in your
public morals last night was not accompanied by a
corresponding change in your private morals."

"What do you mean?" asked Merriam quickly,
and his voice faltered ever so little, a fact which
the other did not miss.

"Oh, you were known, you know, at Reiberg's
Place. You told everybody who you were, I understand. You must have been pretty gay. Celebrat-
ing your new virtue, I suppose! But handing
fifty-dollar bills to dance-hall girls isn't quite the
line for a Reform League hero, Senator! And we
know where you went afterwards. She's a pretty
little thing, but she's not in the Reform League picture! Suppose we say nothing about the United
Traction stock or the Kankakee County vote or the
Interstate Commerce business or any other little incidents of the past like that, but just start with this
little affair of last night. How will that mix with
pure politics, Senator?"

It was Thompson's turn to enjoy himself. He could not refrain from following up this new vein.

"Your old friends are liberal-minded, Senator. But your new friends, the great American people, are a little inclined to be narrow in matters of private morality."

Thompson's follow-up attack was a mistake. It gave Merriam time to think and decide upon his course.

"I was *not* at Reiberg's last night," he said, recovering his loftiness and adding coldness thereto. "Nor anywhere else. I spent the night in this hotel."

Thompson stared. For a moment it almost seemed that his jaw would fall and his precious cigar drop out. But he recovered himself with a sneer.

"You did, did you? In the company of your wife, I suppose! And that thing about your head is really to keep you from catching cold and not to keep your head from splitting open with the headache? You're pretty fresh this morning, considering. I hand it to you there. But "—his rising anger got the better of his unnatural affectation of suavity, which he had maintained up to the limit of his endurance—"but that lie won't go! You don't know what you did last night. You were stewed right. You told every Tom, Dick, and Harry, and Mary and Jane at the dance hall that you were Senator Norman. You fool!"

"After that," said Merriam, playing his part

regally, or, let us say, senatorially, " I can only
suggest to you that behind you is a door which I
wish you would make use of as soon as possible."

Thompson seemed decidedly nonplused at this.
The real Norman had always been amenable to
threats and on the whole patient under abuse.

" Do you mean," he burst out, " that I'm not to
be your manager? You turn me down cold? "

At this juncture there came a quick, light knock
at the door to which Merriam had just referred so
grandly.

Simpson looked quickly at Aunt Mary and then
at Merriam.

" Let me know who it is," said the latter, realising that he must seem to be in command.

When Simpson opened the door it was Rockwell
who pushed past him. He stopped short before
Thompson (with his cigar) in hostile confrontation.

Cautiously Merriam peered around the off side
of his high backed chair.

" Mr. Thompson," he said, " you know Mr. Rockwell, I believe. My new manager! "

For a moment Thompson stood. Once his mouth
opened, almost certainly to frame an oath. It is
strange evidence of the survival of chivalry in
American life that Aunt Mary's presence restrained that outburst. Instead, we must suppose,
he took the stub of his cigar from his mouth and
dashed it on the carpet.

" I'm through! " he said. Then to Merriam:

" I'll use your door all right—for the last time—till
you send for me! "

He caught up his hat and walked past Rockwell,
within an inch of brushing against him but not
looking at him.

At the door he turned.

" You've read your morning papers, I suppose!
Have you read *Tidbits?*   Take a look at it! "

The door slammed behind him.

CHAPTER XIV

HOLDING THE FORT

THE reverberation of Thompson's slamming still echoed in the room when the bedroom door opened and Alicia sailed in, followed more demurely by Mollie June.

"Good morning, Philip," said Alicia to her fiancé.

Then she turned to Merriam.

"Oh, you did splendidly!" she cried.

"Did I?" said Merriam, awkwardly trying to get the woolen scarf off his head.

"Indeed you did. We listened to every word. I through the keyhole. And Mollie June lay down on the floor and listened under the door. It was mean of me to take the keyhole, but I'm too old and fat for the other position."

Possibly Mollie June's recent prostration accounted for the color in her cheeks.

"Help him off with that thing, dear," Alicia added, and herself advanced to Rockwell and took his hands, offering to be kissed—an offer of which Rockwell took advantage with some fervour.

"Yes, I'll help you," said Mollie June, moving somewhat timidly in Merriam's direction.

He met her more than half way.

141

"Please," he said.   "I'm all bound round with a woolen string."

Mollie June drew the ends of the scarf down off his shoulders and untied the loose knot under his chin.

"There!" she said, looking up at him.

Merriam snatched the thing off his head, ruffling his hair.

"Thank you!"

Rockwell's voice reached them across the room. Aunt Mary had been hurriedly narrating the happenings with Thompson. He now looked approvingly at Merriam.

"That's all right," he said, reflectively.   "Very good.   Yes.   Just as well to defy him at once. Could hardly have been better.   Ah, there's Hobart now, I suppose," for a discreet knock had sounded at the hall door.

Rockwell himself admitted the house physician, a bald, youngish man, with nose glasses over slightly shifty eyes and a quite unprofessional manner—the manner of a "smart" young business man.

Merriam and Mollie June joined the others for the introductions.   These formalities over, Dr. Hobart confirmed the report of Norman's condition which Rockwell had given them over the telephone. He "was getting along all right"—with a sidelong glance at Mollie June—"except for a touch of bronchitis."

Mollie June betrayed an embarrassed uneasiness.

Merriam wondered just how much she knew of her
husband's whereabouts—of his escapades in general.

"Very well," said Aunt Mary briskly, "you must
go right to bed, Mr. Merriam, before some one else
comes. You're ill with bronchitis, of course. That
scarf was a splendid idea, Alicia, but it was a close
shave. We mustn't run any more risks. You will
attend him, Dr. Hobart?"

"Of course," said the young physician, evidently
much amused. "Mr. Rockwell has told me the
story. It's as good as a play. Mr. Merriam—I
mean, Senator,—I order you to bed at once."

"Very well," said Merriam and turned towards
Senator Norman's bedroom.

"I'll show you where things are," said Rockwell,
accompanying him. "I explored a bit last night."

In the bedroom with the door closed behind them,
Merriam hesitated.

"Better get your things off at once," said Rockwell, going to the bureau and stooping to open the
bottom drawer. "It's nearly ten o'clock," he continued, rummaging. "The reporters will be here
any minute. I'm surprised some enterprising chap
hasn't arrived already. We'll try to keep them off,
of course. But some of those fellows are mighty
clever. Here we are—pajamas," he added, pulling
out the garments for which he had been searching.

Then he crossed to a closet, from which in a
moment he emerged with a bath robe and a pair of
bedroom slippers.

"I'll put these by the bed so that if there's any reason for you to get up you can do so easily. But unless something happens to change our plans, you're much too sick to get up to-day."

A knock sounded at the door into the sitting room. Rockwell answered it and returned grinning.

"Aunt Mary says that Simpson shall bring you some ham and a cup of coffee as soon as you're in bed. Why didn't you tell me you have had nothing to eat but grapefruit?"

"I had forgotten," said Merriam, realising nevertheless that he was very hungry.

Rockwell dropped into a comfortable chair. "It's rather good fun," he said. "This conspiracy business. I do hope we can pull it through."

By this time Merriam was inside the senatorial pajamas. He approached the bed, turned down the covers, and awkwardly climbed in, feeling for all the world like a little boy who has been sent to bed in the daytime for being naughty.

"Now about lights," said Rockwell rising. The window shades had not been raised; they were using the chandelier. "Not these center lights, nor the night lamp. Both are too bright on your face in case —— Let's try this side light."

He turned on a light on the wall on the other side of Merriam's bed, switched off the ceiling lights, and surveyed the effect.

"That's good," he said. "If we have to bring any one in, you can lie looking this way and still

your face will be in shadow.   Lie well down in with
the covers up to your chin.   Now I'll bring you
some breakfast."

Merriam, left alone for a minute, wished he had
been permitted to finish his breakfast in the sitting
room before being sent to bed. He had counted on
that breakfast, and the first course had been fully
as delightful as he had pictured it.

Rockwell soon returned, carrying a tray on which
was a plate of really fine ham, with rolls and butter
and a cup of coffee.

" I guess I'm not too sick to sit up to eat, so long
as only you're here," said Merriam, suiting his
posture to the word and falling to with appe-
tite.

Rockwell drew up a chair and for several minutes
sat smoking in silence.   Then he said:

" Did you catch Thompson's parting shot about
Tidbits? "

" Yes," Merriam replied, without interrupting
operations.   " What did he mean? "

Rockwell drew a clipping from his pocket.
" Listen," he said, and read the following:

The Senator's Night Off

There was a dance last night at Reiberg's
Place on the West Side. Most of our readers
do not know Reiberg's. It comprises a dancing floor over a saloon, with a bar attached for
the convenience of patrons who may not be
willing—or, as the evening advances, able—to
go downstairs to the saloon; also certain small

rooms where one may drink or otherwise enjoy oneself quite privately. Its patrons, male and female, are chiefly employees in the neighbouring factories.

But last night Reiberg's was honoured, we are credibly informed, by a guest from quite a different sphere—no less than a Senator of the United States. We are not able at present to give his name with certainty, and of course we are not willing to give names in such a case until we have verified our information with scrupulous care. But he certainly announced himself as Senator ———, and he looked the part, and distributed money, presumably from the salary paid to him out of public funds, with lavish abandon.

Having tried to kiss one of the prettier girls and been knocked down by her escort—who evidently knew naught of "senatorial courtesies,"—he emphasised the sincerity of his tipsy apologies by handing the lucky insulted one a fifty-dollar bill.

Later, it is said, he attached himself to another young woman, unaccompanied, it would seem, by any pugnacious swain, with whom he spent several hours, partly on the dancing floor and partly elsewhere.

Finally, with we fear little of his money left about him, he was charitably carried off by the chauffeur of his waiting taxi.

Well, well, after the arduous strain of legislative labours, one doubtless feels the need of a little relaxation. We hope the Senator enjoyed himself.

Rockwell folded up his clipping. "A tolerably

close paraphrase of Simpson's story," he remarked.
" They have the facts pretty straight."

"What is this *Tidbits?* " asked Merriam, sitting
on his pillow with the tray in his lap. He had
stopped eating.

" Oh, a dirty little sheet of scandal. Twice a
week. But it's pretty widely read. And they
know his name, of course. In fact any one can
guess it, because Senator Norman is known to be
in the city, and there is no other United States
Senator stopping here now, so far as any one
knows. It will be a bit nasty if they push this sort
of thing. They'll put it in the regular newspapers
next—a straight news item with his name in
it."

" That article doesn't say where he went afterwards," said Merriam. " But Thompson knew."

" They're keeping that in reserve. Listen! "

Male voices were audible from the sitting
room.

" The reporters! " exclaimed Rockwell. " I'll
take that tray. Lie down and cover up. I must
go and help Aunt Mary hold the fort! "

Merriam finished his coffee in a gulp, and Rockwell set the tray on the seat of a chair and hastily
entered the sitting room.

There followed a long period—more than an
hour, in fact—during which Merriam lay in bed
and listened to varied voices from the other room,
and speculated as to what was going on, and wondered what he should do if the door should open

and some irresistibly aggressive reporter or irresistibly important political friend of Norman's be ushered in.

But Rockwell and Aunt Mary, with the occasional support of Dr. Hobart, successfully withstood the army of reporters and a few minor politicians who called, and at length the loud masculine voices from the other room ceased, and Merriam lay still, somewhat fatigued by his prolonged strain of apprehension, and waited.

Presently the door opened, and Aunt Mary and Rockwell entered. Merriam had closed his eyes, but Rockwell speedily opened them.

" Oh, you can wake up," he said. " It's all right. The coast is clear."

Merriam rolled over so as to lie on his back. " Well, what next? " he said.

Aunt Mary and Rockwell looked at each other. Rockwell spoke:

" Miss Norman and I are going out. We shall drop in at the Mayor's for a few minutes and then go on to a Reform League luncheon at the Urban Club. I am due to act as toastmaster or chairman for the speeches afterwards, and it will be just as well to have Miss Norman present. She will symbolise the prospective new alliance. We are going to leave you under the care of Alicia and Mrs. Norman. No one else is likely to come for several hours now. We shall be back at about half past two or three. Meanwhile luncheon. You didn't get a very big breakfast after all. Simpson shall

serve it here by your bed, and Alicia and Mollie
June can eat with you."

This disposition suited Merriam excellently well,
but he made no comment. He tried to decide
whether Aunt Mary was really eyeing him sharply
or whether he only imagined it.

In any case she almost immediately added a
rather formal " Good morning," and returned to
the sitting room.

Rockwell lingered a moment.

" We're going to try to bring Norman back here
this evening, you know. If it's at all possible. If
it shouldn't be—if he's too sick or something, I suppose you *could* stay over another day still? "

Merriam thought with a panic of his school.

" Not unless it's absolutely necessary," he replied
with a good deal of emphasis.

" It probably won't be," said Rockwell reassuringly. " We're quite as anxious to get rid of you,
you know," he added smiling, " as you can be to get
away from us. A double's a horribly dangerous
thing to have around. Well, so long."

In less than five minutes after Rockwell's departure there came a knock at that door upon
which Merriam's attention was concentrated—a
distinctly feminine knock.

Merriam disposed himself as discreetly as possible under the bedclothes and answered it.

Alicia opened the door and peeped. " May I
come in? " She opened it wider and came through.
" I'm the chaperon, you know."

" Are you? " asked Merriam smiling.

Alicia was pleased by his smile and said so.

" I always like it when people laugh at the idea of my being a chaperon."

" Why? " said Merriam.

. " Oh, so long as it seems funny for a woman to be a chaperon she's young."

" It seems funny for you," said Merriam.

" That's very nicely said," returned Alicia. " Come in, Mollie June."

As Mollie June did not appear, Alicia looked into the sitting room.

" Why," she said, " she must have gone into her bedroom. I do believe she's doing her hair over." And Alicia raised her eyebrows.

In spite of hope deferred Merriam was made happy. He recalled the supreme necessity of shaving earlier that morning.

Alicia dropped into the chair by the bed in which Rockwell had sat and pretended to scan the invalid's face solicitously.

" I should say, Senator," she remarked, " that you do not *look* like a very sick man. Your condition must be improving. We can hope you will be able to take a little nourishment."

" You can hope that all right," grinned the invalid.

" I've ordered ——" Alicia, making talk, plunged into the details of a quite elaborate refection.

By the time she had finished and had replied to

one or two humorous comments from Merriam,
whose spirits were certainly rising, Simpson presented himself with the substantial fulfillment of
her prospectus. And not until then did Mollie
June join them. Her coiffure, though simple, was
certainly faultless and so far as a masculine eye
could judge newly arranged.

Alicia caught Merriam's glance and read his
thoughts and smiled.

"What is it?" asked Mollie June suspiciously.

"What is what?" said Merriam, lamely.

"The Senator has been very humorous over the
meal I have ordered," explained Alicia more
deftly.

"Don't call him the Senator!" cried Mollie June.
"His name is "—her eyes met Merriam's for an
instant—"Mr. John."

"I see," said Alicia. In the dim light Merriam
was not sure whether she raised her eyebrows again
or not, but he was afraid she did.

Simpson, intent only on the proper illumination
of his carefully laid cloth, but unwittingly conspiring with the elder gods (Fate and Destiny and the
like), had turned on the night lamp and set it on
the corner of the table next to Mollie June, and its
radiance fell full on her slender, erect figure, now
arrayed in—Merriam had not the slightest idea
what kind of fabric it was, but it was creamy white,
and at her waist was one of the red roses he had
helped to freshen. The circle of bright light ex-
tended up to her white throat. Occasionally when

she leaned forward her face dipped into it, but for the most part showed only dimly in the fainter glow that came through the shade of the lamp. He could see her eyes, however, and not infrequently they rested on him. His, it is to be feared, were on her most of the time.

When at length the luncheon was finished and Merriam had expressed himself as disinclined for cigarettes and Simpson had removed his dishes and his table and finally himself, Alicia, who was really a most good-natured person—a pearl among chaperons,—yawned and announced that she had a novel which she desired to finish, and that, if they didn't mind, she proposed to retire to the sitting room to prosecute that literary occupation.

"You can amuse him for a while, Mrs. Norman," she said, with a humorous smile; Merriam did not venture to question what more subtle thoughts that smile might veil. "He's your guest more than mine, seeing it's your husband he's impersonating. If he gets too boring, you can come for me and I'll spell you."

Neither Mollie June nor Merriam replied, but Alicia, still with that amused smile, rose and calmly departed. She left the door open, of course, between the two rooms.

Upon the two young people, thus abruptly left alone together, there descended an embarrassed silence. For a minute or so they heard Alicia moving about in the sitting room and then the small sounds which one makes in adjusting one's

self comfortably in an armchair with a footstool
and a book, ending in a pleasurable sigh.

Merriam was overwhelmed by the necessity of
finding talk. He could not lie there in bed and
stare at Mollie June, however beatitudinous it
might have been to do so. Several seconds of pro-
digious intellectual labour brought forth this polite
question:

"Do you hear often from the girls in Riceville?"

"Not very often," said Mollie June.

We can hardly describe this reply as helpful.

Again he struggled mightily, with the banal kind
of result that usually follows such paroxysms of
conversational topic-hunting:

"You must find your life here and in Washington wonderful."

"It seemed so, at first," said Mollie June.

"But it didn't last?"

Merriam was conscious of danger on this tack,
but he must have a moment's rest before he could
wrestle with the void again.

"No," said Mollie June.

Merriam waited, not shirking his responsibilities
but conscious that she meant to continue. She
was always deliberate of speech—a fact which gave
a piquant significance to her simplest words.

"You see," she said, "I didn't really care very
much for George. I thought I did at first, but I
didn't. Papa really made me marry him. And
you know he is untrue to me."

Merriam could have gasped. He felt himself

falling through the thin ice of mere "conversation," on which he had tried so hard to skate, into the depths of real talk. But it was good to be in the depths. And after his first breathlessness he was filled with love and pity. How much the brief, girlish sentences portrayed of disillusionment and tragedy!

"You know about that then?" he asked gently.

"Of course," said Mollie June, almost scornfully. "Before company Aunt Mary and Alicia and Mr. Rockwell keep up the pretence that I can know nothing about such things. I keep it up too! But Aunt Mary knows all about them. George never can conceal anything from her. And I make her tell me everything. Everything!"

Merriam, I suspect, hardly sensed the amount of intellect and character which Mollie June's last statement betrayed—I use the word advisedly, for, of course, intellect and character detract from a young girl's charm, and if she desires to be pretty and alluring she should, and usually does, carefully conceal whatever of such attributes she may be handicapped with. But to "make" Aunt Mary disclose things she wished not to disclose was no small achievement.

"You know about this Jennie Higgins?" Merriam asked.

"Yes. I've seen her and talked with her."

"How?" was Merriam's startled question.

"She's a manicurist, you know. She's employed at ——" Mollie June mentioned a well-known establishment on Michigan Avenue, the name of which for obvious reasons I suppress. "When I found that out, I went there to have my nails done. I just asked for—Madame Couteau, and waited till she was free. She didn't know me, of course. She's pretty," said Mollie June, with judicial coldness.

After a moment she added, "And sweet and—warm."

"But how any man can leave you ——" cried Merriam, treading recklessly on several kinds of dynamite.

"You haven't seen her," said Mollie June.

Merriam was silenced. It was true he had not seen her. And he remembered with confusion that he had talked with her over a wire and, as Rockwell put it, had not "needed much prompting."

He stole a glance at Mollie June. The purity of her white-clad figure, its brave erectness, and the impassive sadness so out of place on her young face caught at his heart.

"How can you stand it?" he cried, and would have put out his hand to her had he not remembered that he was in bed and that his arm was clad only in the sleeve of a suit of pajamas.

Mollie June looked at him.

"I don't know," she said. "What else can I do?"

Merriam lay still, now openly staring at her. Of all intolerable things of which he had ever heard it seemed to him the worst that Mollie June—"the

prettiest girl,"—with all her loveliness and sweetness and courage and youthful joy in life, should
be so slighted and wronged and saddened and de-
graded. It was like seeing a rose trampled under
foot. (Merriam's mental simile was not very original perhaps, but to him it was intensely poignant.)

For a moment she met his gaze, then looked
away. In the subdued light Merriam could not be
sure, but he thought there was a new brightness of
tears in her eyes, released perhaps by his very apparent though inexpressive sympathy.

Presently the thought which had inevitably come
to him forced itself almost against his will to expression:

"You could divorce him."

"I've thought of that." (Somehow this shocked
Merriam.) "But it would be too horrible. Have
you read the divorce trials in the papers? With a
Senator they would make the most of it. And
Aunt Mary won't let me do that. It would ruin
him politically, she says."

"Well, what if it did? How about you?"

"Oh, she loves him, you know. She thinks he
can be brought to change his ways. She believes
in him still."

"Do you?"

"No," said Mollie June, with the clear-eyed,
cruel simplicity of youth.

"He may die," was the thought in Merriam's
mind, but this could not be said.

Full of pity, he gazed at her again, and some-

thing in the profile of her averted face overcame
him. He started up on his elbow—all this time he
had lain with his head on his arm on the pillow.

"Mollie June!" he cried, his voice softly raised.
She did not look at him.

"Dear Mollie June! You must know I love you.
I loved you three years ago in Riceville. There's
nothing wrong about that. When you're in such
trouble I must tell you. It can't do you any good.
There's nothing we can do. But—I do love you!"
She turned her eyes upon him.

"Why didn't you tell me that—in Riceville?"

"Oh!" he cried.

Mollie June rose and came to the bedside.

"I know," she said with womanly gentleness.
"You couldn't, of course. Because you were so
poor. I ought to have waited—John!"

For a moment her hand hovered above his head
as if she would have stroked his ruffled hair. But
it descended to her side again.

"We mustn't talk like this. I must go. I'll tell
Alicia we are—bored!"

There were tears not only in her eyes but on her
cheeks now. Undisguisedly she wiped them away
and carefully dried her eyes with a small handkerchief.

"I shall see you at dinner," she said with a brave
smile, and, turning, walked quickly out of the
room.

CHAPTER XV

COUNCIL OF WAR

IT was some time before Alicia, with something more, if possible, than her usual aplomb, covering, let us hope, a guilty conscience, entered the bedroom, presumably to "spell" Mollie June in amusing the supposed invalid.

Alicia made some remark which hardly penetrated the invalid's consciousness, but scarcely had she sat down in Mollie June's chair before a quick knock sounded at the hall door of the sitting room, almost immediately followed by the sound of the opening of that door, and Alicia sprang up again and hurried away, to be before Mollie June in receiving the newcomers. It began to irritate Merriam to perceive how they all treated her as a little girl, when as he now thrillingly realised she was very much a woman in spite of the youthfulness of her face and figure.

The arrivals in the other room proved to be Rockwell and Aunt Mary returned. Recognising their voices, Merriam glanced at his watch under his pillow and was amazed to find that it was nearly four o'clock.

Rockwell appeared in the doorway.

"Come into this other room," he said. "We must hold a council of war."

"Shall I dress?" asked Merriam, gladly getting out of bed.

"No, no," said Rockwell impatiently. "Just put on your bath robe and slippers."

Having followed this instruction, Merriam stepped to the glass and with a few quick strokes of the brush smoothed his hair, Rockwell watching him without comment. Then they went into the sitting room.

Merriam blankly perceived that the sitting room was empty—of Mollie June.

"She has a slight headache," said Alicia kindly —suffering still, we may hope, from pangs of conscience.

Aunt Mary was sitting in the senatorial armchair, which had been turned about to face the rest of the room. She looked long and hard at Merriam —an intensification of that close scrutiny with which, it seemed to him, she had always distinguished him. Merriam, in his bath robe, sustained it awkwardly but manfully. Alicia and Rockwell were standing. The silence was rather portentous.

"Sit down, all of you," said Aunt Mary suddenly.

The three younger persons present—even Rockwell seemed youthful beside Aunt Mary in her dominant mood—rather hurriedly found seats.

"Is the door locked, Philip?"

Rockwell rose, went to the hall door, turned the key, and returned to his chair.

"Tell him," said Aunt Mary.

Rockwell's budget of news was certainly considerable and important.

In the first place, George Norman was " better." Rockwell and Aunt Mary had gone to see him at Jennie's after the Reform League luncheon. That was why they were so late. He undoubtedly had a touch of bronchitis, with some fever and a cough, but seemed to be improving. He could be brought back to the hotel that evening. Aunt Mary had sat down by his bed and told him briefly but plainly of the happenings at the hotel the previous evening, and had extorted a feeble, amazed acquiescence in the astonishing turn which had been given to his career—an acquiescence which she had immediately communicated by telephone from Jennie's to Mayor Black.

In the second place, the story of Norman's evening at Reiberg's was all over the city—not among the populace, of course, but among the politicians and business men and clubmen—the men who know things. Not only the story in *Tidbits,* which everybody seemed to have read and to have assigned unhesitatingly to Norman, but the further fact that from Reiberg's he had gone in the taxi to " a certain little flat "—that seemed to be the approved phrase,—and had spent the night there, and was still there. The simple truth, in short, was known. Rockwell had taken his cue perforce from Merriam's impulsive denial to Thompson and had flatly contradicted the whole story. Senator Nor-

man had spent the evening, after his interviews
with Mr. Crockett and with Mayor Black, at the
hotel with his wife, and was there now, slightly in-
disposed with a severe cold which had threatened
to turn into bronchitis. His downright assertions
had, Rockwell believed, shaken the confident ru-
mours and would probably delay any further pub-
lication of them for at least a day. But it was
necessary to produce evidence.

"We shall have to use you again to-night," he
said to Merriam. "I have invited the Mayor and
Mr. Wayward to dine with you here at the hotel—
downstairs in the Peacock Cabaret."

"Shall I have to play the Senator there?"
gasped Merriam—"in public!"

"Semi-public," said Rockwell. "I have reserved
a table in an alcove. We shall put you in the corner. All the rest of us will be between you and
the general gaze. Oh, we shall get away with it.
It's much less dangerous than trying to impose at
close range in a private interview on some one who
really knows the Senator—as you did on Thompson
this morning."

"Does Mr. Wayward know?" asked Merriam.

"Of the impersonation? Not yet. But Alicia
shall prepare him in advance."

Alicia nodded. "That's all right," she said.
"Daddy will enjoy it. He'll think it's a huge
joke."

"Moreover," continued Rockwell, with rather
apprehensive eyes on Merriam, "I have accepted an

invitation for Senator Norman to speak at the Reform League luncheon to-morrow."

"Do they have luncheons and speeches every day?" asked Merriam, sparring for time, for of course he saw what was coming.

"Not usually, but they've been having a series. To-morrow is the last one. It's the perfect opportunity for Norman to come out openly for the League. When the invitation came, I simply had to accept it."

"But if George Norman isn't able to speak?" queried Alicia, fearlessly coming to the point.

"Then you'll have to make the speech!" said Rockwell bluntly to Merriam.

"But how can I?"

"You were a debater in college."

"Yes, but the speech itself ——"

"Oh, Aunt Mary will fix you up with a speech."

Merriam turned to that silent mistress of the situation, sitting calmly in the senatorial armchair.

"George is so very busy that I often write his speeches for him," she said, as if it were the most natural arrangement in the world. "I have several sketched out now. We can make a choice among them. I will write it out in full and you can learn it, or I will turn over the outline to you and you can work it up in your own words—if you have to make it."

"You probably won't," Rockwell hastened to say. "Norman is really much better. After a

comfortable night here at the hotel he will be all
right. If he's a little hoarse, we can't help it. But
you must stay over, you see," he added deter-
minedly,—"to make sure. That speech must be
made."

"But my school!" cried Merriam.

"You'll have to send another telegram," said
Aunt Mary.

"What's a day or two of school?" asked Rockwell impatiently, with a layman's insensibility to
the pedagogical dogmas of absolute regularity and
punctuality. "Besides, if you really were sick,"
he added more tactfully, "they would have to get
along without you, wouldn't they?"

"So much is at stake," said Aunt Mary.
"George's future, and all that that may mean to
the State and Nation. If we can bring him to
throw the weight of his popularity and leadership
on the right side!"

"You can't desert us now, Mr. Merriam," cried
Alicia. "When it means so much to Aunt Mary
and Philip and Mollie June!"

Crafty Alicia! Her guile was, of course, clearly
apparent to Merriam. But it is perfectly possible
to perceive that an influence is being deliberately
brought to bear on one without being able to resist
that influence.

"Very well. I'll telegraph again," he said.

"Better do it now," said Rockwell, promptly
clinching this decision. He rose, went to the writing table, got out a telegraph form, and sat down.

"What shall I write?"

Merriam collected himself as best he could under Alicia's admiring, expectant eyes and Aunt Mary's steady regard.

"Better," he dictated, "but doctor won't let me leave to-night. Expect to be down to-morrow night."

"That's good," said Aunt Mary, in a tone of quiet approval which gratified Merriam more probably than he realised.

Rockwell finished writing and turned in his chair.

"I'll be going down in a few minutes. I'll send it then. Now you'll need to dress for dinner—Senator! Pack up your things too. After dinner you and I will leave the hotel together in a taxi. We shall drive over to the University Club. There we shall simply go up to the Library for a few minutes and then come down again, walk up Michigan Avenue for a block or two and catch another taxi, and drive to the Nestor House. There you can register under your own name. Simpson will send your things over. I shall go on and get Norman and bring him back here. You see? Senator Norman leaves the hotel about nine o'clock with his new manager—me. Within an hour or so he returns, still in my company, and goes to his room. If he's all right, you can go down to Riceville on the morning train if you like. I'll come to see you before you go."

"We'll *all* go over to see you," said Alicia, with

an unmistakable emphasis on the "all." "We shall have so much to thank you for!"

Merriam did not reply to this cordial remark.

"Why do we go to the University Club?" he asked.

"And not directly to the other hotel?" said Rockwell. "Well, I'm afraid we may be rather closely watched. To tell the truth, I suspect that the driver of the taxi we take here may be questioned afterwards as to where he set us down. The University Club will tell them nothing."

To Merriam's excited mood this explanation, with its hint of powerful hidden enemies intently watching every move which he and his friends could make, added a touch of piquancy to the situation that was nothing short of delightful.

He could not well express this, however, and Rockwell, who was all business with no such romantic nonsense in his head, immediately sent them about their several parts. He himself was first to take Alicia to her waiting limousine.

When Alicia and Rockwell had departed Merriam sought to return to his—the Senator's—bedroom. But Aunt Mary detained him.

"Sit down, Mr. Merriam," she said, kindly enough but in a manner that demanded unquestioning obedience.

Then she rose and entered Mollie June's bedroom but immediately returned.

"Mollie June is dressing for dinner," she said.

An instant's pause. Then, looking hard at Merriam, " She's a lovely child."

Both the look and the final word provoked Merriam to a sort of resentment.

" I don't believe she's as much of a child as you think," he said boldly.

" It depends on the point of view, no doubt," said Aunt Mary drily.

Then she began to ask him about himself, his family, his own life, on the farm of his boyhood, at college, and at Riceville—all those facts which Alicia had so much more tactfully elicited in the private dining room off the Peacock Cabaret the night before and some others in which Alicia had not been interested. Merriam had nothing to be ashamed of and spoke up promptly and manfully in his replies, wondering in the back of his mind the while what inscrutable thought or purpose prompted Aunt Mary in her catechising. He little dreamt that the whole course and happiness of his life turned on the showing he was able to make in this odd examination.

There is no doubt that Aunt Mary—whatever her idea may have been—was satisfied. When at length she had no more questions to ask the expression of her eyes, though they still rested on him, was almost one of absence. She drew a deeper breath than was her wont—suggestive, at least, of a sigh.

" You give a good account of yourself," she said. " You are worthy of the Norman blood."

Greater praise than that no man could have from Aunt Mary, as Merriam dimly realised.

"I wish George were more like you."

Immediately she added, with a conscious return to dominating briskness:

"You must dress.   So must I."

And she rose and without looking again at Merriam went into Mollie June's bedroom.

CHAPTER XVI

A T last, at twenty-five minutes after six, Merriam sank, exhausted but immaculate, into
an easy chair and lit a cigarette, in an effort to
compose his nerves and regain the *sang froid* he
needed for his imminent rôle of a particularly debonair senator of the United States acting as host
to a brilliant dinner party.

At half past six precisely, Aunt Mary knocked
on his door and he opened that door and announced
himself ready.

Aunt Mary wore another black evening gown,
very similar, in masculine eyes, to the one in which
she had appeared the night before, except that it
was less conspicuously burdened with jet. Tall and
erect, with her gray hair plainly but carefully
dressed, she looked every inch a senator's sister and
—this would have pleased her—a Norman.

Advancing into the sitting room, Merriam encountered Mollie June, standing again beside the
bowl of roses. She was in pink—tulle over satin,
though Merriam could not have described it so.
But the vivid colour and the dainty softness of the
fabric he could appreciate quite well enough, at

168

least in their contiguity to the slender figure, white
throat and shoulders, and charming complexion of
Mollie June. There is no doubt that he looked a
moment longer than he should. The debonair senatorial outside of him was moved to say, "How
lovely you are!" But the Ricevillian pedagogue
underneath blocked the utterance. Perhaps his
eyes said it plainly enough to satisfy Mollie June,
for she evinced no disappointment.

"We must go right down, mustn't we?" she said,
raising her eyes from the roses.

"Yes," said Aunt Mary, in a tone of jarring
briskness.

A male figure which Merriam had not perceived
stepped out of the background, moved to the hall
door, and opened it. Merriam saw that it was Dr.
Hobart, quite as point-device as himself and rather
more at ease but not nearly so handsome (though
of this, I assure you, Merriam never thought at
all).

Aunt Mary and Mollie June passed through the
door.

"Come along, Senator," said Dr. Hobart, in excellent spirits, and Merriam mechanically followed
and mechanically paused and waited while the
physician closed and locked the door.

"This must be great fun for you," said Dr. Hobart as they went down the hall towards the
elevators.

"Yes," returned Merriam without conviction,
his eyes on a girlish figure in pink that moved

ahead of him. "Fun" did not strike him as exactly the word.

Fortunately at this point a small incident occurred which served to bring Merriam out of the brown study—or perhaps we may say the roseate study—into which he had fallen.

As they approached the elevator lobby he became aware of the pretty floor clerk who on the previous evening had been wearing Senator Norman's violets. He was, of course, entirely unmindful of the fact that on his way to Norman's rooms that morning he had passed her rudely by without a glance, but he did notice that this evening she wore no flowers and that she studiously avoided seeing him and smiled her best smile upon Dr. Hobart instead. That gentleman, with a shade too much alacrity, stepped aside so as to pass close to her desk and, leaning down, spoke to her. The pretty floor clerk, from the toss of her head and the pleased smile on Hobart's face, had said something saucy in reply.

"Good enough," thought Merriam, as they all stepped into the elevator. "I'm glad she has more interests than one," and thought no more of the incident at the time.

In a moment or two more they had reached the basement floor, which was their destination.

Opposite the elevators on this floor was a small reception room or parlour, and here Senator Norman's other guests were awaiting him—Rockwell, Murray, Mayor Black, Alicia, and Alicia's father.

To the last-named gentleman Merriam was imme-

diately presented. He was a stoutish, jovial man of
fifty or so, bald of pate and humorous of eye, and
the amused particularity with which he surveyed
Merriam and the gusto with which he addressed
him as " Senator " showed both that Alicia had performed her task of enlightening him and that she
had been right as to the attitude he would take.

" Splendid! " he whispered to Merriam. " You
would have fooled me all right," and he beamed delightedly.

Alicia gave him only a minute. " They are
ready," she said. " We are to go right in. You
are to walk with me." (This last to Merriam.)

In a moment, therefore, Merriam found himself
escorting Alicia down a sort of central aisle among
the tables of the Peacock Cabaret, behind an excess-
ively urbane head waiter, conscious that the rest
of his guests were making a more or less imposing
procession after them, and intensely conscious of
suspended conversation throughout the great restaurant and of countless curious eyes staring
across rosebuds and water bottles at himself.

" Say something to me," whispered Alicia. " You
mustn't look self-conscious."

Merriam glanced at her and realised for the first
time that evening her vivid, vigorous, peony-like
beauty.

" What can I say," he asked smiling, " except
' How lovely you are '? " and he wondered why it
was so easy to say this to Alicia when he had been
unable to say it to Mollie June.

"Bravo, Boy Senator!" applauded Alicia, and then they reached the haven of that alcove which Rockwell had promised.

It was really a small square room quite separate from the main part of the Peacock Cabaret except that there was no wall between. The head waiter guided Merriam to the seat at the far end of the table. Thus when he sat down he would be facing the main dining room, visible to all its occupants, yet screened from them by the table and his own guests about that table. It was really an excellent device for displaying him in public and still protecting him from close inspection.

In a moment the whole party had arrived and been seated.

A canapé was being served, and Alicia at his end of the table and her father at the other end were starting conversation. Merriam glanced across the board at Mollie June. For some reason a charming girl never looks more lovely than at table. She looked up and caught his gaze. Her face was grave. He thought she looked wistful. For a moment only he met her eyes, then turned to reply to a remark of Alicia's. Somehow his spirits soared. He plunged into the conversation with a zest which he had hardly known since his fraternity days. Mollie June said little, but she laughed at the stories and seemed to become excited and happy. She was content, perhaps, to enact the rôle of the gallery to which Merriam was playing with such excellent effect. As for Rockwell and

Aunt Mary, they sat by in serene content: the affair was going well; as long as that was the case they need not exert themselves.

The mildly uproarious party undoubtedly attracted the desired amount of attention from the main dining room. Eyes were turned and necks craned, and couples and groups that passed the alcove almost invariably slowed their steps to stare. Some dozens of men who had heard the stories of the real Norman's whereabouts were convinced that these were false, at least in part; by the witness of their own eyes they knew that the Senator was that evening at any rate in the bosom of his family at the hotel. They could be relied upon to assert as much in all parts of the city on the following day.

Only one outsider ventured to intrude upon the party and submit Merriam to the ordeal of closer inspection, and he got no nearer than the length of the table. This was the Colonel Abbott whom Merriam had so perilously encountered at the very beginning of his play-acting the night before. Merriam remembered him vividly, called him by name, and replied cordially to his expressions of pleasure at finding him recovered from his threatened indisposition. So that danger passed, and the table, after a brief exchanging of relieved glances, recovered its gayety, perhaps with some accentuation.

A little later came a reporter. Merriam professed that he had "nothing to say." Asked if it was true that he was to speak at the Reform League luncheon on the morrow, he replied, with an inner quailing but with outward composure, that he was.

The reporter turned to Mr. Wayward. Was it true that he intended to make a contribution to the campaign fund of the Reform League? Mr. Wayward's joviality suffered an eclipse. His eyes fell. But on raising them he encountered a glance from his daughter that can only be described as stern, and promptly admitted that it was true.

The reporter tried Rockwell, but the latter shook his head so indomitably that the interviewer at once abandoned him and passed to Mayor Black. That gentleman promptly and as it were automatically gave utterance to several eloquent phrases, too meaningless to be recorded. Even the reporter neglected to make notes of them, and looked about the table for other prey. Finding none, he excused himself with the remark, " I am making note of the names, of course," and disappeared.

Once more the conspiratorial table drew a long breath and endeavoured to recover its festive mood, but before much progress had been made in that direction a bell boy came with a note addressed to Senator Norman and asking that he and Mr. Rockwell come to Room D, one of the private dining rooms.

Merriam passed the note to Rockwell and then to Aunt Mary, and the three prime conspirators stared at one another. None of them knew the handwriting, which was poor and hurried and in pencil.

"I'll go," said Rockwell. "You stay here."

The rest of the party did not know what had happened, but in their situation the most trivial incident was, of course, sufficient to cause uneasiness. The conversation during Rockwell's absence was forced and fragmentary. In fact, it was almost a solo performance on Alicia's part. Merriam caught Mollie June's eyes upon him, and was grateful for their expression of self-unconscious solicitude.

Presently the boy returned again with the same note, at the bottom of which was scribbled: " Come —Room D. Rockwell."

Merriam showed it to Aunt Mary.

"Is that his handwriting? "

"Yes, it is."

"Then I suppose I must go."

He rose, murmured an " excuse me " to the table at large, and made his way towards the open end of the alcove. As he did so he glanced at Mollie June. Alarm stood in her eyes. Coming opposite her chair, he bent down and said gently:

"It's all right. I probably shan't be long."

It was perhaps a little too much in the tone and manner that Mollie June's real husband might properly have used. Mollie June herself did not seem to notice this; she appeared duly comforted. But Mr. Wayward, at her left, undoubtedly stared after Merriam with an odd expression in his genial eyes.

Following the bell boy, Merriam tried hard to think what might be in store for him. "Thompson" and "Crockett" were the only ideas his blank mind could muster. Had they discovered the trick and come to threaten him with exposure? Well, Rockwell would be present. He leaned heavily on Rockwell.

The boy stopped before a curtained door.

"This is it, sir," he said and waited expectantly.

Merriam fumblingly produced a dime, and the boy departed. Drawing a deep breath, he pushed aside the curtain and entered Room D.

To his great relief the only persons present were Rockwell and Simpson. They were both standing, beside a bare table. Merriam vaguely remembered that Simpson had not appeared in connection with the serving of the last two or three courses.

"Now tell it again," said Rockwell promptly.

The waiter looked steadily at Merriam.

"It's this way, sir," he said. "Mr. Thompson, as was the Senator's manager until this morning, has found out where the Senator really is, at ——" the man looked away. "Jennie's," he finished, without expression in his tone. "There's a girl she lives with, Margery Milton, who's a milliner's assistant at one of the department stores. He got it from her. Straight from her he came here to have dinner with Mr. Crockett, out in the Cabaret. When I saw them come in, I turned your party over to another man and served them myself. I managed to hear a lot of what they said. Mr. Crockett had learned of your dinner party, of course. Putting that together with what Mr. Thompson had got from Margery, they saw the game. Mr. Crockett would hardly believe it at first. But Mr. Thompson means to make sure. He's going to Jennie's himself about ten o'clock to-night—they have some kind of a committee first,—and force his way in, if necessary, and see the Senator himself. Then they'll have proof, you see. I thought I'd better let you and Mr. Rockwell know."

"You did just right," said Rockwell warmly, "and we'll make it worth your while."

He turned abruptly to the younger man.

"Merriam! You're the only one who can save us in this fix."

"How?" said Merriam, to whom it seemed that all was lost.

"Listen, man. You go back to our table and excuse yourself and me. 'Important business.' Don't tell them anything more. Not even Aunt Mary. We haven't time. Better bring Murray. We may need an extra man, and we can trust him best. We three will take a taxi at once. We shall have to circle about a bit, to throw off possible trailers. But in less than an hour we'll be at Jennie's. You shall take Norman's place there, and we'll take Norman and bring him back to the hotel, to his room. Just as we planned, only a bit sooner. When Thompson arrives, Jennie shall let him in. He'll insist on seeing you. Let him. You're not Senator Norman. Tell him so. Jennie

shall tell him so, too. He'll see it himself, of
course, as soon as he looks close with his eyes open.
You and Jennie must make him think you played
off the resemblance on this Margery Milton for a
joke. We'll fix her, too, of course. You'd better
tell him your real name, so he can look you up if
he wants to. He won't expose you in Riceville.
He'll have no motive to. And he won't think anything of your little escapade in itself. You came
to Chicago on school business—went out to see the
sights—got a little more liquor than you were used
to. Your taxi driver took you to some dance hall.
He'll interpret ' Reiberg's.' You stayed there a
while—don't know what you did—met Jennie there
—and she brought you home. You were pretty
sick in the morning and stayed over all day. You
see? It all hangs together, and relieves Norman
entirely of the Reiberg incident and Jennie, and
cinches his blameless presence at the hotel all last
night and all to-day. It'll save everything! Better than we planned. Couldn't be better!"

Rockwell had worked himself up to exultant enthusiasm.

Merriam's emotions while this new plot was unfolded were sufficiently complex. There was an
opaque background of sheer bewilderment. There
was also a sharp sense of alarm at the thought of
having his own name appear in this business. But
other sentiments, less acute individually, but of
some potency none the less, joined their voices with
Rockwell's to silence that alarm. There was the

mere love of adventure, of playing a dangerous game, which is strong in any healthy young man. Then there was the thought of Mollie June: he would be doing it for her—making a real sacrifice, of his reputation, possibly of his position, his pedagogical career, for her sake. And, oddly enough, quite simultaneously with this thought of Mollie June, there was a recollection of " Jennie's " voice over the telephone. He was not conscious that he was curious to see " Jennie," but I am afraid he was.

Scarcely half a minute had passed when Rockwell, eagerly scanning his face, cried, " You'll go! "

" Yes," said Merriam, looking at Simpson's impassive countenance and surprised at his own words, " I suppose I will."

CHAPTER XVII

A DEVIOUS JOURNEY

ROCKWELL, as usual, gave Merriam no time for reconsideration.

"Go and make your excuses at the table then."

But Merriam was still looking at Simpson. He had perceived that the impassivity of the waiter's countenance covered a blank misery.

"Simpson," he said, "we'll try to see that this works out to your advantage—at Jennie's. Shake on that." And, in violation of all codes on which the social system rests, he held out his hand as one man to another.

Simpson, much more rigorously trained in those codes than Merriam had been, hesitated, glanced at Rockwell. But a light came into his eyes. He seized the hand, gripped it, gave one spasmodic shake.

"Thank you, sir!" he said.

He dropped the hand and as quickly as possible regained his servitorial manner.

Merriam smiled at him and then spoke to Rockwell:

"Where shall I join you—Murray and I?"

"At the Ladies' Entrance," Rockwell replied. "It's less likely to be watched than the other."

Merriam turned and passed through the curtained doorway, down the hall, and along one side
of the Peacock Cabaret. The curtain being up on
the small stage and the moderately comely demoiselles of the chorus executing a dance which involved a liberal display of white tights, he reached
his alcove comparatively unnoticed.

He stopped beside Mollie June's chair, which was
nearest the open side of the alcove. All the members of the dinner party regarded him anxiously;
Aunt Mary's face was more than usually grim.
Carefully pitching his voice so that it should be
audible to all at the table yet should not carry to
the main dining room without, he said:

"I am tremendously sorry to have to desert this
pleasant company, but Mr. Rockwell and I are
called away on important business. We should be
very glad if you will come too, Father Murray.—
Can you come at once?" he added as the priest
stared.

Aunt Mary's lips opened.

"I'll explain later," said Merriam hurriedly.

As he spoke, however, he realised that no opportunity to "explain later" would probably be af-
forded him. Alicia had said they "all" would go
to see him in the morning at the Nestor House.
They could not "all" come to Jennie's.

He looked down at Mollie June. She was looking up at him. His view of her from above—the
contour of her face and throat, the recalcitrant
wave of her soft hair, the brightness of her lifted

eyes—might have moved older and colder blood than Merriam's. He was close enough to catch a faint, warm sense of her in the air. He desired to envelop her in love. What he might do he could not resist. He laid his hand gently over one of hers that rested on the edge of the table and bent to her ear.

"Mr. Rockwell will tell you to-morrow what I have done," he whispered. "It is for your sake, Mollie—June."

He straightened up. He was not flushed outwardly. He looked almost cold. Father Murray was making his way down the side of the table.

"Good night, all," said Merriam. "This way, Father Murray."

He glanced once more at Mollie June—his last sight of her, he thought. Her face was rosy and her eyes glistened. It was a picture for which a man—a very young man, at least—might do anything, even sacrifice his love. He smiled at her almost gaily, turned, and passed out of the alcove, Father Murray following.

They skirted the sides of the Peacock Cabaret in an effort to reach the exit as little observed as possible. Unfortunately, before they attained that goal, the curtain of the small stage descended, the white legs of the chorus, kicking at it as it fell, were hidden from the attentive eyes of the male diners, and not a few of these observed the famous senator's escape. This probably mattered little, however, because of Father Murray. The well-known High Churchman was enough to shield the name of Norman. He could hardly be bound for Reiberg's, or even, it would be argued, for "a certain little flat," in Father Murray's company.

They got their coats from the checkroom, went up the stairs to the first floor, and made a détour through passages to the Ladies' Entrance.

Rockwell was already there with a taxicab. He motioned to them to enter it.

Merriam was a little surprised, and Father Murray probably more so, to find Simpson already within. Father Murray greeted him with clerical suavity. Merriam said nothing. He was listening to Rockwell's colloquy with the chauffeur:

"This cab will probably be followed. Your first job is to shake off pursuit. Circle around through the Loop—twist and turn—until you're absolutely sure you've lost anybody who is after us. Then make for the Eighteenth Street Station of the Alley L. If there's no one behind us when you get there, it will be worth twenty-five dollars to you above the fare."

"Right, sir," said the man. "Jump in, sir."

Rockwell stepped in and slammed the door, seating himself with Simpson, his back to the driver. In a moment he was staring intently through the peephole window in the back of the taxi.

"See!" he said.

Merriam, turning to look over his shoulder, perceived a yellow cab about sixty feet behind them, also starting, at about the same pace as their own.

They went west to Fifth Avenue and turned north along the car tracks under the Elevated. A moment later the yellow cab also turned north on the car tracks.

They swerved east on Randolph Street. For a minute or two the yellow cab did not appear. It must have been caught behind some car or truck. But presently it rounded the corner and sprinted till it was again within about thirty yards of them, when it slowed down to their own pace.

Rockwell spoke through the tube to the chauffeur:

" That yellow cab! "

" I'll lose 'em! " the man replied, with reassuring confidence.

At the second corner he turned north again and sped across the Clark Street Bridge. The yellow cab also had business north of the river.

Their subsequent maneuvers were at first decidedly puzzling to Merriam and his fellow passengers, with the possible exception of Simpson. They sped around and around a rectangle of streets enclosing half a dozen squares, with one of its sides only one block from the River. On the shorter sides they sometimes lost the yellow cab, but on the longer stretches it always appeared in full and open chase behind them.

" What the devil! " cried Rockwell as their driver turned west for the fourth time on the southern side of the rectangle—the street nearest the River.

Simpson spoke: " He's all right.   It's the bridge trick."

No further explanation was necessary.   Their chauffeur suddenly swerved south on Dearborn Street, making in a burst of speed for the River. The bridge bell was jangling its warning that traffic must stop for the opening of the bridge to let a steamer pass.   Theirs was the last vehicle on the bridge.   The bars dropped behind them. Looking back through the peephole window, our passengers had the satisfaction of seeing the yellow cab caught behind the bars, unable to follow them, unable even, because of other vehicles crowding behind, to turn out and make a détour to another bridge.

Rockwell excitedly seized the tube.   " Good work! " he called.   " I'll give you another ten for that."

" Thank you, sir," came the complacent reply.

With a sigh of relaxing tension Merriam sank back in his corner, abandoning the peephole.

" Who do you suppose it was? " he asked. " Thompson? "

" Oh, no, not Thompson himself.   One of his henchmen.   He and Norman have all kinds of— assistants! "

" Where are we going? " asked Father Murray.

Rockwell laughed.   " I'd almost forgotten that you don't know yet.   I'll tell you," and he entered upon an explanation of Thompson's discovery and proposed method of verification and their own counterplot.

Father Murray was feebly protesting against the difficulties and dangers of the counterplot, but these complaints were interrupted by the stopping of the taxi. They had reached the Eighteenth Street Station of the Elevated.

Rockwell looked quickly through the peephole window and then opened the door and jumped out. The others followed. They scanned the street in both directions. There was no other taxicab in sight.

Rockwell stepped up to the smiling chauffeur, asked the amount of the fare, and paid it with the thirty-five dollars bonus.

" You did the trick very neatly," he said. " Now, scoot! "

" Thank you, sir. Yes, sir."

There was still no trace of curiosity in the man's tone or glance.

" Come! " said Rockwell, and he led them to the entrance of the Elevated Station.

At Forty-Seventh Street they left the Elevated and, walking to the corner, waited for a cross-town surface car.

" What's the idea? " Merriam asked, his mind becoming active again.

" Well," said Rockwell, " the first thing our late chauffeur will do after getting back to town will be to gather in another twenty-five dollars or maybe more for telling some one of Thompson's men where

he left us. So it's best to muss up our trail a bit
more before we strike Jennie's."

. He was hailing an east-bound car.

As they sat silent again inside, Merriam's
mind took its cue from Rockwell's last word.
" Jennie's ! " Phrases from his one brief telephone
dialogue with Jennie sounded in his ear, oddly
clear and melodious :

" Georgie, boy! Don't you know me?—You
ought to ! " with a thrilling little laugh. " You
must be careful, Georgie," in a lowered tone.
" Can you come anyway?—You'll telephone again?
—Georgie, boy ! " and the sound of a kiss !

These phrases—surely nothing in themselves—
echoed in his mind with the same unaccountable
piquancy and warmth with which they had first
come to him over the telephone. He flushed a little, sitting there in the stuffy, bumping, jangling
car, as he recalled the way he had involuntarily
" played up " to them. He had promised to go to
her if he could get away, to telephone her again if
he could. That was mere trickery and deceit, a
part of the game he was playing; that was all right.
But his final whispered " Dearie, good night ! "
Had that been necessary? He remembered Rockwell's dry comment: " You don't need much
prompting ! " But his thoughts ran away with
him again. Now he was going to see her—to spend
a night in her apartment. What would she be like
—tall or short, slender like Mollie June or plump
like Alicia, fair or dark, with blue eyes or brown or

black, curly hair or straight? He could not frame
an image that satisfied him as the instrument of
that voice.

"Well, what is it to me?" he demanded roughly
of himself, suddenly realising the tenor of his medi-
tations. "See here, my boy, you must be careful.
She's probably a regular chorus girl—or worse."
(But he did not really believe that of her.) "She's
nothing whatever to me," he asserted sternly to his
truant fancy. "She belongs to—Simpson. And
I belong to Mollie June."

The car stopped at last, and Rockwell was getting up.

When they had descended into the street Merriam found that they were at the end of the line
by the Lake.

"Illinois Central next," said Rockwell, grinning,
and marched them to the Forty-Seventh Street
Station of that railway. None of the others spoke.

Their guide bought tickets to the City. "Are
we going back to the Loop, then?" thought Merriam.

In a moment they were on the platform. Merriam walked back and forth apart from the others,
drawing deep breaths of the Lake air and looking
up at the stars, dimly bright in the April night.
"I belong to Mollie June," he said firmly to himself.

Presently one of the odd little suburban trains
drew up, and they entered.

But they had scarcely sat down and yielded up

their tickets when Rockwell routed them out—at Forty-Third Street. Evidently his buying tickets clear to the City had been a part of his elaborate ruse.

Rockwell went at once to a telephone to call up a neighbouring garage.

Merriam took a cigarette and lighted it and again walked up and down. His thoughts now ran unbidden upon Mollie June. Images of her crowded his mind: Mollie June rosy and bright-eyed as he had seen her last at the dinner table in the alcove of the Peacock Cabaret; Mollie June by his " sick " bed, standing over him after he had impulsively declared his love, her hand hovering above his hair, tears upon her face, turning bravely away from him; Mollie June above the roses, as he had first seen her that morning—was it only that morning? —lifting the wet stems from the bowl; Mollie June confronting Mayor Black, refusing in angered innocence to leave the room; Mollie June in the Peacock Cabaret the night before; Mollie June in the front row in " Senior Algebra " back in Riceville. Ah, he *did* belong to Mollie June, heart and soul. There was no doubt of that, and all the Jennies in the world were of no account whatever.

So it was a young man in a very laudable frame of mind indeed—waiving the fact that Mollie June was a married woman!—whom Rockwell presently bundled into the taxi he had summoned. Father Murray was already inside. Rockwell followed, leaving Simpson to speak to the chauffeur.

It puzzled Merriam to find Simpson thus placed in command, as it were, and his thoughts came back to the present adventure. He listened closely.

"Stop first at Rankin's Hardware Store," Simpson said to the chauffeur, "on Forty-Third Street."

In a couple of minutes, it seemed, they stopped before Rankin's emporium. Simpson alone descended. The other three remained in the taxicab, Rockwell openly smiling at the puzzled inquiry on Merriam's face but vouchsafing no enlightenment. Merriam would not ask questions.

The hardware shop was closed, but there was a light within and a man. Simpson pounded at the door till he gained admittance, and in a few minutes returned bearing—a small stepladder!

"What on earth——?" The words were almost starting from Merriam's lips, but he managed to swallow them, and listened again for Simpson's direction to the driver.

It was an address: "612 Dalton Place." That meant nothing to Merriam.

Again a brief drive, Merriam laboriously cogitating, with bewildered eyes on the small ladder—an affair of some six steps,—which Simpson had brought into the cab and was holding upright between them.

Father Murray asked the question which Merriam had so manfully (and youthfully) repressed:

"What's that for?"

"You'll see," said Rockwell, grinning, enjoying the mystery.

Simpson remained as silent and grave as an undertaker.

The taxicab had turned several corners and covered perhaps a couple of miles of streets. Now it slowed down, stopped.

" There ain't no 612," said the driver through the tube.

Rockwell took command again.

" Isn't there? " he said. " Let's see."

He got out. Peering through the open door of the taxicab, Merriam could see that the house before which they had stopped was numbered 608.

" 612's a vacant lot," he heard the chauffeur say.

" So it seems," Rockwell replied. " Well, we'll get out here anyway."

Merriam eagerly took this cue, and the other two followed, Simpson bringing his ladder. Rockwell was handing a couple of green bills to the driver.

" Drive on opposite where 612 ought to be," he said, " and wait. We'll be back by and by."

" This way," he added, and started with Merriam and Father Murray down the street past the vacant lot. Simpson, carrying his small stepladder as unobtrusively as possible at his side, followed laggingly behind.

The square beyond the next avenue seemed to be occupied entirely by a huge block of apartments. They did not cross the avenue but turned the cor-

ner and walked on down one side of the great flat
building but on the opposite side of the street.
Their side held a miscellany of small detached
houses.

Merriam glanced at Rockwell. He was slowing
his steps and seemed to be watching a couple of men
who were moving in the same direction as their
own on the other side of the street immediately
under the apartments.

A moment later these two men turned in at one
of the entrances of the flat building. After perhaps
twenty feet more Rockwell glanced over his
shoulder. Merriam involuntarily did likewise.
Half a block behind them was Simpson with his
ladder. There was no one else in sight.

Rockwell stopped for a second, then said,
"Come!" and quickly crossed the street and entered another door of the flat building.

Within the vestibule he stopped again.

"We must wait for Simpson," he said.

He began reading the names below the battery
of bells. Merriam and Father Murray stared at
each other.

In a moment Simpson joined them with his ladder. Rockwell promptly opened the inner door of
the vestibule and proceeded to ascend the stairs.
Simpson trudged after him, and Merriam and the
priest followed perforce.

They reached the second floor and the third and
continued on up to the fourth, which was the top
floor.

Arriving there, Merriam found Rockwell pointing to a sort of trapdoor in the ceiling above the
landing at the head of the stairs.

"Right!" he whispered.

Simpson calmly set his ladder down, separated
its legs, and planted it firmly beneath the trap.
He and Rockwell paid no attention to the doors of
the two apartments which opened off the landing
within a few feet of them. Simpson ascended the
ladder and, exerting his strength, pushed the trapdoor up. It moved with a grating sound, start-
lingly loud in their quasi-burglarious situation.
The night air rushed in. The trap gave upon the
roof of the building.

Simpson did not hesitate but pulled himself up
on to the roof.

Rockwell followed.

"You're to come too," he said as he looked down
at Merriam gleefully and winked. He was evidently pleased with himself. "You wait here,
Father Murray. Remember, if any one comes
you're a roof inspector. That's next door to a sky
pilot anyway!"

The priest groaned but made no protest, well
knowing, doubtless, that rebellion now would avail
him naught, and Merriam quickly followed Rockwell on to the roof.

It was a flat tar-and-gravel roof—not an unpleasant place to be in the starry April night. They
circled about chimneys and miscellaneous pipe
heads and stepped across brick ledges, which

seemed to separate different sections of the building from one another.

Presently they were approaching the opposite side of the building, having circled the interior court and light wells. They came to another trapdoor, a twin of the one by which they had ascended.

Simpson was about to open this second trap when Rockwell spoke:

" Wait a minute! "

Stooping lower and lower till at last he seemed to be almost sitting on his heels as he walked, he made his way to the edge of the roof on the new street and peeped over the parapet—a dozen feet perhaps beyond the trapdoor. For a moment only he looked, then returned in the same cautious and laborious manner.

" We were right," he said to Simpson.

" Watchers? " Simpson asked.

" Two of them. And half way down the block a taxi."

But now Simpson was carefully raising the trapdoor. After listening for a minute he put his head down and looked.

" Coast is clear," he reported.

" Go ahead, then," said Rockwell.

So Simpson put his legs down inside, hung, and dropped into the vestibule. Rockwell and Merriam followed.

Straightening himself up inside, Merriam found Rockwell facing the door of the right-hand apartment.

" This is Jennie's! " he whispered.

CHAPTER XVIII

JENNIE

ROCKWELL knocked twice. A girl with a thin, dark face peeped out.

"Hello, Margery," said Rockwell.

"Oh, how d'you do?" said the girl, recognizing the speaker. Relief was mingled in her tone with continuing caution. "Who's with you?"

"Friends," said Rockwell. "Mr. Merriam, the Senator's double. And Simpson."

"Simpson can't come here!" said Margery sharply.

Merriam glanced at Simpson and was amazed to see how moved he was. He had a sense that the man could hardly keep himself from trembling.

"He's come to help take Norman away," said Rockwell. "He need go no farther than the hall. Come, Margery, let us in. We can't stand here all night. I'll explain to both of you inside. I'm George's friend, you know."

"Well!" Still unwillingly Margery released the chain and moved back, opening the door for them.

As they stepped inside she stared at Merriam.

"The devil!" she exclaimed.

"No," said the young man, "my name's Merriam. How do you do, Miss Milton?"

195

He looked at Margery almost as curiously as she was looking at him. He was really as innocent as Mollie June—more so, in fact, not being married,—and Margery was the first member of the *demimonde* or the near *demimonde* with whom he had ever had personal contact. He found her disappointing. She was thin to the point of angularity, in a trying yellow negligee, with straight black hair, black eyes that were unpleasantly direct, and a lean dark face that was undeniably hard.

For a moment only she stared. Then she shut the door and spoke to Simpson:

"You stay here!"

"Yes," said Simpson, with more than servitorial humility.

Rockwell was advancing into the sitting room, which opened immediately off the tiny hall, and Merriam, feeling himself dismissed by Miss Milton, followed.

Merriam's sole first impression of the sitting room was of a soft, rather agreeable harmony in yellow. The wall paper, the hangings, the upholstery of chairs and davenport, the shades of lights were all in mild tints of that pleasant colour. Probably Margery's yellow negligee was intended to fit into this ensemble.

But he had no time for detailed observation. For as they stepped forward the yellow portières at one side of the room parted, and another girl appeared between them—undoubtedly Jennie.

This time he was surprised but hardly disappointed. The figure between the portières was that of a stage parlour maid—just the right height for a soubrette and just pleasantly, youthfully slender, yet rounded, in a trim-fitting dress of some black material, cut rather low at the throat and edged with white, with a ridiculously small, purely ornamental, white apron with pockets. Black-silk-stockinged ankles and black, high-heeled satin pumps completed a picture that was both chic and demure. Merriam remembered that it was as a parlour maid that Norman had first known Jennie and guessed that this costume had been assumed for his benefit.

In a moment the portières closed behind her. She was looking at the older man, having barely glanced at Merriam.

"How do, Mr. Rockwell," she said.

Merriam, almost with alarm, recognised the tones that had so piqued him over the telephone.

Then she turned to him.

"This is —— Gee, but you're like him! I wouldn't have believed it."

"Miss Higgins, Mr. Merriam," said Rockwell tardily.

Merriam responded awkwardly:

"How do you do, Miss ——"

"'Miss Jennie' will do," interrupted Jennie.

(Merriam remembered uncomfortably how Mollie June had hit upon a similar "compromise.")

"I ain't partial to 'Higgins,'" Jennie added.

"I'm thinking of changing it to 'Montmorency.' Wouldn't 'Jennie Montmorency' be nice, Mr. Rockwell?"

"I don't think it fits very well," said Rockwell. "You'd better change it to Simpson."

Jennie coloured. She coloured easily, as Merriam was to learn. Now that she had turned again to Rockwell he had a chance to look at her face. She was an exceedingly pretty blonde. Her throat was attractively rounded, her shoulders also. Those shoulders might be unpleasant when she was older and stouter, but at present they were charming. Her chin and cheeks were also daintily full— quite the opposite of Margery Milton's. The cheeks were pink, slightly heightened with rouge perhaps but not with paint. The eyes were softly, brightly blue. The hair fair and smoothly wavy, if one may attempt to express a nuance by combining contradictory terms. In short, she was, as some of her admirers undoubtedly expressed it, "not a bit hard to look at."

For a moment Jennie's colour flooded. Then came her retort to Rockwell:

"Mind your own business," she said.

The words were sharp, but somehow the tone was not. The voice was still soft and—warm. It is the only word. It was the voice one might attribute to a kitten, if a kitten were gifted with articulate speech.

Rockwell only laughed. At the same moment Margery Milton entered from the hall, where she

had presumably been impressing upon Simpson the
necessity of remaining in strict hiding.

Jennie glanced at her friend.

"Well," she said, "may as well sit down."

She dropped into a chair and crossed one leg
over the other.

"You've come to take Georgie away," she continued as the others sat down.

"Yes," said Rockwell. "Listen, Jennie. You
too, Margery," and he began to explain the new
situation which had resulted primarily from Margery's confidences to Thompson. He did not soften
this point in his relation.

"See what your gabbling's done," said Jennie,
without anger, to her friend when he had finished.
"You always talk too much."

"I can talk if I please," said Margery sullenly.

"It will pay you better to keep still this time,"
said Rockwell.

"Pay me? How much?" demanded Margery
promptly.

"Say a hundred dollars."

"A hundred ——! I'm mum as a stone image.
When do I get it, though?"

"Here's twenty now on account." Rockwell
held out a yellow-backed bill, which Margery
quickly accepted. "You get the rest when this is
all over."

"How do I know I get the rest?"

"Shut up, Marge," said Jennie. "You know
Mr. Rockwell."

"We've no time to lose," Rockwell continued, looking at his watch. "It's twenty-five minutes to ten now. Thompson said ten, but he might come a bit sooner. We must get Norman away at once. You understand that you're to let Mr. Merriam go to bed in his stead. When Thompson comes you must admit him. You can pretend to be unwilling to do so, but you must let him in without too much fuss. You're to tell him that Norman's not here and has not been here—that there's a man here who looks tremendously like Norman and that at first you fooled Margery into thinking it was Norman."

While Rockwell was issuing these instructions Jennie's cheeks had grown hot.

"I'm not that kind," she cried. "I've never had any one but George." Margery also glowered.

"I know that, my dear," said Rockwell, mendaciously perhaps but promptly. "But you've got to do what I tell you to-night. You don't care what a fellow like Thompson thinks. He always thinks the worst anyhow. It's to save George. He'll be ruined unless we can fool Thompson completely to-night. It's for George," he repeated. "You'd do a lot for George."

Jennie's colour was subsiding. She had uncrossed her legs and was sitting erect. She looked fixedly at Rockwell.

"I *have* done a lot for him," she said.

"I know," said Rockwell. "And you'll do this to-night." He was using his most persuasive tones.

Jennie stole an almost timid glance at Merriam.
The latter's youthful chivalry was aroused. He
was filled with pity for her, mingled with something like admiration on account of her prettiness.
He saw her, more or less correctly, as a pathetic
victim of real love and a false social system. He
smiled at her reassuringly.

"It'll be all right," he said. "I shan't trouble
you at all."

Jennie's glance lingered on his face—the face
that was so much like Norman's. She saw him for
the clean, innocent, naïve boy that he was. He
was what George Norman might once have been,
long years ago. I am afraid that something akin
to interest crept into her look. She dropped her
eyes.

"All right," she said curtly to Rockwell. "I
suppose I will."

"Jennie, you're a fool!" cried Margery.

"Shut up, Marge," said Jennie, with whom this
seemed to be a frequent locution.

Rockwell had already risen.

"Is George dressed?" he asked.

"No," said Jennie. "He's too sick."

"Come, then," said Rockwell to Merriam. "We
must help him into his things."

He crossed the small room and passed through
the yellow portières. Having been at the apartment earlier in the day with Aunt Mary, he was
acquainted with its geography.

Merriam rose to follow, but he felt that something more ought to be said to relieve the half-hostile awkwardness of the situation. Jennie's eyes were still cast down.

"Is he pretty sick?" he asked as he moved across the room. He was not much concerned about Senator Norman, but he could think of no other remark.

Jennie raised her eyes and looked at him—an unreadable glance.

"Pretty sick," she said, almost indifferently.

Merriam paused a moment before the portières, looking back, still meeting her eyes.

Then he turned his own away and pushed the portières aside. He found himself in a dining room, done entirely in blue, as the sitting room was in yellow. Rockwell was already opening a door on the further side. Merriam quickened his steps and was close behind the older man in entering a small white bedroom.

On a single bed therein lay Senator George Norman. Evidently he had heard their voices in the sitting room, for he had raised himself on his elbow.

He and Merriam stared at each other in the amazement that is inevitable to two men who find themselves really bearing a striking physical resemblance to each other, however much they may have been forewarned. We are so accustomed to the idea that each of us has a sort of exclusive copyright on his own particular exterior that we cannot seriously believe in anything approaching a replica unless actually confronted with it.

The Senator did not look especially "boyish" as he lay there. His ruffled hair was indeed practically untouched with gray, but his cheeks were haggard and feverish, and there were many little wrinkles about his mouth and eyes. For all that Merriam could hardly believe he was not looking into a mirror. The experience was hardly pleasant for either man. "This is what I shall be like some time when I am old and ill," Merriam thought; and the Senator can hardly have escaped the bitter reflection of the man who has left many years behind him: "That is what I was once." Looking closer, Merriam could detect slight differences. The lips and nostrils of his distinguished relative were undoubtedly a little fuller than his own, and—yes, he surely was not flattering himself in thinking that the chin was rounder and weaker. But above all such trivial points the likeness rose overwhelmingly, incredibly complete. Merriam even recognised a similarity of movement as the sick man impatiently twisted himself on the bed.

Rockwell was standing silent, also no doubt inspecting the resemblance of which he had made such remarkable use.

The Senator was the first to find his tongue.

"So you're my virtuous double," he said, with a sort of petulant scorn.

"The voice, too!" Rockwell thought. He almost dreaded to hear Merriam's reply, which would echo the very quality and timbre of the other's speech, as if he were mocking him. But Merriam

did not seem to notice. The fact is one cannot
judge the sound of one's own voice nor appreciate
the similarity in another's tones or in an imitation.

"I'm the double," Merriam was saying.

For a moment longer the Senator stared. Then
he laughed. He evidently laughed more easily than
Merriam, and somewhat differently. Merriam
made a mental note that if he should be involved in
any further impersonation he must be careful of
his laugh.

"Well, it's rather convenient just this minute,"
said Norman, none too courteously, "though it may
be damned inconvenient in the end."

"We'll help you dress," said Rockwell. "We've
come to take you to the hotel, you know."

"Yes, I know that all right," said Norman. "If
I'm to be a damned reformer, I must get out of
this." He laughed again. "Hand me those trousers, will you?"

He put his legs out of the bed. He had already
dressed himself as far as his shirt. Then he had
apparently given the job up and got back into
bed.

"I'm weak as a kitten," he continued, "and I've
the deuce of a fever, but I guess I can make it.
You've a taxi, of course?"

"Yes," said Rockwell.

He did not tell Norman that the road to the taxi
lay through two trapdoors and across a roof.
Neither did he mention the fact that Merriam was
to stay at Jennie's or allude to Thompson's com-

ing. Perhaps he feared that if Norman knew of Thompson's approach he would prefer to stay where he was and join forces with him again.

In a very few minutes Norman was fully dressed—in the evening clothes in which he had left the hotel the night before, on his way, as he supposed, to Mayor Black's. Rockwell tied his white bow for him.

During the process of dressing he and Merriam were continually glancing at each other. Neither could resist the attraction. Several times they caught each other at it.

At about their third mutual detection, which happened during the tying of the bow, Norman laughed again.

"We're certainly a pair," he said. "Whether aces or deuces remains to be seen, eh?

"Gad, but I'm weak," he added, sinking on to the bed as Rockwell finished his job. "You may have to carry me downstairs."

"We'll carry you all right," said Rockwell. "We're all ready, aren't we?"

"I suppose so," said Norman.

Rockwell stooped and picked him up in his arms, exerting himself only moderately, apparently, in so doing. The Senator was light on account of his carefully preserved slenderness, and Rockwell was really very strong.

"Bring his hat, Merriam," said the latter.

Rockwell carried him through the blue dining room into the sitting room, Merriam following with the silk hat. Both Jennie and Margery were standing.

Norman waved his hand limply to Jennie over Rockwell's shoulder.

" Bye-bye, pet," he said. " I'm all in, you see. Sorry to have bothered you like this when I wasn't fit."

" Georgie boy! " cried Jennie.

With a little run she came up behind Rockwell, caught Norman's hand, and kissed it.

" You'll let me know how you are? You'll come back? "

" Course I will," said Norman, though he had promised Aunt Mary that afternoon that he would " cut out " Jennie and the whole of that part of his life to which she belonged.

It may be that Jennie suspected something of the sort. There were tears in her bright, soft eyes, and her cheeks were pale enough to make her slight rouging obvious.

" You will, won't you? " she said. " Come soon, Georgie boy! "

Norman only smiled at her and feebly waved again. Rockwell meanwhile was moving towards the hallway. Jennie followed closely, though Margery tried to prevent her.

" Let them go, Jen! " whispered Margery.

" Shut up, Marge! " said Jennie almost fiercely.

And then the catastrophe which Margery had been trying to forestall, and which Rockwell had not sufficiently foreseen or else had not cared to prevent, occurred: Jennie came face to face with Simpson in the little hallway. She stopped short.

"You!" she said.

"Yes, Miss Jennie," said Simpson, looking at her steadily. "I didn't mean you should see me. I came to help take Mr. Norman away. It was me that discovered the plan to catch him here."

Jennie knew from Rockwell's earlier explanation that this was true. She tried to give Simpson what she herself would probably have called the "once-over"—a scornful survey from head to foot. But her histrionic purpose failed her. Her eyes fell too quickly.

"Well, be quick about it," she said. For the first time her voice was harsh.

Rockwell meanwhile had carried Norman on into the outer hall—for Simpson had already opened the door—and set him down leaning against the banister.

"Margery!" he called sharply.

Margery, glad of any diversion, advanced quickly:

"What do you want?"

"A stepladder. Got one?"

"Why—yes!"

"Go with her, Simpson, and get it," Rockwell commanded.

"Yes, Mr. Rockwell."

"This way," said Margery, and she and Simpson passed by Jennie and Merriam, who stood a little behind Jennie, and disappeared into the flat.

Jennie gave one quick look at Norman, who was leaning weakly against the railing staring in front of him, turned away with eyes that were very bright and a little hard, brushed past Merriam, and went back into the sitting room and sat down.

Almost at the same moment Simpson returned, carrying a rather tall stepladder and followed by Margery.

Norman came out of his apathy and stared. Simpson set the ladder up in the center of the hall, mounted it, and climbed through the trap, which they had left open when they descended.

"Here. Catch!" said Rockwell. He tossed Norman's silk hat up through the trap, and Simpson caught it.

Then he stooped, picked Norman up again, and began to mount the ladder with him.

"What in hell!" said the sick man.

Rockwell did not reply but continued to mount and then hoisted the Senator up so that Simpson could catch him under the arms and draw him through the trap.

Finally he spoke to Merriam:

"Take this ladder inside. Then you must go straight to bed. He'll be here any time now. I'll 'phone from the hotel when we get there."

He swung himself up on to the roof. The trap closed.

"Well, I'll be damned!" said Margery Milton.

Merriam did not like profanity in women, even in Margeries.

"Very likely you will," he said.

Margery looked at him sharply:

"You think you're smart, don't you? Are you going to bring that ladder in?"

CHAPTER XIX

A NEW ANTAGONIST

MERRIAM shut the stepladder together, lifted it into an oblique position, and carried it through the inner hallway into the sitting room, where he stopped, not knowing where to go with it.

Jennie was still sitting. She looked up at him. The same expression of interest which had showed in her eyes once before returned to them. She smiled and shifted her position, crossing her knees. But she volunteered no information as to what he should do with the stepladder which he was awkwardly holding.

Meanwhile Margery had followed him into the inner hall, closed the door, and put up the chain. She now came past him and pushed aside the portières into the dining room.

"Bring it this way, please," she said, quite politely.

He carried the ladder through the blue dining room into a kitchenette, and thence through a door which Margery held open on to a narrow back porch, from which he had a glimpse of a sort of orderly labyrinth of steep wooden stairs and narrow back porches around the four sides of an inner court.

210

He returned into the kitchenette, which was almost entirely filled up with a gas stove. Margery shut the door.

"Go into the sitting room and talk to Jen," she said. "I want her to forget about Simpson. I'll change the bed for you."

"Thank you," said Merriam, who began to perceive that Miss Milton, in spite of her profanity, had certain admirable qualities.

He went through the dining room, hesitated for a moment before the portières—he could not have said why,—and then pushed them open.

Jennie had risen and was standing beside a table between the windows. The table held a parchment-shaded lamp, a newspaper, a small camera, and a bowl of violets. Merriam had not noticed the flowers before. He remembered the violets worn by the floor clerk at the hotel, and wondered whether George Norman had saved himself trouble at the florist's by ordering two bunches from the same lot, to be sent to different addresses.

Jennie was looking down at the flowers. She must have been aware of his presence. If so, she was apparently content that he should have the benefit of a good look at her trim figure and at her face in profile, which was its best view. She had a pretty nose; the artificially heightened colour of her cheeks was charming in this light; and the bright knob of her fair hair over her ear was a most alluring ornament.

In a moment she bent gracefully down to smell

the violets. As she straightened up she turned to look at him—a serious, appraising look that was somehow intimate. Then she smiled brightly.

"Come in, Mr. ——" (she seemed to forget his name and let it go) "and sit down."

She tripped across the room to the davenport and sat, indicating that he was to sit beside her.

Merriam wanted both to take that seat and not to take it. He took it.

She crossed one leg over the other and looked at him, smiling. One small, squarish, plump hand lay on her knee, ready, Merriam half divined, to be taken if any one should desire to take it. He wondered if it were true that she had "never had any one but George."

"I forget your name," she said confidentially.

"Merriam." It was not said stiffly. He was too much attracted to be stiff. He realised that he was answering her smile.

"What's your first name?"

"John."

"Then I shall call you 'John.' I don't like last names—and 'Mister' and 'Miss.'"

"They're stiff," he said, "playing up" alarmingly as on a former occasion.

She scrutinised his face, growing grave.

"You're awfully like George," she said, "except here."

She raised her hand, and with the tip of her forefinger touched his chin.

"You're sterner," she added.

It was the very point Merriam himself had noted.
He admired her acuteness of observation. And of
course he was flattered. But he realised that he
was not being particularly stern at that moment.

"I expect I am," he said, trying to look, if not to
be, more so.

Jennie moved an inch or two farther away from
him, as if a little frightened by the iron qualities
of this male.

"Where's Margery?" she asked.

"Here," said Margery's voice, with disconcerting
patness.

She came through the portières and surveyed the
two of them with an ironical look that was by no
means lost on Merriam. He felt ashamed of himself.

But Jennie gave him a quick glance with a little
pout in it, as if to say, "What a nuisance! When
we were just beginning to get acquainted!"

And straightway his shame fled and he smiled at
her.

Margery, however, was speaking in her most
businesslike tones:

"I've changed your bed, and you'd better get into
it as quick as you can. It's late now."

"Yes," said Merriam, rising. "What time is it?"

Before he could get out his own timepiece Jennie
raised her arm and glanced at a small gold wrist
watch.

"Oh! Five minutes after ten!" she cried. She
rose too. "You must hurry."

"Yes," said Merriam.

He moved to the portières—hesitated. He did not know how to take leave under these novel circumstances.

"Good night, ladies," he ventured in rather ceremonious tones.

To his chagrin both girls burst out laughing.

"Good night, gentleman!" Jennie called merrily after him, and their renewed giggling pursued him as, in painful confusion, he crossed to the door of the bedroom.

He shut that door behind him and rapidly undressed, stimulated to speed in his operations by a vigorous mental kicking of himself as an ass and a "boob." A suit of pajamas, apparently quite new, was laid out on a chair. He got into these and slipped into bed.

The moment he was recumbent he realised that he had forgotten to turn out his light. No matter. He had no idea of sleeping. Besides Thompson would be there any minute.

Ah, Thompson! With relief his mind seized upon this topic. It was sufficiently absorbing. Any minute now Thompson would burst in, demanding Senator Norman. He, Merriam, would pretend he had never seen Thompson before, never even heard of him. "My name is not Norman," he would say. "My name is Merriam. Who are you? And what do you want?" Thompson would stare, falter, begin to apologise and explain. It was pleasingly dramatic. He pursued the interview. His own conduct therein displayed the quintessence of composure and *savoir faire.* Jennie and Margery—yes, both of them were present— would be impressed; they would laugh at him no longer. Thompson was sacrificed mercilessly.

But the minutes passed and nothing happened. There was no sign of the real Thompson. What was wrong? The silence of the small, lighted bedroom began to get on Merriam's excited nerves. Had Thompson somehow, in spite of Rockwell's elaborate precautions, got wind of the real situation, discovered their trick before it was played? Had he remained at the hotel, seen the real Norman return, and perceived the whole imposition?

A light knock sounded on his door. Merriam jumped and then lay still.

" Can I come in? "

It was Jennie's voice.

" Yes," he said, embarrassed; but what other reply could be made?

Jennie opened the door and came to his bedside. She had changed her attire completely. She now wore the costume of a *ballerina*—a tight pink corsage, very low and sleeveless, with the slightest of pink loops over her shoulders, a short, fluffy pink skirt barely to her knees, pink tights, and pink dancing slippers. Over one of the bright knobs of her hair was a pink rose. She was much more brilliantly rouged than before, and he was conscious of a warm scent of powder and perfume.

Merriam lay staring at her without speaking,

subconsciously shocked perhaps, but openly bewildered and fascinated.

She smiled at him and seemed to be inspecting
him in return. Her left hand hung at her side,
holding something heavy, but she put out her right
and touched his hair—with a single little movement ruffled it.

"You look very nice lying there," she said in the
most natural tones in the world. "How do I
look?"

She stepped back and pirouetted, turning completely around on her toes. The fluffy pink skirts
swung out and circled with her in a most entranc-
ing manner. Merriam was quite dazzled. The
white gleam of her back as she turned, the slender
white arms, held gracefully away from her sides,
in spite of that heavy something in one hand, the
tight slimness of the waist, the glimpse of pink legs
beneath the circling skirt—he had seen the like
only on the stage. It was rather overpowering so
close at hand.

But in a single rosy moment her revolution was
completed. She was facing him again and relaxing down off her toes.

"How do I look?" she repeated, smiling, with
the slightest natural augmentation of her artificial
flush.

Merriam swallowed. "Stunning!" he ejaculated.

She beamed. "Of course I do," she said.

Then her face seemed to harden. She stepped

closer to the bed so that she was almost bending over him.

"I've got a part to play," she said. "Well, I'm going to play it." There was a touch of something like defiance in her voice now. "I've cooked up a plot for Mister Thompson. Marge don't like it, but she'll help. I'll show him! You've got to help too."

She raised her left hand, displaying the heavy object held therein, which he had not yet identified. He was somewhat startled to see that it was a small revolver.

"Take it," she said.

As he did not instantly put out his arm she tossed it across so that it fell on the bed on the other side of him.

"It's loaded," she said, "with blanks. Mister Thompson shall see you first. But afterwards Marge and I will see what we can do with him. We'll get him to stay for a little supper, and I'm going to play up to him. I'll do a dance on the table. But when he tries to catch me I'll scream. That's where you come in. You rush out with your revolver and drive him out of the house. Won't it be fun?" she demanded, glowing with excitement. "We'll have the goods on him. He'll keep his face shut after that. Whatever he knows or thinks about George! We'll have a fine story for Mrs. Thompson, if he don't. Oh!"

A doorbell had rung loudly in the kitchenette.

"There he is now. Remember! When I scream!"

She was gone from the bedroom, closing the door behind her.

Merriam lay as if dazed. This "high life" was proving almost too fast for his bucolic and pedagogical wits. He jumped when the bell rang again more violently. Then he heard the sound of the hall door being opened and a loud masculine voice. Was it Thompson's? A moment or two later the voice became more distinct, and he could hear the girls' voices too. He could not be sure it was Thompson. Was it some one of his "henchmen" instead? Whoever he was, he was in the sitting room. In a moment or two he would almost certainly be coming out to the bedroom.

Merriam suddenly remembered the revolver and reached for it and slipped it under the bedclothes.

He had several minutes more to wait. The voices became lower. Then they were raised again. Suddenly he heard the rings of the portières clash— the curtains had been sharply flung aside. Margery's thin voice came to him.

"See for yourself, then!" it said.

"That's better," said the masculine voice in tones half amused, half irritated. *Was* it Thompson?

Light footsteps and heavy footsteps crossed the dining room together. The bedroom door was opened.

"Sir," said Margery to Merriam, in tones a little shrill with excitement, "this is a Mr. Crockett. He has some crazy notion about your being Senator Norman. See for yourself, Mr.—Crockett!" She spoke his name as though it were an insult. "Remember, he's sick," she added warningly. Margery was not a bad actress.

Crockett! Crockett himself! So much the better! With an effort Merriam steadied his nerves. Mr. Crockett advanced to the bedside—a tall, imposing gentleman in evening clothes with keen blue eyes and a thin remnant of lightish hair.

"Well, George," he said blandly, "glad to see you. Your little friends are very loyal. But they couldn't keep me away from you."

Merriam instantly disliked Mr. Crockett. He plunged with zest into his part.

"George?" he inquired coldly. "My name's not George!"

"Oh, come, come, Norman! You're caught. Fess up."

But he looked closer. At the same moment Margery lifted a silk shade off the electric bulb by the bureau, and the cold hard light fell full on the younger man's face.

"Who do you think I am?" said Merriam. "And who are you?" he added in an insolent tone.

The impressive financier stared. He bent down and stared harder.

"Well?" Merriam demanded with all the hauteur he could muster. And then: "Got an eye-ful?"

He had preconceived this colloquy in much more dignified phrases, but the insulting tag of boyish slang popped out of him unawares. However, he could not have done better. Probably he could never, by taking thought, have done as well. Senator Norman would assuredly not have used that expression; it had been coined long since his day in Boyville.

Mr. Crockett was convinced. But he was a gentleman of considerable imperturbability. He merely straightened up and asked:

"Who *are* you? "

The younger man suddenly decided not to give his name. There was that in Mr. Crockett's blue eyes that suggested an uncomfortable pertinacity and ruthlessness in following up any clue he might get hold of.

"What business is that of yours? " said Merriam.

Mr. Crockett blinked. He was doubtless unaccustomed to such replies. But he merely asked another question:

"Where are you from? "

"Down State," said Merriam. That was both insolent and safe: Illinois is tolerably sizable.

"How old are you? "

Merriam saw an advantage in answering this query truthfully.

"Twenty-eight," he said. "What of it? "

"You don't happen to be a young nephew or cousin of Senator Norman's, do you? " asked Mr. Crockett, hitting the bull's-eye with his first arrow.

Merriam, somewhat startled, countered with a flat denial:

"No, I'm not. I've been told I look like him," he added. "Somebody took me for him last night.

But I'm only related to him through Adam and
Eve—so far as I know."

Mr. Crockett scanned him narrowly:

"Somebody took you for Norman last night?"

"They sure did." Having struck the slangy note
by accident, Merriam was enough of an actor to
keep it up.

"I should be much obliged if you will tell me
about that."

Merriam's self-confidence returned. He had
been realising how little this dialogue was develop-
ing in accordance with his pleasing anticipations.
Instead of the rôle of a polished man of the world,
delivering brilliant thrusts of irony and reducing
his interlocutor to apologetic confusion, he had
stumbled inadvertently on that of a slangy youth,
submitting to be catechised by an individual who
remained singularly composed and had proved dan-
gerously shrewd. But at last he had led up ad-
roitly enough to the story which Rockwell had
charged him to tell. He set himself to tell it in
character:

"Well, if you want to know, I came up to the
City on business—yesterday. When I got my work
done I thought I'd have a little fun—see the sights,
you know. I don't know this town much, but I got
hold of a taxi man who took me around. I looked
in at several places. I guess I had a pretty good
time. I don't remember much. I had more high-
balls than I'm used to. We ended up at a dance
hall somewhere. There were some pretty girls

there. Somebody said, 'You're Senator Norman, aren't you?' That struck me as funny. 'Sure, I am,' I said, and I kept it up. Soon everybody in the place was calling me 'Senator.' I treated the gang. Then I got into a fight. I don't remember how. Somebody knocked me down, I think. But I wasn't hurt any. After that I picked up this little girl that lives here—the one in pink,—and she brought me home with her. I had a bad head on this morning and a bad cold besides. The little girl is a good sport. She let me stay here all day. I'm going down home in the morning."

" I see," said Mr. Crockett slowly.

Merriam had need of all his self-command to conceal his elation as he perceived that his formidable antagonist had swallowed bait, hook, and sinker, as the idiom goes. He was obviously piecing Merriam's narrative together in his mind with the *Tidbits* story about Norman. Margery, who had remained standing unobtrusive and silent by the bureau, flashed Merriam a commendatory glance.

Stimulated thereby, he pertly followed up his advantage:

" Care for any more of my personal memoirs? "

" No, thank you," said Mr. Crockett with a rather sour smile. " Good night, Mr.—Mr.——"

He was angling for the name again, but with a feebleness unworthy of a great financier.

" Mr. Blank," said Merriam. " I've a bit of a reputation to keep up in my own home town."

"I see," said Mr. Crockett again. "Well, I'm sorry to have intruded. Take care of your reputation!"

He turned away towards the door.

In that open door Jennie had stood listening. Now her cue had come. She took it promptly. She advanced into the bedroom, stepping lightly on her toes, her pink skirt waving prettily. She smiled her brightest smile at Mr. Crockett.

"He isn't Senator Norman, is he?" she cried gaily.

"He certainly isn't," said Mr. Crockett, looking at her. No man could have helped looking at her.

"You were awfully rude about it," said Jennie, pouting. She had stopped about two feet in front of him.

"Was I?"

"I should say you were. Awfully! You ought to do something to make up for it."

"What ought I to do?" asked Mr. Crockett.

"You might stay for a little supper with Margery and me."

"Might I?"

Unexpectedly Mr. Crockett looked away from Jennie. He looked at Merriam, thoughtfully—a disconcerting thoughtfulness. Then he turned back to Jennie.

"Perhaps I might," he said, with a faint smile.

Merriam read his mind. He was sure he did. The man might or might not be slightly attracted by Jennie's prettiness, but what he was thinking was that he would be able to get more out of her than he had been able to get from Merriam. The latter at once perceived that Jennie's melodramatic scheme was dangerous and silly. It might have been all right with Thompson, but not with this man. She hadn't sense enough to see the difference. But he could do nothing to stop her.

Already she had cried, "Oh, goody!" like a little girl.

She stepped past Mr. Crockett, brushing him with her skirts, put her hands on his shoulders, and began playfully to push him towards the dining room.

"It's all ready," she was saying. "We got it for the man inside, but he says he isn't hungry. We have sandwiches and olives and cheese and beer—and there's whiskey, if you like."

"I'll take beer," said Mr. Crockett, mustering a certain lightness and allowing himself to be pushed.

Merriam looked at Margery, still standing by the bureau. She too had changed her costume. She now wore an evening dress of black and gold, in which she looked very well, rather brilliant, in fact. But what Merriam noticed was the understanding look in her eyes. She had read Mr. Crockett's purpose as clearly as he had.

"We'll be careful," she said. "You did fine. Shall I turn out the light?"

"No," said Merriam. "Leave it, please."

She walked out of the room and closed the door.

CHAPTER XX

AN EVENTFUL SUPPER PARTY

THOUGH Margery had closed the door Merriam could hear practically everything that went on in the adjoining room—as one commonly can in an apartment.

"Get the food from the ice chest, will you, Marge?" cried Jennie, in tones whose gaiety sounded genuine. "I'll set out the drinks. Let's have a cocktail to start with, Mr. ——"

She interrupted herself:

"What's your first name?"

"Well," said Crockett, "one of my first names is Henry."

"Then I'll call you 'Harry.' I hate last names—and 'Mister' and 'Miss'!"

Merriam in his recumbent solitude made a cynically humorous grimace. She had used those very words with him—had begun the same way. Her regular formula doubtless.

"I'm 'Jennie,' you know," she continued. "Now, what kind of cocktail?"

"I'll stick to beer, please."

"But I want to start with a cocktail! Have one with me! Please!"

The tone was that of a teasing child. In his

mind's eye Merriam could see vividly the trim pink figure (as it had pirouetted before him) and the pretty pouting face. But Crockett was apparently unmoved.

"Bye and bye," he said suavely. "Go ahead with your cocktail. We don't all have to drink the same things, do we? I'll start with beer and work up to cocktails."

"Well, then," said Jennie, with a swift return to unpetulant gaiety, "Marge is bringing your old beer. Oh, goody! See! Cheese sandwiches and chicken sandwiches and lettuce-and-mayonnaise sandwiches!"

Evidently Margery had returned well laden from the ice chest.

"Which kind will you have, Harry?"

"Cheese, thank you," said "Harry."

"There! With my own fingers!"

Jennie spoke with some confidence that the touch of her fingers would render bread and cheese ambrosial.

"Thank you," said "Harry" again, with the barest nuance of dryness in his tone. "I'll open the beer. What will you drink, Miss Milton?"

Undoubtedly he was snubbing Jennie! Those blue eyes of his might perhaps be attentive enough to white arms and tight waists and pink legs when he himself had sought them out, but they were not to be distracted by any such frivolous phenomena when serious business was afoot. Jennie would fail! Merriam was sure of it.

But at any rate she was not easily snubbed.

"Her name's Margery," she cried, consistent in her antipathy to surnames.

"Well, Margery?" said Crockett, complaisantly.

"Beer," said Margery.

It was the first word Merriam had heard her speak. Her taciturnity comforted him. Jennie was a little fool, but Margery would keep her head. They would waste their time and their sandwiches and beer on Crockett, but perhaps she would foil any inquiries he might presently attempt.

"Don't set things in the middle of the table, Marge," cried Jennie. "Set 'em around the edge. I'm going to do a dance for you, Harry. Wouldn't you like to see me dancing on the table?"

"It would be very charming," said "Harry." But the tone was merely gallant; it betokened no quickening of pulse.

"I must have a sandwich first, though," said Jennie quickly. Even she perceived that she was not making progress.

There followed eating and drinking, accompanied by a patter of gay, disconnected sallies from Jennie, relating chiefly to the eatables and drinkables. "Harry," continually appealed to by that name, remained calmly polite. Margery, when addressed, responded in monosyllables. Ripe olives and cold tongue and mustard were produced. Jennie had her cocktail, and then another. She needed stimulant, poor girl, to keep up the gay vivacity which was meeting with so little encouragement. A second bottle of beer was opened for "Harry" and Margery.

Meanwhile Merriam, still listening, was engaged also in active cogitation. He saw well enough into Crockett's thought. The latter had been momentarily convinced by his, Merriam's, well-told tale. (Margery had said he had "done fine.") But the keen, realistic mind behind those blue eyes had almost immediately rebounded and seized upon the overwhelming inherent improbability of that yarn. That there should be a man without close relationship to Norman who resembled him so strongly was in itself decidedly remarkable. That this man should encounter Norman's mistress, by pure chance, at a public dance and go home with her was even more curious. And that all this should happen, merely fortuitously, on the very night on which Senator Norman had unaccountably broken, before nine o'clock, solemn promises given with every appearance of sincerity and willingness shortly before eight, and suddenly gone over to a party for which throughout a score of years he had expressed nothing but dislike and contempt—the mathematical chances against such a series of coincidences were simply incalculable.

It was a quick, clear perception of this abstract, apriori incredibility that Merriam had read in Crockett's final glance before Jennie playfully pushed him out of the bedroom. Doubtless he was still revolving it in his mind as he sat at Jennie's table, responding with merely mechanical polite-

ness to her rather pitiful attempts to pique his interest and desire. Well, let him revolve it. The
story all hung together. What could he make of
it? Little enough, probably, with the data he had
now. But that was why he was lingering here at
Jennie's—in the hope of getting more data. After
another cocktail or two Jennie would not know
what she was saying. Then he would begin to hint,
to ask questions. Could Margery keep her quiet?
A single word might give him a clue.

Merriam became conscious of a wish that Rockwell were at hand to help. But that wish instantly
gave birth to further fears. Rockwell had said he
would telephone from the hotel as soon as they
arrived. That message might come any minute
now—with Crockett there! Whereabouts in the
flat was the telephone? He had not noticed it anywhere. He looked about the bedroom. But it was
not there, of course.

Ought not that message to have come already?
Surely they should be at the hotel by now unless
something had gone wrong. He suddenly envis-
aged all the perils of discovery, which he had hith-
erto been too much occupied to realise, involved in
the transportation of the sick Senator across the
roof—down through the other trapdoor into the
other hall—down three flights of stairs—along
two blocks of city street to the taxi. They
might so easily have been noted by some of
Thompson's, or Crockett's, watchers, and followed
to the hotel. Then they would be caught in-

deed—in the very fact. Verily, the paths of the impostor are perilous!

Then Merriam's mind was brought sharply back from these alarming excursions to his own scarcely less dangerous situation. Crockett had for the first time volunteered a remark. It was just such a remark as Merriam had anticipated.

"Nice boy you have in there."

His voice was slightly lowered but only slightly. Perhaps he did not realise the perfection of the acoustic properties of flats.

"Very nice boy!" agreed Jennie cordially.

Merriam noticed with alarm just the faintest touch of the effect of cocktails in her accent. How many had the girl had by now?

"So you met him at Reiberg's, did you?" Crockett pursued.

"Reiberg's?" said Jennie doubtfully, "Reiberg's?"

"Yes," Margery cut in. "Picked him up there and brought him home. I call it a shame. Jen's never done that sort of thing before."

"I expect you took to him because he looks so much like Senator Norman," suggested Crockett, rather skillfully persistent.

"Yes," said Jennie, "looks very like George. But he's *not* George. He's John!"

"John what?" asked Crockett mildly.

"John Blank!" said Margery sharply. "He told you he didn't want to give his name. Jen, keep your face shut!"

"I beg your pardon, I'm sure," said Crockett.

"Have a cocktail now!" said Jennie, quite unabashed.

Crockett at last agreed to a cocktail, and it was fixed for him, and the conversation, if such it could be called, again concerned itself with incidents to the consumption of food and drink.

Thank God for Margery! She had won the first trick. But Crockett would try again. And Jennie would grow more and more difficult to handle. Aside from the danger, Merriam hated to think of Jennie's getting really drunk. Could not Margery get rid of the man? The trouble was he had stayed at Jennie's invitation. Could not he, Merriam, do something?

He felt under the bedclothes until he found the revolver. He drew it out and looked at it. But of what use was it, really? Would Crockett blench at the mere pointing of a pistol? He doubted it. It was loaded only with blanks, Jennie had said. And he dared not fire it anyway. The occupants of a dozen adjoining flats would hear the report. People would come bursting in. The police would be called. Well, was not that the solution? To have Crockett caught in that flat by the police in connection with a shooting? Perhaps, but not a nice one for himself. Not to be tried except as the very last resort. Besides, would it serve their purpose? A public exposure of Crockett would do no good. What they needed was a threat of possible exposure to hold over him—not the exposure itself.

If only Jennie could succeed in her purpose of enticing him into some display of amorousness, of which he and Margery might be witnesses. It would be pleasant to "have the goods on him," to use Jennie's phrase. Why did she not dance for him? But Crockett would not be enticed. He might, however, pretend to be. He might decide to "play up" in that way if through Margery's watchfulness he could get nothing out of Jennie without doing so.

But now there flashed into Merriam's mind a doubt of the efficacy of Jennie's scheme even if they should succeed in carrying it out. Suppose Crockett should catch hold of her after her dance and try to kiss her, and she should scream, and he should rush out with his revolver, and Crockett should be intimidated thereby into ignominious exit? That would be very good fun, but would it give them any hold over him in case of need? He could deny it. Against his word the only witnesses would be Jennie and Margery, whose testimony would not be taken very seriously, and himself—a nobody and an impostor. No wonder Margery, the clearheaded, had disapproved. They ought to get more tangible evidence—something in writing, or a photograph.

He suddenly remembered the camera on the table in the living room, and recalled also a certain college episode, a rather lurid incident of his fraternity days, in which a camera and a girl and a priggish freshman had figured. It suggested to him a decidedly picturesque and venturesome procedure against Crockett. But he shook his head. It was too violent, too rough. All very well for a parcel of boys with a freshman. But with Mr. Crockett, the mighty capitalist! No! Hardly!

Just then he heard Jennie say:

"Get your mandolin, Marge. I'm going to dance now."

"Fine!" said Crockett. But he was still cool, amused.

Margery made no reply, but she evidently complied. In a moment there came a preliminary strumming on the mandolin.

"Help me up, Harry," said Jennie.

"With pleasure," said "Harry."

He was helping her to mount on to the table.

"Move that siphon off," Jennie said. "I might kick it over."

There was gay excitement in her voice. Cocktails had made her indifferent to appreciation. As for Merriam, the conscience of a realist compels me to report a sense of disappointment: he wanted to see the dance.

"Now sit down again," cried Jennie. "You can see better."

At this frankness Crockett laughed. There was the sound of his dropping into a chair.

"Now, Marge!" Jennie commanded.

But Margery did not strike into her tune and the dance did not begin, for at that instant the telephone rang.

It was in the dining room, then!

There was a quick movement of chairs and feet. Then Crockett's voice said, " Hello! "

He was answering it!

" That's not fair! " cried Margery. " It's not for you! "

" Keep off! " said Crockett in a quick, stern whisper, and then, evidently into the telephone, " Yes! Yes! "

Merriam leapt out of bed, revolver in hand, in his pajamas and flung open the door.

Crockett was standing by the wall at the telephone. Jennie, in her ballet costume, stood transfixed in the center of the table. Margery was rushing at Crockett.

" You—you spy! " she screamed.

Merriam, in the door, pointed his revolver.

" Drop it! " he cried, meaning the telephone receiver. " Hands up! "

But Crockett, catching Margery by the shoulder with his free hand, held her powerfully at arm's length and only smiled at Merriam's revolver.

" Why? " he asked into the telephone, and added quickly, " Nothing! These girls are romping so! "

But his words could hardly be heard for Margery's screaming. He dropped the receiver and put the hand thus freed over the mouthpiece.

" Shut up! " he said fiercely to Margery, and gave her shoulder a violent wrench.

" O—oh! " she groaned.

Something had to be done instantly, for Crockett

was turning back to the telephone. With a sort of impulsive desperation Merriam threw the revolver at Crockett's head. The man dodged, and the revolver struck the opposite wall and fell to the floor. But the movement took him away from the telephone, and Merriam, rushing forward, added the impetus of a straight-arm thrust, which sent him staggering against the table.

Then Merriam caught up the receiver.

"Hello! Hello!" he cried into the mouthpiece.

For an instant no reply. Then Central's voice said sweetly:

"Your party's hung up." And added, in tones of unwonted interest: "What's the row there? Shall I send the police?"

"No, no!" said Merriam. "There's nothing wrong here."

He hung up and turned to face the room.

Crockett was still leaning against the table. Margery was clutching the arm which a moment before had gripped her, and Jennie had jumped down from the table and caught hold of his other arm. But the financier appeared very little ruffled. He even smiled at Merriam, not unpleasantly.

"Well, Mr. Merriam," he said, "suppose we sit down and talk it over—if these ladies will release me, that is."

"Mr. Merriam!" Then the message *had* been from Rockwell, and Crockett had got the name after all. How much more had he learned? Merriam was quite willing to talk in the hope of finding that out.

"Very well," he said. "Let him go, Margery,—Jennie."

"I'll dance for both of you!" cried Jennie, whose cheeks were decidedly flushed.

"No!" said Merriam. "Sit down, please."

"Sit down, Jen!" seconded Margery, viciously.

"Oh, well!" Jennie plopped petulantly into a chair.

The others sat, Merriam and Crockett across from each other. The financier looked steadily at the younger man.

"Miss Milton was right," he began quietly. "The message was not for me. It was for you, Mr. Merriam. I think I ought to give it to you."

"If you please," said Merriam.

"It was that you should 'come at once to the hotel.' "

Merriam managed not to blink.

"What hotel?" he asked.

For an instant Crockett weighed his answer. Then:

"The De Soto," he said.

But Merriam had read the meaning of the momentary pause: Rockwell had not named the hotel —he wouldn't, of course—Crockett was guessing.

"De Soto?" he asked, looking as puzzled as he could. "I thought it might be from the Nestor House." (He was using the first name that popped into his head.)

"Oh," said Crockett lightly, "Mr. Rockwell would be much more likely to telephone from the De Soto."

Merriam was startled, but he could only go on as he had begun.

"Rockwell?" he echoed, as if still further mystified.

"Come, come," said Crockett, "I recognised his voice. I know it perfectly."

"No friend of mine," Merriam persisted. There might be no advantage in continued denial, but certainly there could be none in admission.

"Really, Mr. Merriam, hadn't you better tell me the whole story? You'll not find me ungenerous. I'll let you down easy."

"The whole story?" said Merriam. "Thought I told you my whole story in the bedroom a while back. What more do you want?"

Crockett shrugged his shoulders. He smiled blandly:

"What I want is another cocktail, I guess. You'll join me, Mr. Merriam? You've had nothing all evening. It must have been dull for you, lying in there, while these pretty ladies have been entertaining me so charmingly. I understood you were sick, you know," he added slyly, "or I should have insisted on your coming out long ago." Then, quickly, so as to give Merriam no chance to reply: "Jennie, my dear, let's have your pretty dance now. We were interrupted."

"No," said Jennie, rather sleepily, "I'm tired."

"Have a cocktail," said Crockett promptly.
"Then you'll be all right again."

Jennie looked up with interest. "Well," she
said.

Crockett rose to mix the drinks.

"You'll have one, too, Mr. Merriam?"

But during the brief interchange between Crockett and Jennie, Merriam had been doing some quick
thinking—wild thinking, perhaps. The plan suggested by his college memory, which before he had
rejected as too violent, his mind now seized upon
and was eagerly shaping to the present situation.

When Crockett addressed him, he rose.

"No," he said. "I'm tired too. I *am* sick."
He simulated a slight dizziness. "I'll go lie down
again. If you'll excuse me."

He moved to the bedroom door, affecting uncer-
tainty in his steps. As he passed into the bedroom
he called: "Margery!"

CHAPTER XXI

FLASH LIGHTS

IN a moment Margery had followed him.

"Shut the door." He barely formed the words with his lips.

She obeyed.

"That camera—in the sitting room," he whispered. "Can you take a flash light with it?"

"Sure," came the whispered answer. "That's what we use it for."

"Have you any rope?"

"Rope?" echoed Margery's whisper. "There's a clothesline on the back porch."

"Bring it to me!"

Margery looked at him. But a high degree of mutual confidence had been established between these two. She nodded.

"Right away?"

"Yes. *He* mustn't see it."

"No."

She opened the door and closed it behind her. Merriam sat on the edge of the bed, thinking hard.

"He wants a drink of water," he heard her say to the others in the dining room.

With one ear, so to speak—that is to say, with so much of his mind as could attend to one ear,—

he listened to Crockett and Jennie, engaged still in the business of mixing drinks. With the rest of his mind he was making plans, with a rapidity and confident daring that astonished himself.

In a moment Margery had returned. In her right hand she carried a glass of water. Her left hand, hanging at her side, seemed to hold carelessly only a newspaper, folded in two. But as soon as she had closed the door she produced from between the folds a fairly stout clothesline, loosely coiled.

Merriam tried its toughness and surveyed its length.

"All right," he whispered. "Now go back. Drink with them. Jennie must dance. And have Crockett sit where he was before."

This was at the end of the table nearest the telephone and nearest also to Merriam's door.

Again Margery looked at him. She glanced at the rope. But she asked no questions. Without a word she went out and closed the door behind her. Admirable girl!

Merriam's next actions were rather remarkable. He felt hastily in the pockets of his trousers, which lay over a chair, and produced a penknife. With this instrument he cut off four pieces of rope, each about four feet long. This left about ten feet in the main piece. With this main piece he proceeded to manufacture a slip noose, carefully testing both the strength of the slipknot and the readiness of its slipping. Then he gathered the noose and the four other pieces of rope into his left hand and rose and stood before the door, drawing a deep breath and listening.

He had, of course, kept track more or less of the happenings in the other room. Margery, on returning, had demanded another glass of beer and had yielded to insistence that she have a cocktail instead. Then she had suggested that Jennie dance. Jennie had already been assisted on to the table again, and Margery was picking tentatively at her mandolin.

"R-ready!" cried Jennie, a little unsteadily.

Merriam stepped back and turned the button of his electric bulb, so as to have no light behind him.

Then, as Margery struck into a bright quick tune, he softly opened the door with his right hand, holding his left hand with the ropes behind him, and stood looking at Jennie, whose pink toes had begun to patter merrily on the polished table.

Jennie saw him and laughed to him, her eyes and her cheeks bright.

"Come in, Johnny," she cried, and for a second one pink leg pointed straight at him as she turned.

"Couldn't resist, eh?" chuckled Crockett, who was leaning back in the heavy chair Merriam had wished him to occupy. He was apparently really pleased for the first time. "Don't blame you," he added. "Come on in."

His eyes, quite unsuspicious, returned to the circling skirts and the flushed face bobbing above them.

This was Merriam's moment.

He stepped quickly behind Crockett's chair, dropped the short pieces of rope on the floor, raised the noose with both hands, slipped it over the man's head, and pulled it suddenly tight about his neck.

Crockett emitted a strangled oath and started to rise, but Merriam with one hand on his shoulder thrust him down again, and with the other tightened the noose about his throat.

"Sit still," he threatened, "or I'll choke you!"

Margery's tune had stopped abruptly, and Jennie stood still on the table, staring down in frightened bewilderment.

"Margery!" Merriam commanded, "take one of these pieces of rope and tie his arm to the arm of the chair."

The arm referred to was immediately raised away from the chair, but the noose tightened with a further jerk, and the arm fell limply back. In fact Crockett was gasping and choking so desperately that Merriam was compelled to loosen the rope a little.

"Take it quietly," he cautioned, with perhaps a trifle more of youthful ferocity and exultation than the romantic hero should exhibit, "or I'll hang you sitting down!"

Margery, obedient as usual, had stepped quickly forward, picked up a piece of rope, and begun to bind the arm nearest her to the chair.

Crockett, somewhat eased, though still gasping a little, turned his head to look at Merriam. His first involuntary startled alarm was passing. The

blue eyes looked steadily at the young man. A
trace of their earlier cool amusement returned. He
looked away again and sat perfectly still, acquies-
cent.

Merriam, however, remained warily at his post
in charge of the slip noose while Margery tied both
arms.

"Now tie his feet to the legs of the chair," said
Merriam. "Jennie, you can help. Jump down
and tie his right foot while Margery ties the
left."

But Jennie, still on the table, shook her pretty
head.

"I'd rather dance," she said, and regardless of
the lack of music she folded her arms and began to
do the steps of the Highland Fling.

"Let her alone," said Margery, who had gone
down on her knees and was at work on the left foot.

Jennie tossed her head and quickened the tempo
of her dance, keeping her eyes on Crockett, who,
though still swallowing with difficulty, affected to
regard her with interest.

Margery crossed to Crockett's other side and
knelt again. In a moment she completed her labours and rose, her cheeks a little reddened by her
posture and vigorous work.

"There!" she said, looking straight at Merriam,
as if she were a soldier reporting to his officer.

"Thank you very much," said the young man.

He loosened the noose, leaving it still in place,
however, about Crockett's neck. Then he stepped

to the side of the table and held out his arms to
Jennie.

"Come!" he said, "I'll lift you down."

She stood still. "You don't like my dancing,"
she pouted. "*He* likes it!" She pointed at Crockett, who, twisting his eased neck about, smiled.

"I'll like lifting you down," said Merriam.

Jennie smiled and approached the edge of the
table. For a moment he held a rosy, fragrant bur-
den in his arms, and in that moment Jennie raised
her face to his as if to be kissed. She was really
rather incorrigible.

On a different occasion the young man might
have been irresistibly tempted (he had not thought
of Mollie June for a long time), but just now he
was no more in a mood to be enticed than Crockett
had been an hour before.

He set her lightly and quickly on her feet.

"There!" he said.

She made a face at him and dropped petulantly
into a chair.

Merriam turned to face his well-trussed victim.

The said victim was now sufficiently at ease to
open the conversation.

"Well, Mr. Merriam," he said, "you've managed
it rather cleverly. Very neat, in fact. You have
me a prisoner all right. But what's the big idea?
It seems to me you've only given yourself away.
Before I only knew your name and that you were
in connection with Rockwell and that your presence was desired at some hotel—the Nestor House,

we'll say, to avoid argument. Now it's very clear that you are deeply implicated in the extraordinary events that have been happening. Otherwise you would have had no sufficient motive for this rather violent, not to say melodramatic, line of conduct." He glanced, with a smile, at his pinioned arms.

This point of view, however, had already occurred to Merriam; and the answer was that Crockett, knowing already of a direct, confidential connection between Senator Norman's double and Senator Norman's new manager, would in a few hours at most be able to work out the whole truth of the situation.

So he only answered his victim's smile with another smile equally good-humoured.

" I don't think I've given away anything much," he said. " And I felt it was time to take out a bit of insurance."

" Insurance?" repeated Crockett.

" Yes. Insurance that you will treat me with that generosity which you half promised a while ago."

" I promised nothing!" said Crockett, the smile fading out of his eyes. " I refuse to give any promise whatever."

" That's all right," said Merriam, still good-humouredly. " In fact, I shouldn't count much on promises anyway.

" You're married, I believe? " he continued to Crockett.

Crockett did not reply.

"And a church member, I presume? And a member of a number of highly respectable clubs? "

He paused and waited, smiling.

The smile was too much for Crockett. After a moment of holding in, he said sharply:

" Well? "

" Well, a gentleman who is all those things ought to be careful how he accepts entertainment from unattached young ladies, like our pretty Jennie here—in their flats at midnight." And then to Margery, " Go and get your camera ready.

"When I was in college," Merriam continued, " the fraternity I belonged to initiated a freshman who turned out to be goody-goody. He wouldn't play cards, wouldn't dance, wouldn't go to the theater, wouldn't smoke. Even refused coffee and tea. Above all he simply wouldn't look at a girl. All he would do was study and go to class—and to church and Sunday School. To make it worse he was a handsome cuss with loads of money and his own motor car. He got on the fellows' nerves. Then a show came to town with a girl in the chorus that two of the fellows knew. So a bunch of us went to the show, and afterwards the two fellows who knew the girl brought her back to the chapter house in a taxi, with an opera cloak over the black tights which she wore in the last act. We gave her a little supper, and then four of us went upstairs to get the good little boy. He hadn't gone to the show. He was studying his trigonometry. We didn't have to lasso him, of course, because there were four of us. When we brought him into the dining room, the girl stood up and dropped off her cloak. It was worth something to see his face. Then we tied him into a chair, just the same way you're tied now. We set a beer bottle and half-emptied glass handy, and the girl sat on his knees and cocked one black leg over the arm of the chair and put one hand under his chin and put her lips to his cheek. And then we took the flash."

"Oh, goody!" cried Jennie, ecstatically pleased by this climax. But Crockett by this time was staring at the story-teller with really venomous eyes.

Merriam avoided those eyes and addressed himself to Jennie, the appreciative.

"That was all," he said. "We gave the girl a twenty-dollar bill and the roses and sent her back to the hotel in the taxi. We could only show the picture to a few chaps, of course. One of the fellows did finally tell the story to one girl whom a lot of us knew and showed her the picture. It worked fine. The good little boy's reputation was made, and he had to live up to it, to the extent at least of becoming human. He became one of the finest fellows we ever had. The year after he graduated," Merriam finished reflectively, "he married the one girl who had seen the picture, and the chapter gave it to her with their wedding present."

During this sequel Margery had returned with the camera and with some flash-light powder, for which she had had to search, in a dust pan.

"Damn you!" cried the great financier viru-
lently, straining helplessly at the ropes which con-
fined his arms and legs. "If you think it will do
you any good to take an indecent picture of
me ——"

"Cut that!" said Merriam sharply. "Do you
want me to tighten that noose again?"

Crockett subsided with a snort that might have
made whole boards of directors tremble.

"Indecent!" said Merriam, enjoying himself
hugely, as if he were still in college. "Certainly
not! Only pretty. Very pretty. Come, Jennie!
How about the pose?"

"I'll show you!" cried Jennie. Half dancing
on her toes, with skirts fluttering, and eyes spark-
ling the more, it seemed, because of Crockett's bitterly hostile regard, she tripped around the table
and stood by his side, facing the same way he faced.
She plucked the rose from her hair and stuck it behind Crockett's ear. It drooped grotesquely over
his thin hair. Then, laughing at the rose, she put
one bare arm about his neck, her hand extending
beyond his face on the other side.

"Give me a cocktail glass in that hand!" she
cried. "Never mind what's in it. Anything!"

Merriam filled a glass from the siphon and put it
into the hand referred to.

Then Jennie raised a pink leg and put it on the
table, stretching straight in front of herself and
Crockett towards the center of the board, amid the
plates and glasses and crumpled napkins. She put

her other hand under Crockett's chin as if about to
tickle him, dropped her face close to his, and looked
at Merriam with eyes of laughing inquiry.

"Fine!" said Merriam. "Are you ready, Margery?"

Margery was already pointing the camera.

"Not yet," she said.

He addressed himself to the victim:

"Mr. Crockett, you can, of course, wink or twist
your face to spoil the picture. If you do, I'll simply have to choke you a little before we try again.
So you'd better look pleasant!"

"Ready!" said Margery.

Merriam set the dust pan, with the little heap of
powder in the center of it, on a plate on the sideboard beside Margery, lit a match, and, with a last
glance at Jennie's extraordinary pose and laughing
face, switched off the lights and touched the
powder.

CHAPTER XXII

IMMEDIATELY after the flash Merriam switched on the lights, and his eyes sought Crockett. Apparently the man had faced the camera stolidly—a grotesque figure surmounted by the dangling flower and enveloped as it were in Jennie's acrobatic pose.

"All right!" said Merriam, coughing in the smoke which filled the small room. "But we'll take one more. You never can be sure of a single film. Got some more powder, Margery?"

"Yes," said Margery, who had set the camera down and stepped aside to open a window. She passed into the sitting room.

Jennie gingerly removed her leg from the table and her arm from about Crockett's neck. In the latter process she spilled a little of the water from the cocktail glass—unintentionally, let us hope—on Crockett's head.

"Damn!"

Jennie, quite regardless, eased herself on her two legs again.

"Gee!" she said. "I couldn't have held that pose much longer. In another second I'd have split at the waist!"

Merriam laughed. "Look what you've done,"
he said.

Jennie caught up a napkin and mopped the face
and head.

"Sorry!" she cried sympathetically. "I didn't
mean to wet him! There!" and she dropped a
light kiss on the cleansed cheek and smiled her
rosiest smile at the trussed victim.

Crockett answered Jennie's smile with a glare
that might have caused a panic on the Stock Ex-
change.

It had no very serious effect, however, on Jennie.
She shrugged her pretty shoulders and daintily
chucked him under the chin.

"That isn't a nice look!" she said.

At this point Margery returned with a package
of flash-light powder and began to pour a second
little pile on the dust pan.

"Take your pose!" said Merriam to Jennie.

"Not that one," said Jennie. "It's too hard.
Look!"

She picked the rose from above Crockett's ear
and stepped behind his chair. Then she stooped
till her chin rested on the top of his head and let
her two bare arms drop past his cheeks till her
hands came together on his shirt front. In her
hands she held the rose pointing upward so that the
blossom was just below his chin.

The effect was distinctly comical—Crockett's
dour countenance, with its angry eyes, framed
above by Jennie's pretty laughing face, resting on

the very top of his head, at the sides by her round white arms, and below by the rose under his chin.

"Fine!" Merriam laughed. "It's better than the other. Ready, Margery?"

"Yes."

A second time he switched off the lights and touched a match to the powder.

Again Crockett had not even blinked so far as Merriam could judge. Well satisfied, the latter spoke to Margery:

"Put that camera away, will you, please, where it could not be easily found except by yourself."

Margery picked up the camera and departed into the kitchenette.

Then, "Let him alone, Jennie," he said. For Jennie had left the back of Crockett's chair and perched herself on the edge of the table beside him and was flicking him under the chin with the rose.

"All right," she said. "He's no fun. He's very cross!"

She slid off the table and dropped into a chair, transferring her attention to Merriam, as though in the hope that he might be less obdurately disposed.

But Merriam addressed himself to the other man.

"Now, Mr. Crockett," he said, "this little supper party and entertainment are over, I believe. If you wish to leave, I shall be glad to release you and permit you to do so."

Crockett's reply was a sound between a grunt and a growl.

Merriam walked around the table and picked up the revolver where it had fallen by the wall.

"I don't believe," he continued, "that it will do you any good to start any rough-house when I have freed you. If you do, Jennie and Margery will scream, and I shall fire this revolver. That will bring in neighbours and probably the police, whose testimony would thus be added to that of the pictures we have taken as to your manner of spending your evening. You will understand that while I shall have those pictures developed the first thing in the morning I shall not show them to any one except Mr. Rockwell unless you compel me to do so."

By this time Crockett had become articulate.

"Compel you to do so?" he repeated stiffly. "May I ask what you mean by that?"

"Well," said Merriam, "you see I am an enthusiastic supporter of the Reform League as led by Mr. Rockwell and Senator Norman and Mayor Black. You, I understand, are opposed to the League and its policies. So long as your opposition relates itself only to those policies and involves only open public discussion of their merits, I shall, of course, have no reason to interfere. But if your opposition should take the form of any personal attack, on Senator Norman, let us say, I should feel compelled to retaliate by a personal attack upon you, making use of these pictures we have taken to-night and the story that will readily weave itself about them. Do you see?"

"See!" Crockett cried. "Of course I see. Blackmail! How much do you want for that camera? Name your price."

"It has no cash price," returned Merriam steadily. "Now if I release you, will you leave quietly?"

For a long moment the financier stared at the younger man who had worsted him. Then:

"At this moment," he said acridly, "I certainly have no other desire than to get away from this place and to be rid of my present companionship."

Merriam was tempted to laugh at the stilted dignity of this phraseology, but he managed to keep a straight face.

"Very well," he said. "Margery,"—for Margery had just returned from the kitchenette minus the camera,—"help me untie him, will you? Feet first."

Margery and Merriam knelt for a moment at the two sides of Crockett's chair and released his two legs. Then Merriam again put the table between himself and Crockett and stood waiting, revolver in hand, leaving to Margery the work of unbinding the arms. He was afraid that his own near presence to Crockett when the latter found himself free might tempt him irresistibly to personal assault.

In the moment during which he stood waiting he became conscious that Jennie, half reclining in the chair into which she had dropped, was smiling at him—a pretty, confidential smile which he did not understand.

But he had no time to consider Jennie just then, for Margery had completed her work. The last piece of rope fell on the floor, and she lifted the slip noose from about Crockett's neck. He had been rather tightly bound and did not instantly have the full use of his limbs. Margery took his arm to assist him.

"My coat and hat!" he said, not looking at Merriam.

"In the sitting room," said Margery.

He turned himself in that direction and in a jerky walk, with some support from Margery, moved towards and through the portières. He had disdained to cast so much as a glance at either Merriam or Jennie.

Jennie resented this. "Old crosspatch!" she cried.

Merriam stepped hastily to the portières and peeped through. Crockett had caught up his light overcoat and silk hat from a chair. He refused Margery's offer to help him on with his coat and made, already moving more naturally, for the hall door. Margery followed him. The door opened— closed again. Margery returned from the hallway.

Merriam advanced through the portières into the sitting room.

"Well!" he exclaimed.

"Well!" returned Margery, with a dry laugh— the first laugh Merriam had heard from her during the whole evening.

"See what he does in the street," she added.

"Raise the shade about a foot. I'll turn off the light."

Merriam acted promptly on this excellent hint. In a moment the room was in darkness, and he was kneeling by the window watching the street below, which was fairly well illuminated from arc lights at either corner. Part way down the block on the other side of the roadway a car, presumably a taxi, stood by the curb, with a man walking up and down beside it. Jennie's flat was too high up for Merriam to be able to see the sidewalk immediately below. If, therefore, Crockett on emerging from the building merely walked away, he would see nothing. But this was hardly likely.

Presently, sure enough, the taxi showed sudden signs of life. The man hastily got in, and the car rolled forward, crossing the street diagonally, and stopped directly below Merriam's window. Crockett had come out and signalled it. A moment later it shot away down the block and turned the corner.

Merriam still knelt by the window, peering into the street. He was looking for signs of any remaining watchers, for he had his own exit to think of: Rockwell had wanted him to "come at once to the hotel."

As he knelt there in the dark he suddenly sensed a warm fragrant body close beside his own. A pair of soft bare arms slipped about his neck.

"It was fine!" Jennie's voice whispered in his ear. "You're a nice boy!"

She had crept up behind him in the dark. Margery must have left the room.

For a moment Merriam knelt in fascinated silent rigidity. When he moved it was only to turn his head. And the turning of his head brought his face close to Jennie's, which, with the dim light from the street upon it, smiled at him with a kind of saucy tenderness. It was the face of a pretty child, with the lure of womanhood added, but with nothing else of maturity in it.

Her lips puckered. "Kiss me!" she whispered.

As he still only stared she quickly leaned forward a couple of inches more—her lips rested on his.

I am very much afraid that for an instant Merriam's lips responded. He half turned on one knee. His arms involuntarily closed about the seductive little body. He felt the short silk skirts crush deliciously against his legs.

And then a grotesque sort of composite picture of all the things he ought to remember, including Rockwell, Norman, Mollie June, and the members of the Riceville School Board, rushed across his mind. He struggled to his feet, pushing Jennie—not roughly—away.

"Margery!" he called.

"Yes?" came Margery's voice from the dining room.

"Turn on the lights!"

By the time Margery had stepped through the portières and pushed the switch Jennie had thrown herself face downward on the davenport, crying.

"Nobody loves me!" she sobbed.

Margery, standing by the switch, looked from Merriam at the window to Jennie on the couch and back again. Her expression indicated no bewilderment—rather a humorously cynical comprehension. She knew her Jennie.

At any rate, that glance steadied the young man. After meeting it for a moment he turned to Jennie. Poor little girl! He felt that he understood her perfectly. There was a side of himself that was like that. Only he had other sides powerfully developed, and Jennie had no other sides. All his young chivalry rose up, in alliance with the missionary spirit of the teacher. He desired greatly to help her.

After an instant's hesitation he crossed the room and drew up a chair beside the davenport.

"Jennie," he said, "listen!"

"Go away!" said Jennie.

"I *am* going away in a minute. But I want to tell you something first."

Her sobbing ceased, but he waited till she asked:

"Well, what?"

"There *is* somebody who loves you."

Hopefully Jennie raised her head and turned her face to him—still oddly pretty in spite of the tear-streaked rouge. But after a moment's look she said resentfully:

"It isn't you!"

"No," said Merriam, "it isn't I."

Even at this rate the discussion was apparently

interesting enough to rouse her. With a sudden
movement she curled herself up, half sitting, half
reclining, in a corner of the davenport, and
smoothed the crumpled skirts over her knees.

" Do you mean George? " she asked.

" No," said Merriam, " I mean Mr. Simpson."

" *Mister* Simpson! " She laughed derisively,
not prettily at all. "A waiter! "

" Listen, Jennie. Simpson is a fine fellow, with
lots of brains and lots of courage. He has shown
both within the last twenty-four hours. He's rendered a very important service to Mr. Rockwell and
Senator Norman, and they're going to give him a
lot of money for a reward. I don't know how
much—maybe five thousand dollars. And he's
crazy about you. He'll marry you in a minute if
you'll let him, in spite of—George. He'll take you
away on a fine trip—anywhere you want to go.
And afterwards he'll set up in a business of his
own—a café or whatever he likes. You'll have a
real home and a husband and money enough and
friends. It'll be a lot better than this stuff—like
to-night. It really would. Think it over, Jennie! "

On the last words he rose.

" He's right! " cried Margery, who had drawn
near.

" Shut up, Marge! " said Jennie.

But Merriam, looking closely at her with the
sharp eye of a teacher to see whether or not his
point had gone home, was satisfied. He was sure
that she would think it over in spite of herself.

He looked at his watch. It was ten minutes after one.

"I must telephone at once to Mr. Rockwell in Senator Norman's rooms at the Hotel De Soto," he said to Margery.

"Yes," said Margery. "The hotel number is Madison 1-6-8-1."

"Thank you."

Without looking again at Jennie, he went to the telephone in the dining room. In a moment he had the hotel and had asked to be connected with Senator Norman's rooms. It was Rockwell's voice that answered, "Hello!"

"This is Merriam."

"Thank God! Where are you?"

"At Jennie's."

"Still? What the devil was the ruction there when I called up?"

"I'll tell you about that later. Do you still want me to come to the hotel?"

"Certainly. As fast as you can."

"You got the Senator back all right?"

"Yes. But he's pretty sick. Caught more cold, I guess. Hobart's worried about him. You'll have to stay over another day all right. And make that speech."

Merriam groaned.

"Listen!" said Rockwell. "You'll have to be mighty careful about getting into the hotel. You aren't Senator Norman just now, you know. The Senator has already returned to the hotel, openly, with me, three hours ago, and is sick in his rooms. We'll have to smuggle you in without any one's seeing you. But I have a plan—or rather Simpson has. You'd better come down on the Elevated. That'll be better than a taxi this time. No chauffeur to tell on you. Be sure you get away from there without being followed. Margery'll show you a way. Get off at Madison and Wabash. Simpson will meet you there and smuggle you in the back way. You can come right away?"

"Yes."

"Then for Heaven's sake come! We'll talk after you get here." He hung up.

Merriam stared at the instrument as he slowly replaced his own receiver. Another day. "And make that speech!" Would this kaleidoscopic, unreal phantasm of adventures never end? When would he wake up? He perceived suddenly that he was very tired. But he must brace up sufficiently to get back to the hotel. There doubtless he would be permitted to go to bed and snatch at least a few hours' sleep—before the speech!

He turned and found Margery standing between the portières, watching him.

"Well!" she said sharply.

"I must—must—get dressed," he finished, realising for the first time since he had leapt out of bed with his revolver to divert Crockett from the telephone that he was attired only in pajamas. "Rockwell says you can tell me a way to get away from here without being seen by any watchers."

"Yes," said Margery. "Go and dress. I'll attend to that."

He went into the bedroom and began to get into his clothes, working mechanically.

Presently he was ready—though with such a loose and rakish bow as he had never before disported—and emerged into the dining room.

There he encountered a cheering spectacle. Margery was seated at the table between a coffee percolator, efficiently bubbling, and an electric toaster. She was buttering hot toast. Jennie sat at one side of the table. A pale blue kimono now covered her dancing costume, and she looked quite demure. She raised her eyes almost shyly as Merriam entered.

"Well!" he exclaimed. "This is grand. Margery, you certainly are a trump!"

Margery's rather sallow cheeks flushed slightly. "You'll need it," was all she said, and proceeded to fill a cup for him from the percolator.

"How do I get away?" Merriam asked as he sipped.

"Back stairs," said Margery succinctly. "I'll show you."

Munching toast, he enquired the whereabouts of the nearest Elevated station and was duly instructed.

He had a second cup of the black coffee. Margery did not take any and would not give Jennie any.

"We go straight to bed," she said decidedly.

From time to time Merriam cast an unwilling glance at Jennie, sitting downcast and out of it on Margery's other side. About the third time Jennie intercepted his glance and answered it with a small wistful smile. After that he would not look again.

In a few minutes, of course, this very early breakfast—it was somewhere around two o'clock—was over, and Merriam rose.

"I must be off," he said, and hesitated. "I am very much indebted to both of you for—all the help you have given me this evening!" (Inwardly he abused himself for his stiltedness; it was like his telling Mollie June he was glad to have helped her in algebra.)

Jennie rose too and came around the table towards him. She had suddenly summoned back a smile, and she moved daintily inside the blue kimono. Above the stalk of that straight, demure, Japanesy blue, her head nodded like a bright blossom—with its fair, wavy hair, blue eyes, and childishly rounded cheeks, still gaudy with the remains of rouge.

She tripped forward till she was almost touching Merriam, stopped, and suddenly raised her eyes to him.

"Kiss me good-bye!" she said.

We may suspect that it was a sort of point of honour with Jennie to retrieve the rebuff she had received in the sitting room. As for Merriam, in spite of the obvious deliberateness of this assault, I am not perfectly sure I could answer for him if it had not been for Margery. But Margery's presence saved him from serious temptation.

Instead of stooping to kiss the lifted lips he caught Jennie's hand that hung at her side, and, stepping back half a step, raised the hand and kissed it.

Sometimes the inspirations of youth are singularly happy. It seems to me that this one was of that kind: it involved neither yielding nor discourtesy.

Jennie was somewhat taken aback, yet she could not be hurt by a gesture so gallant.

" Good-bye, Jennie," he said. " I hope to be the best man at your wedding before long."

" Oh ! " she said, and withdrew her hand. Then: " Good-bye ! "

After a moment's hesitation and a last quite shy glance at Merriam she suddenly gathered up the skirts of the kimono and ran into the sitting room.

"Are you ready? " said Margery dryly.

" My coat. I haven't a hat," he added, remembering that under Rockwell's instructions he had left this article in the taxi in which they had come to the flat.

" Your coat's in the hall," said Margery. " I can get you a hat too."

The dining room was connected directly with the hallway, and in a moment Margery had returned with Merriam's light overcoat and with a man's derby—probably Norman's property.

" Thank you," said Merriam, taking them.

"This way," she replied, moving towards the kitchenette.

In the kitchenette he was momentarily surprised to see Margery opening a tin box labeled "Bread." Was she going to equip him with a lunch? But she drew out, not a loaf, but the camera.

"You'll want to take this along," she said.

"Indeed, yes."

Then he followed her out on to the back porch, where earlier—ages ago, it seemed—he had deposited the stepladder.

"Now," said Margery, "you go down these stairs and diagonally across the court to that archway. See?" She pointed. "That brings you out on the other side of the block. Nobody will be looking for you there. And the Elevated station is three and one-half blocks west. Put on your hat and coat. I'll hold it."

"Thank you so much," said Merriam, as the coat slipped on.

Then he turned, took off his hat again, and held out his hand.

"Good-bye, Margery," he said, shaking hands heartily. "Thank you—for everything."

For a moment they looked at each other with mutual respect.

Then Merriam said:

"I'm going to send Simpson around to see Jennie. Shan't I?"

"You can try it," said Margery. "Good-bye."

She went back into the kitchenette and closed the door.

CHAPTER XXIII

"**M**ADISON and Wabash!" shouted the guard. Merriam started, picked up his camera, and made for the door. He had scarcely heard the other stations called and thanked his stars that he had waked up for this one.

He descended the stairs from the Elevated platform and found Simpson waiting.

"Good morning, Simpson."

"Good morning."

"Mr. Rockwell says you can get me into the hotel unnoticed."

Simpson looked at him sideways, hesitated, then turned and started slowly west.

Merriam fell into step beside him and for a moment wondered obtusely what ailed the man. Then he understood. Of course! He wanted news of Jennie. Perhaps he was suspicious as to how Merriam might have spent his time in that apartment. Perhaps he, like Margery, knew his Jennie only too well.

To set his mind at rest, Merriam plunged at once into a sketchy summary of the events at the flat—Crockett's arrival—"almost as soon as you had left," he placed it—his own telling of his story—

266

Crockett's being half convinced—Jennie's plan—
the supper party (without reference to Jennie's
change of costume or the dancing on the table)—
Rockwell's telephone call—the tying up and the
flash lights.

" I have the films here," he added, exhibiting the
camera as tangible evidence that he was not yarn-
ing. " Can you get them developed for me in the
morning? "

" Yes," said Simpson, in a much less frigid tone
than before. He took the camera.

"After Crockett had gone," Merriam continued
smoothly, " I talked to Jennie about you. I told
her she ought to marry you, and how well you've
shown up in this affair, and that Senator Norman
and Rockwell are going to pay you a bit of money
for it, which you've certainly earned, and that you
would take her away on a little trip any where she
wanted to go, and then set up in a busine s of your
own somewhere, and that she would be a lot hap-
pier that way than now."

An older man, more sensitive to the dynamite in
the situation, would probably have spoken less
freely and less successfully. Whatever else Simpson may have felt, he could not question his companion's youthful candour and good will. After
perhaps a dozen steps he spoke in a carefully controlled voice:

" What did she say? "

" She didn't answer me," lied Merriam. " I told
her to think it over. She was impressed all right,

And when I left I told Margery I was going to send you around."

"What did Margery say?" asked Simpson quickly.

"She said yes, you should come."

Simpson drew a deep breath and stopped short at a corner.

"I'm very much obliged to you, sir," he said, looking quickly at Merriam and quickly away again.

Merriam held out his hand.

"Good luck!" he said.

Simpson grasped the hand and shook it intensely. Then, resuming his really admirable self-control, he said:

"We turn down here. I'm going to take you up a fire escape. It's the only way. You can't go into a hotel in the regular way even at this time of night without being seen."

They turned into an alley which ran behind the Hotel De Soto, and presently came to a door—a servants' entrance—in the ugly blank wall of yellow brick.

Simpson opened the door, and they passed into a bare hallway, pine-floored, plaster-walled, lighted at intervals by unshaded, low-powered incandescents.

Many doors of yellow pine opened on both sides of this hall, but Simpson, walking rapidly and quietly, passed them all, turned into a further stretch of hallway, narrower and still more dimly lighted, and stopped before a door of iron—evidently a fire door. He got out a key and unlocked this door, and they emerged into the air again in the inner court of the hotel, a great dismal well, the depository of drifts of soot, accentuated here and there by scraps of paper and other rubbish, and the haunt, for reasons difficult to understand, of the indomitable, grimy wild pigeons of the Loop.

Simpson closed the iron door behind them and began a searching scrutiny of the rows of windows. All but half a dozen or so were dark. It looked safe.

Satisfied, Simpson walked twenty feet or more along the side of the court and stopped below a fire escape. The platform at the lower end of the iron stairway was placed too high for a man to reach it from the ground unaided.

" Give me a boost," said Simpson. He stooped and placed the camera on the ground.

In a moment Merriam had hoisted him up, so that he could catch hold of the end of the platform and pull himself on to it. Then Simpson lay down on his stomach and dropped his arms over the edge of the platform. Merriam first handed up the camera and then with a little jump caught his hands and was drawn up until he in his turn could get hold of the edge of the landing and scramble on to it.

A moment later they were erect and had begun stealthily to mount the narrow stairs.

It seemed to Merriam that they went up inter-
minably—a short flight—a turn—another short
flight—along a platform past sleeping windows—
another flight. He got out of breath, and began to
feel very tired. The effect of Margery's coffee was
wearing off.

But at last Simpson stopped on one of the plat-
forms and peered through a window. It was one
of which the shades were not drawn at all and was
open about two inches at the bottom.

"This is it," said Simpson, and he stooped,
opened the window, and climbed in.

As soon as Merriam had followed, Simpson
closed the window and drew the shade. Then he
crossed the dark room and pushed a switch.

"Where are we?" asked Merriam.

"This room is next to Senator Norman's bedroom," said Simpson, "on the other side from the
sitting room. The couple who had it left this
evening, and Mr. Rockwell has taken it for you under the name of Wilson. Mr. Rockwell will be expecting us."

He moved to a door at the side and knocked
softly four times—once, twice, and once again.

Almost immediately a key was turned on the
other side, the door was opened, and Rockwell stood
surveying them.

There was only a dim light in the room behind
him. With a glance over his shoulder at the bed
where the sick Senator lay—the same bed in which
Merriam had played at being sick on the previous

afternoon,—he entered the new room and closed the door.

"You've made it!" he said. "Thank Heaven! You weren't seen, Simpson?"

"I think not, sir."

He looked closely at Merriam. "You're tired," he said.

"I sure am."

"Well, so am I. What a day! And to-morrow will be as bad. Maybe worse. Never again will I father an impostor. But we've got to see it through this time. Sit down. Have a cigarette, and tell me what happened at the flat. Then I'll let you go to bed and snatch a few hours' sleep. You must be in fighting trim to-morrow, you know—for the speech!"

Merriam took the proffered cigarette and dropped gratefully into a chair. Rockwell and Simpson also sat down.

"How's Senator Norman?" Merriam asked.

"Sick. Hobart looks serious, but he says he'll pull around in a day or two. He's dosing him heavily. You've simply got to stay by us and play the game until he's on his feet again."

"I suppose so. Well——"

He was about to repeat the summary of the events of his evening which he had already given Simpson, so as to get it over and get to bed. But before he could begin a knock sounded at the side door through which Rockwell had entered.

Simpson went to the door and opened it. It was Dr. Hobart.

"Miss Norman and Mrs. Norman want to come in," he said.

Rockwell hesitated. No doubt he would have preferred to hear Merriam's story himself first, without even Aunt Mary present.

Merriam meanwhile sat up, suddenly forgetting his fatigue: he was to see Mollie June still that night. He had not hoped for that.

"I supposed they would have gone to bed," he said, to cover his involuntary show of interest.

"No," said Rockwell. "After the dinner party they waited for me to come back with Norman, of course. Then he was so ill that Hobart kept us all busy for a couple of hours doing things. We didn't want to get in a nurse on account of—you, you know. And then they wanted to wait till you came. We expected you a long time ago. Well," he added, turning to the physician, " tell them to come along."

It was at least a minute before they arrived. Merriam was oddly nervous. He had been through strange scenes since he had left Mollie June in the Peacock Cabaret, and she must have divined as much.

They entered, Aunt Mary first with Mollie June behind her, and Merriam and Rockwell rose. The two women were dressed just as they had been at the dinner party—Aunt Mary in the black evening

gown and Mollie June in the filmy rose. Mollie
June looked just a little pale and tired, but Aunt
Mary had not turned a hair.

"Well, young man," began the older woman
briskly, "you've kept us up till a pretty time of
night. What was happening there where you were
when Mr. Rockwell telephoned? Sit down and
tell us."

Evidently Aunt Mary, conscious of the ungodly
hour, did not think it necessary to allow Merriam
time for even a formal greeting of her young sister-
in-law, who had stopped uncertainly in the doorway.

But Merriam was not to be hurried to quite that
degree, whatever the time of night or morning
might be. He turned to Mollie June.

"You're coming in, aren't you? Take this
chair."

He pushed a rocker towards her, concerned at
her evident fatigue.

She came forward and sat down, then raised her
eyes to him with a grave "Thank you."

For a moment Merriam did not understand that
steady, unsmiling look. Then he thought he did
understand. It had a questioning quality. Mollie
June's mind was at ease now about her husband,
since he was back and not supposed to be seriously
ill, and she, like Simpson earlier, was wondering—
not that it concerned her, of course—how Merriam
had spent the night—so large a part of it—at
Jennie's flat. She, too, knew Jennie, to the extent

at least of having seen and in a measure comprehended her. Perhaps even in a Mollie June there
is that which enables her to understand a Jennie
and her lure for a youthful male. He remembered
Mollie June's description of her and the cool de-
tachment with which it had been uttered: " She's
pretty and sweet, and—warm."

For just an instant Merriam was slightly confused. He had verified that description—all of it.

It is to be feared that his embarrassment, slight
and merely instantaneous though it was, did not
escape Mollie June. She dropped her eyes, still
unsmiling.

Merriam's second sketch of his evening's adventures differed from the one he had given Simpson in being fuller and in two particular points:
first, of course, in omitting reference to his missionary efforts in Simpson's behalf, which, however laudable, were hardly for the ears of Mollie
June; and, second, in including mention of Jennie's
change into her ballet costume—because he realised as he talked that the pictures, to be developed
in the morning, would exhibit that detail most
unmistakably and that he would do well to prepare
Mollie June's mind—and Simpson's, for that
matter—in advance. But he laid his emphasis on
the more dramatic episodes—the hurled revolver,
the tying up, the flash lights, and Crockett's angry
exit. He told it humorously and well, and was
rewarded by Mollie June's interest. Her questioning gravity disappeared, and she followed him with

eager attention and with a return of pretty colour to her cheeks.

Aunt Mary and Rockwell—not to mention Simpson—also listened attentively. When Merriam had finished they looked at each other.

"Well," said Rockwell, "I'm not sure but that it would have been better to let him go as soon as you had told him your yarn, but on the whole I think you did mighty well. Those pictures may come in handy."

Aunt Mary rose. "You certainly are an enterprising young man, Mr. Merriam," she said dryly. "Now go to bed and get some sleep. You make your début as an orator at noon, you know! Come, Mollie June."

"Good night, Miss Norman," said Merriam, and he advanced to Mollie June, who had also risen.

"Good night, Mrs. Mollie June." He dropped his voice for the last three words and held out his hand.

She took it with an unconscious happy smile.

"Good night—Mr. John," she said.

Whatever she may have feared or suspected his story had established an alibi for him.

CHAPTER XXIV.

THE REFORM LEAGUE

"QUARTER to ten," said Rockwell cheerily. "I've let you sleep to the last possible moment. Here's your breakfast on the stand. Better eat it and drink your coffee first. Then a shave and get at this." He indicated a small pile of manuscript on the writing table. "Your speech, Senator!" he grinned.

"Good Lord!" groaned Merriam, remembering everything. He perceived also that he was to breakfast alone—no Mollie June. But the sight of the manuscript fascinated and aroused him. He realised, as he had not done before, that within a few hours he was to make a public address in a great Chicago club before many of the city's most prominent men and women—on what subject, even, he had no idea!

"Good Lord!" he said again and put his feet out. "How's Senator Norman?" he asked.

"Sleeping now," said Rockwell. "Hobart thinks he can get him on his feet by night. He's due to start for Cairo this evening, you know, on a stumping trip." Then quickly: "You'll find these sliced oranges refreshing. Have your bath first if you want to."

Merriam was in the midst of his breakfast when Rockwell returned. " By the way," he said, " here are your pictures," and he took some unmounted prints from an envelope.

Merriam reached for them with curiosity and something like trepidation. They were not good flash lights—a little blurred,—but the faces and attitudes were unmistakable. Jennie's foot and leg extending forward across the table were very much in evidence in the first of them.

" Rather striking poses," commented Rockwell.

" Jennie's invention," said Merriam defensively.

" No doubt. Well, they could hardly be better for their purpose. I think Crockett will go slow all right."

" Have—has Miss Norman seen them? "

" Yes. And Simpson, of course." For a moment Rockwell quizzically regarded Merriam's face, in which a further unspoken question was anxiously plain. Then he answered it: " No one else. Mrs. Norman is still sleeping. I'm not sure Aunt Mary will consider them proper pictures for her to see anyway. Come," he added briskly, " you've eaten only one piece of toast. You must get outside of at least one more piece. And then shave. I'll strop your razor for you. I'm your valet this morning, Senator."

With a sigh Merriam glanced at the waiting speech and tackled a second piece of toast, with the feeling that its mastication was a task of almost impossible difficulty. He achieved it, however, to the rhythmic accompaniment of Rockwell's stropping, consumed another cup of coffee—his third, I regret to say,—and proceeded to shave.

At last Merriam was collared and tied and was slipping into his coat. Rockwell rose and laid down the manuscript.

"Ready?" he said. "Very good. You can get to work. It's a quarter past ten. The luncheon is at twelve-thirty. But we shan't appear at the luncheon itself. Too dangerous. You'd have to meet a lot of men who know the Senator—meet them face to face in cold daylight and talk to them. We'd never get away with it. So I'll telephone that you've been detained by important business but will be in for the speeches. That way we'll come in by ourselves, with everybody else set and no opportunity for personal confabulations. You'll have to run the gauntlet of their eyes, of course. But you can do that."

Earnestly for a moment he scrutinised Merriam's face and figure, as if to reassure himself that the astounding imposture had been and was still really possible.

"Yes," he continued confidently, "that'll be all right. The speeches are scheduled to begin at one-fifteen. We'll leave here at five or ten minutes after one. That gives you nearly three hours to salt down the speech. You can learn it verbatim or only master the outline and substance and give it in your own words. Perhaps you'd better learn a good deal of it just as it is. Aunt Mary has it chock-full of the Senator's pet words and phrases. Your own style might be too different. Do you commit easily?"

"Fairly so," said Merriam. As a matter of fact the speech itself presented few terrors to him. He had done a good deal of debating and declaiming in college, and of course in his capacity as principal of the high school he was called upon for "a few words" on every conceivable occasion in Riceville.

"Good. Go to it, then. I'll make myself scarce. Here are cigarettes. You won't be disturbed. *Au revoir*, Senator! If you want anything, knock on this door Either Hobart or I will answer."

Grinning, Rockwell departed into the real, the sick Senator's, bedroom, leaving Merriam with the typewritten manuscript.

He worked away for a couple of hours, sometimes sitting down, more often walking back and forth, occasionally refreshing himself with a cigarette, and faithfully learning by heart Aunt Mary's Senator Norman's speech on "Municipal Reform."

By half past twelve he had mastered it to his satisfaction. He decided to go through with it once more by the clock. It was designed, as he knew from a pencil note at the top of the first page, to take thirty minutes. He did so, and came out at the end by five minutes to one.

Evidently his delivery was a little more rapid than Senator Norman's. He must remember to speak slowly.

He had just reached this conclusion when a

knock sounded at the side door and Rockwell entered.

"I've got it by heart," said Merriam.

"Good! Come into the sitting room, then. You're to have a cup of coffee and a sandwich before you start."

"Fine. I *am* a bit hollow. How's the Senator?"

Rockwell looked worried, but answered, "Sleeping again now. Come along if you're ready."

"In a minute."

Merriam bathed his face and hands, folded the speech and put it in his pocket, and followed Rockwell across the Senator's bedroom, with just a glance at the sick man in the bed and a nod to Dr. Hobart, who sat by the window with a newspaper, into the sitting room.

After his morning of intense, solitary labour he was somewhat nonplused for a moment by the size of the company he found assembled there—Aunt Mary and Mollie June, of course, Alicia, Mr. Wayward, and Father Murray. He said good morning to each of them.

Alicia reminded him that it was really afternoon now.

"We shall meet Black in the car," said Rockwell. "Then the roll of the conspirators will be complete!"

Mollie June, who had had no speech to learn, had slept late and was now as blooming as ever.

"We're all going to hear you," she said as she gave Merriam her hand.

"Good Heavens!" he said, with a twinge of
the stage fright which he had thus far had no
time to feel. "I shouldn't mind the others, but
you ——"

He left that dangerous remark unfinished.

To Aunt Mary he said: "I've learned the speech
by heart. I admire it very much," and was pleased
to note that even Aunt Mary had an author's sus-
ceptibility to praise.

Meanwhile Simpson, who was in attendance, had
poured out a cup of coffee, and Mollie June brought
it to him with a sandwich on a plate.

"Won't you sit down to eat it?" she asked, regarding him with a look of awe which flattered him
enormously and served to quiet his rising nervousness.

(Mollie June had taken oratory of all degrees
and on all possible occasions on the part of Norman
as a matter of course, but the thought that John
Merriam, who was only a little older than herself
and had taken her to "sociables" and had wanted
to make love to her but had not dared, was about
to address the distinguished Urban Club of Chicago
at one of its formidable luncheons filled her with
admiration.)

"Thank you," he said, taking the coffee and the
sandwich. "No, I think I'll eat it standing." But
he smiled at her with the confidence which her admiration had given him, thereby increasing the
admiration—a pleasing psychological circle.

But now Rockwell was at his side and barely

gave him time to finish his sandwich and gulp down the coffee.

"Miss Norman and the Senator and I go with Mayor Black in the Senator's car," said that master of ceremonies and conspiracies. "The other four of you are to follow in the Mayor's machine. Here's your coat and hat."

Along the hall—down in the elevator—through the lobby to the pavement—Merriam had only a dazed sense of being part of an irresistible, conspicuous procession which was carrying him whither he had no strong desire to go.

A limousine was already drawn up at the curb, and the hotel starter was deferentially holding the door.

Mayor Black was already within the car.

"Ah, Senator," the Mayor ejaculated, "I'm glad to see you up again, and to have you—really you—coming to the Reform League!"

For an instant Merriam did not understand. Then he realised that the Mayor thought he was addressing the real Senator Norman. It was a good omen for the continued success of his impersonation.

He sank into the seat opposite the Mayor, who was facing forward with Aunt Mary beside him. Rockwell climbed in and sat next to Merriam. The door slammed, and the machine started.

Then, as the Mayor still beamed at him and as neither of the others spoke, Merriam said gently:

"I'm still the impostor, I'm afraid, Mr. Mayor."

"Eh!"

The Mayor leaned forward to scrutinise his face and then turned as if bewildered and still unconvinced to Rockwell.

"Yes," said Rockwell. "I tried to get you on the 'phone this morning, but your line was busy, and I didn't have a chance to try again. The Senator is still sick. Worse, in fact. Mr. Merriam is going to keep the Senator's engagement at the Urban Club for him."

"My God!" cried the Mayor. "Speak before all those people! You never can do it!"

"Yes, we can," said Rockwell, with smiling serenity. "You were fooled again yourself just now," he pointed out.

The Mayor groaned. "Then we still don't know where Senator Norman himself will stand when he's up," he said.

"I telephoned you yesterday that he had agreed to everything," said Aunt Mary coldly. "That was true."

"While he was sick," said Black. "Will he stick to it when he's well again?"

"He'll have to stick," said Rockwell. "Ten times more so after this speech. He can't possibly go back on that."

"If this Mr.—Mr. Merriam," said the Mayor, eyeing him with profound dislike, "is unmasked at the Urban Club, it would be the utter ruin of us all."

" It undoubtedly would," replied Rockwell cheerfully. " All the more reason why we should all keep a stiff upper lip and play up for him."

" No!" cried the Mayor. " It's insane! Stop the car! I'll step into the nearest store and telephone that the Senator has fainted in the cab and can't appear. Anything is better than this awful risk."

He put out his hand for the cord to signal to the chauffeur. But Rockwell roughly struck his arm down.

" Sit still!" he commanded savagely. " Do you want us to choke you again? This car goes on to the Urban Club. Senator Norman has a fine speech, and he'll make it well. No one will suspect. The thing has the one essential characteristic of successful imposture—boldness to the point of impossibility. If any one notices any slight change in his appearance or voice or manner, it will be put down to his illness. It will cinch the whole thing as nothing else could. You've got to go through with it, Mayor."

Mr. Black groaned again and relapsed into a dismal silence.

Fortunately he did not have long to brood, nor Merriam long to work up the nervousness which this dialogue had naturally renewed in him. In a couple of minutes after the Mayor's second and more lamentable groan the limousine stopped before the imposing entrance of the Urban Club.

"Sit tight, Mayor!" Rockwell warned.

Then the doorman of the Club opened the car, and Rockwell descended and helped Aunt Mary out, and Merriam and the Mayor followed.

Inside their coats and the men's hats were quickly taken from them by efficient checkroom boys, and they were guided immediately to the elevator. The speeches had already begun upstairs, some one said.

They stepped out into the hallway outside the Club's big dining room. From inside came the noise of clapping. Some one had just finished speaking.

"This is our chance," said Rockwell, meaning doubtless that they could best enter during the interlude between speeches. "Go ahead, Senator. Take the Mayor's arm!"

In a moment they were passing through a group of tuxedoed servants at the door. Merriam was conscious of a large room in pleasant tones of brown with a low raftered ceiling and many windows of small leaded panes. The tables were arranged in the form of a great horseshoe, with the closed end—the speakers' table—opposite the door. The horseshoe was lined inside and out with guests, perhaps two hundred in all—men who looked either distinguished or intelligent, occasionally both, and women who were either distinguished or intelligent or beautiful—from some points of view the great city's best.

Then came the turning of many eyes to look at

himself and Mayor Black, and the toastmaster at the center of the speakers' table rose and called to them:

"Senator! Mayor! This way."

He pointed to two empty chairs on either side of his own.

Merriam nodded, and, still propelling the semi-comatose Black, circled one side of the horseshoe, giving the line of guests as wide a berth as he could, to avoid possible contretemps from personal greetings to which he might be unable to make suitable response.

Arrived at the speakers' table, he shook hands warmly with the toastmaster—a bald, benevolent-looking man of much aplomb, whose name he never learned—and with two or three other men from nearby chairs—evidently personal acquaintances of Senator Norman's—who rose to welcome him, making talk the while of apologies for being late. Presently he found himself seated at the toastmaster's right, facing the distinguished company. No one had betrayed any suspicion. The imposture was, in fact, as Rockwell had said, so bold as to be unthinkable.

Mayor Black had meanwhile been seated at the toastmaster's left, and Rockwell and Aunt Mary had been guided to two vacant seats at the left end of the speakers' table. The necessity of greeting friends had somewhat roused the Mayor, who had found his tongue and managed to respond, though for him haltingly.

The toastmaster leaned towards Merriam and whispered:

"You're to speak last, Senator. Colonel Edwards is next, then Mayor Black, then you."

With that he rose and felicitated the company on the arrival of the two distinguished servants of the City and the Nation between whom he now had the honour to sit.

He then introduced Colonel Edwards, a stout, quite unmilitary-looking gentleman, who was earnestly interested and mildly interesting on the subject of good roads for the space of fifteen minutes.

Merriam's attention was distracted almost at the beginning of Colonel Edwards' speech by the arrival at the entrance of the dining room, now directly opposite him, of the second taxi-load from the hotel. Alicia caught Merriam's eye and smiled at him mischievously. Evidently she was enjoying the situation to the full. Mollie June, on the other hand, though deliciously crowned with a small blossomy hat of obvious expensiveness, was entirely grave, her eyes fixed almost too steadily and too anxiously on our youthful hero, where he sat in the seats of the mighty, outwardly at least as much at ease as if he had been accustomed for thirty years to find himself at the speakers' table of historic clubs.

Colonel Edwards suddenly sat down. He was one of those rare public speakers who occasionally disconcert their audiences by stopping when they are through.

The toastmaster gasped, but rose to his feet and the occasion and called upon Mayor Black.

As the Mayor slowly rose Merriam was most uncomfortably anxious—uncertain whether the city's chief executive was even yet sufficiently master of himself to face an audience successfully. But Mr. Black was one of those gentlemen, not uncommon in public life, who are apparently more at ease before an audience than in any other situation. His great mellow voice boomed forth, and Merriam relaxed. That speech was hardly, perhaps, one of the Mayor's masterpieces. But that mattered little, of course. He produced an admirably even flow of head tones. It *sounded* like a perfectly good speech.

Merriam, at any rate, was quite oblivious of any lack of strict logical coherence in the Mayor's remarks. He was suddenly smitten by the realisation that his own turn came next. For a moment he fought a panic of blankness, then mentally grabbed at the opening sentences of what he had so carefully committed during the morning. Outwardly serene and attentive to the speaker, inwardly he hastily rehearsed his first half dozen paragraphs, and, winking his eyes somewhat rapidly perhaps, fixed the outline of the rest of it in his mind.

The Mayor rose to a climax of thunderous tone and eloquent gesture and sat. Loud applause followed.

Across the clapping hands Merriam glanced at

Mr. Wayward and Alicia and Mollie June where
they sat at one side of the horseshoe. The other
two were clapping, but Mollie June was not. He
thought she looked pale, but of course he was too
far away to be sure. " She is afraid for me," he
thought, and gratitude for her interest mingled
with a fine resolve to show her that she had no
cause for fear—that he would give a good account
of himself anywhere—for her.

The glow of that resolution carried him through
the ordeal of the toastmaster's introduction and
brought him to his feet with smiling alacrity at the
proper moment.

The applause was hearty. There is magic still,
strange as it may seem, in the word " senator." He
was forced to bow again and again.

Then he struck into his speech—Aunt Mary's
speech. He found himself letter-perfect. He had
at least half his mind free to attend to his delivery.
He gave it slowly, impressively, grandly facing first
one part of his audience and then another. George
Norman himself before packed galleries in the Senate Chamber at Washington had never done better.
And it was a good speech, deftly conceived, clearly
reasoned, aptly worded. Merriam himself in all
his morning's study of it had not realised how perfectly it was adapted to the occasion and the audience. Down at the far end of the speakers' table,
the female author of it sat unnoticed, watching
with tight-pressed lips its effect; her only right
to be there, if any one had asked you, the ac-

cident of her relationship to the wonderful Senator.

He reached the end.   As he rounded out the last sentence his eyes rested triumphantly for a second on Mollie June.   Whether or not her cheeks had been pale before, they were flushed now.   He sat down.

The room rocked.   The applause this time was no mechanical reaction.   It was an ovation.   The toastmaster leaped to his feet with ponderous agility and grabbed for Merriam's hand.   The latter found himself standing, the center of a group of excited men, all of whom he must pretend to know, overwhelming him with congratulations.

Behind him he caught a remark that was doubtless not intended for his ears : "How the devil does he keep his youthful looks and fire?   He might be twenty-five!"

Then Rockwell charged into the group, excited himself, but persistent with the formula, "Pressing engagement," and got him out of the room, and into the elevator, and through the hallway on the first floor, with his hat and coat restored, and into the limousine, which darted away for the hotel.

CHAPTER XXV

SECOND COUNCIL OF WAR

MERRIAM and Rockwell were alone in the Senator's car.

Merriam leaned back against the cushions and closed his eyes. He was at once fatigued and excited. It almost seemed to him that he was still addressing the Urban Club. Then he seemed to be talking still but to a single auditor—a girl with flushed cheeks and eyes that shone with excited pride.

He opened his eyes. Rockwell was regarding him steadily. " I don't wonder you feel done up," he said. " It was splendid, my boy. You spoke like a veteran. You ought to go into public life on your own. Perhaps you will." He seemed to meditate. Then: " You saw Crockett, I suppose? "

" No ! " exclaimed Merriam.

" Didn't you? He was seated six places to your right at the speakers' table. Right in line with you, of course. Not strange you missed him. Just as well, perhaps. It might have shaken even *your* nerve."

The phrase " even *your* nerve " was pleasant praise to Merriam. He had never thought of himself as possessed of any exceptional *sang froid*. But perhaps he had behaved with rather creditable composure in a trying situation.

"*He* was shaken, I can tell you," Rockwell was saying. "Lord, I was on pins! I didn't know but what when you rose to speak he would jump up and denounce you. But not he. He simply lay back and stared and kept moistening his lips. I suppose he couldn't make up his mind for sure whether you were the Senator or the double or whether he himself had gone crazy or not. We'll hear from him, though," he added reflectively.

"I suppose so," said Merriam wearily. "I wish to Heaven we were clean through the thing!" That feeling had come suddenly, and for the moment he meant it, though he was having the time of his life.

"So do I," said Rockwell heartily. "But we're not. Not by a long shot. So you must buck up. Here's the hotel. You shall have a real meal now. That'll put heart into you again."

The machine stopped, and the door was opened.

"Quick time, now!" Rockwell whispered.

Senator Norman and his new political manager, Mr. Rockwell of the Reform League, rushed almost precipitately into the lobby of the Hotel De Soto and made a bee line for the nearest elevator. It was obvious that important business urgently called them, for they merely nodded hurriedly in response to several cordial salutations.

As the elevator shot up Rockwell leaned heavily

against the side of the car, took off his hat, though
there was no one with them, drew a deep breath,
and comically winked both eyes at Merriam.

" What a life ! " he ejaculated.

Stepping out at Floor Three, they were greeted
by the spectacle of Dr. Hobart bending over the
floor clerk's desk and evidently having a delightful
tête-à-tête with the handsome young mistress of
that sanctum, whose eyes were coquettishly raised
to his, though her head was slightly bent—for she
was smelling an American Beauty rose. A large
vase of the same expensive flowers adorned one corner of her desk.

Only a momentary glimpse did Merriam and
Rockwell have of this pretty tableau, for Dr. Hobart at once straightened up as if in some embarrassment and came towards them.

" I was just thinking it was about time for you
to be back," he said, though he surely did not expect
them to believe that he had just been thinking anything of the sort.

The pretty floor clerk, no whit nonplused, bowed
and smiled at Rockwell. But she studiously failed
to observe Senator Norman's presence.

Dr. Hobart walked down the hall with them.

" How's Norman? " Rockwell asked.

" No better, I'm afraid," said the physician apologetically. " He has a high fever, and a while ago
he was slightly delirious. I had to give him more
of the drug. He's sleeping again now. Simpson
is with him, of course."

"Damn!" said Rockwell, with a sort of deliberate earnestness.

They reached the sitting room and entered it. There was no one there. Simpson was apparently in the Senator's bedroom. Merriam dropped into a chair and closed his eyes again. Rockwell walked across to a window and stood staring out. Dr. Hobart stopped uncertainly in the middle of the room and fiddled with a cigarette without being able to make up his mind to light it. For several moments none of them spoke.

But Rockwell was not the man to remain long in any apathy of inaction. He turned suddenly, and Merriam, whom the prolonged unnatural silence had caused to open his eyes, saw that he had made up his mind to something.

"Hobart," he said, "I suppose Simpson isn't practically necessary in there." He indicated the sick room.

"N-no," said Dr. Hobart, "I suppose not. He's just watching. Norman will sleep soundly for some time."

"Then ask him to come here, will you?"

The physician disappeared into the bedroom and in a moment returned with Simpson.

"Simpson," said Rockwell, "we're going to have a meal here, for nine people. A luncheon, if you like. But make it hearty. Choose the stuff yourself, and serve it as quickly as you can, please."

For a moment Simpson stared. Then, as if re-

membering a nearly forgotten cue, he replied sub-
missively, "Yes, sir," and turned to the door.

As that door closed behind Simpson, Merriam
suddenly stood up.

"I must send a telegram to Riceville," he said,
starting for the writing table for a blank.

"Wait a bit," said Rockwell. "You can send it
just as well an hour from now."

Merriam was disposed to argue, but just then the
rest of their party trooped in, having returned to
the hotel in Mayor Black's car.

Alicia walked straight up to Merriam, gay
with enthusiasm, caught his hand, and squeezed
it.

"My dear boy," she cried, "it was perfectly
splendid! I've half a mind to kiss you!"

"Please do," said Merriam.

"I will," said Alicia promptly, and before the
young man could realise what was happening she
had put her gloved hands on his shoulders and
kissed him on one cheek.

Merriam was vastly astonished. In the circles
in which he had moved in Riceville or even at college, his remark could have been taken only as a
daring pleasantry. But he undoubtedly had *sang
froid*, for he concealed his confusion, or most of it,
and said:

"Let me turn the other cheek."

"Oh, I mustn't be a pig," said Alicia. "I'll
leave the other cheek for Mollie June."

At this Merriam's confusion became, I fear, per-

fectly apparent, for the remainder of the party had
followed Alicia into the room and were grouped
about him.

"Kiss him quick, Mollie dear," said the incorrigible Alicia, thereby causing confusion in a second person present.

But Mayor Black, no longer to be restrained,
saved the situation. He seized Merriam's hand
and pumped it.

"One of the best speeches I ever heard the Senator make!" he asserted, in tones which Merriam
feared might rouse the real Senator in the adjoining room.

Mr. Wayward meanwhile was patting him on
the back and murmuring, "Fine! Excellent!"

Merriam turned to Aunt Mary:

"I tried to do it justice," he said.

"You gave it exceedingly well," said Aunt Mary,
with less reserve than he had ever seen her exhibit
before.

"Indeed you did!" cried Mollie June earnestly,
her eyes shining with sincerity.

And that tribute, from the least qualified judge
of them all, was, I regret to state, the one which
young Merriam treasured the most.

Simpson, who had worked with amazing alacrity,
and even inspired his assistants to celerity, had
completed his preparations and announced that he
was ready to serve the luncheon.

Rockwell delayed the meal for several minutes
for the sake of an apparently important conference

into which he had drawn Mr. Wayward and the
Mayor over by the window.

Presently, however, they all sat down, with Merriam beside Mollie June. The luncheon passed, as
luncheons do, in small talk and anecdote.

At last Rockwell, having finished the last morsel
of a piece of French pastry, laid down his fork and
fixed his eyes significantly on Mr. Wayward, who
was in mid-career with something like his fifteenth
anecdote. Mr. Wayward faltered but rallied and
finished his story. It was the best one he had told,
but there was only perfunctory laughter. Every
one about the table was looking at Rockwell, realising that at last the great question that was in all
their minds, " What are we to do next? " was to be
discussed and decided. Simpson, it should be
added, had dismissed his assistants as soon as the
dessert course was served, so that only the initiated
were present.

Three times during the meal Dr. Hobart had left
the table to enter the sick room. On the second
occasion he had remained away some minutes.
Rockwell now turned to him.

" Give us your report, Doctor," he said abruptly.

" Well," replied the physician, " he is better.
Half an hour ago he was awake for perhaps five
minutes. His temperature is lower, though he
still has some fever. He is sleeping again now,
more quietly than at any time since he returned
to the hotel. In short, he is doing as well as could
be expected. But it is out of the question for him

to start on that speech-making tour this evening."

"Undoubtedly," said Aunt Mary, with much decision.

"Just so," said Rockwell. "That being the case, two alternatives present themselves: to announce his illness and call off the trip, or to go on playing the game as we have begun, with Mr. Merriam's help."

Merriam gasped and opened his mouth to protest, but Rockwell waved him down.

"The Mayor and Mr. Wayward and I have been discussing the matter. At first blush, there may seem to be little question as to which of these two courses we should pursue. Having come safely— so far as we know at least—through all the perils of discovery thus far, it may seem that we should tempt fortune no further, but let Mr. Merriam return to his school, publish the fact of the Senator's illness, and cancel the speaking engagements."

"Surely yes," interjected Merriam, and Aunt Mary and Father Murray and Mollie June and even Alicia seemed to assent.

"On further consideration," Rockwell continued imperturbably, "I think you will all see that the thing is not so clear. The course I have just suggested may be—doubtless is—the more prudent one, if prudence were all, but it is decidedly unfair to George Norman."

At this Aunt Mary almost visibly pricked up her ears.

"In his name," Rockwell went on, "we have
thrown over the conservative wing of the party,
with whom he has always stood and who have supported him—have 'betrayed' them, as they will
put it, in this traction matter and in aligning him
with the Reform League. We did so on the theory
that he was to appeal to the people and to come
back stronger than ever as the leader of the new
and growing progressive element, which is sure to
be dominant in the next election if only they can
find such a leader as Norman could be. But if we
cancel this trip and let him drop out of the campaign, if we stop now, where will he be? He will
have lost his old backers and will not have made
new ones. He will be politically dead. We shall
have played absolutely into the hands of Crockett
and Thompson and the rest of the gang, and shall
have accomplished nothing but the political ruin of
George Norman."

All the persons about the table except Mayor
Black and Mr. Wayward stared hard at Rockwell
as this new view of their predicament sank into
their minds. The Mayor and Mr. Wayward smiled
and nodded and watched the effect on the others.
Particularly they watched Merriam, who sat dum-
founded and vaguely alarmed. What new entan-
glements was Rockwell devising for him? He
must get back to Riceville. Involuntarily—he
could not have said why—he cast a quick glance at
Mollie June, and encountered a similar glance from
her. They both looked away in confusion.

Aunt Mary spoke:

"Tell us your plan."

It was like her—that masterful acceptance, without comment, of the situation.

"My plan, as you call it," said Rockwell, fixing his eyes not on Aunt Mary but on Merriam, "is simply that we should go on for another day or two as we have begun—play the game for George until he can take the cards in his own hands. This is Thursday. He is scheduled to leave this evening for Cairo, to speak there at nine o'clock to-morrow morning, to go on to East St. Louis for a talk before the Rotary Club at noon, and then up to Springfield for an address in the evening. Is that correct?"

"Yes," said Aunt Mary. "And he was to speak in Bloomington and Peoria on Saturday and in Moline and Freeport on Sunday."

"The speeches are all ready, I believe?"

"Yes. George and I outlined them together some time ago, and I have them written and typed."

"Exactly. Turn the manuscripts over to Mr. Merriam as you did this morning. He will have time on the train on the way to each place to master the speech to be given at that point. We shall take a special car. Mr. Wayward and I will go with him. You"—he was addressing Aunt Mary —"and the Mayor and Dr. Hobart—and Simpson," he added, glancing up at the waiter, who stood listening in the background,—"and the rest of you will stay here to guard George. That will

be easy when the newspapers are full of his speeches
out in the State."

"Mr. Crockett will know," said Father Murray
timidly.

"He may suspect," said Rockwell with a grin.
"But if you keep every one away from George—
conceal his presence here, — he can't be sure
whether it's George himself or his double who is
speech-making over the State. And if he were
sure, he wouldn't dare denounce him. Thanks to
Mr. Merriam's clever trick last night, he has a particularly strong reason for keeping his mouth shut.
If on the other hand we give up and lie down—cancel the trip,—he can easily start all manner of
nasty stories about his escapades. I'm sorry to say
it, but George has a pretty widespread sporting
reputation." Rockwell glanced apologetically at
Mollie June, but continued. "When a man with
such a character is laid up, people are ready to believe anything except that he is really legitimately
sick. Things will be safer here than they would be
if we abandoned our trick. And our part out in
the State will be 'nuts,' compared to what it was
at the Urban Club this noon, for instance. Very
few people out there know Norman well. There is
no question at all that Mr. Merriam will get by.
And we know from this noon that he will make the
speeches in fine shape."

"The speeches will need to be altered a bit," said
Aunt Mary, "if they are to appeal to the progress-
ives."

"Mr. Merriam can attend to that on the train," said Rockwell. "Soften the standpattism and throw in some progressive dope. Can't you?" He appealed to Merriam.

"I suppose I could," said Merriam, "but—my school."

"I know," said Rockwell, "but it will be only a day or two longer. We'll telegraph again, of course. If you were really sick, as we've been telling them, they'd have to get along, wouldn't they? You've got to see us through. We must keep the ball rolling. It will probably be only one more day. George will be able to travel to-morrow, I presume?" he asked of Dr. Hobart. "By noon, anyway?"

"By noon, I hope," said the physician with cheerful optimism.

"You see?" said Rockwell. "George can catch the noon train for Springfield and get there in time to take on the evening speech. Mr. Merriam will have made the two at Cairo and East St. Louis. He can go back to Riceville from Springfield."

Just then the telephone rang, and I believe every person in the room jumped.

Rockwell rose to answer it.

"Senator Norman? Yes, he is here. But he is engaged. This is Mr. Rockwell, his manager. You can give the message to me."

A moment later he put his hand over the receiver and turned to Merriam.

"He insists on speaking to the Senator. You'll

have to answer. I think it's Crockett. For Heaven's sake, be careful!"

Merriam took the receiver:

"Hello!"

A voice which he remembered only too well from the night before at Jennie's replied:

"This is Mr. Crockett. I have the honour, I believe, of speaking to Mr. Merriam."

"You have the wrong number!" said Merriam and hung up.

But before he had had time to explain to the others or even to wonder whether he had done wisely, the bell jangled again. He turned back to the instrument. Rockwell came quickly to his side, and Merriam, taking down the receiver, held it so that his "manager" too should be able to hear what came over the wire.

"Hello!"

"Ah! Senator Norman, by your voice," said Crockett in tones of elaborate irony. "I wish to congratulate you, Senator, on your speech this noon. It was a magnificent effort. So full of progressive ideas and youthful virility!"

"Thank you," said Merriam.

"And, Senator, I really must see you right away. I am calling from the lobby. I will come up to your rooms at once, if I may. Or meet you anywhere else you say. It is of the utmost importance to you, Mr. Mer ——" (he pretended to correct himself) "to you, Senator, as well as to me."

"Wait a minute," said Merriam. He put his hand over the mouthpiece and looked at Rockwell.

"Tell him you will see him at eight o'clock this evening, here."

Merriam repeated this message.

"At *eight?*" said Crockett, with significant emphasis on the hour. "Very good, Senator. Thank you." He hung up.

Rockwell and Merriam turned to the others. Aunt Mary and the rest had risen. They were standing by their places about the table, looking rather scared.

"*Eight* o'clock?" questioned Aunt Mary, with an emphasis similar to Crockett's.

"Yes," said Rockwell doggedly. "Because "— he addressed Merriam—" your train goes at seven. At seven-thirty Miss Norman shall telephone Crockett, expressing your regret that you overlooked the fact that you would have to be gone by that time. Man alive!" he cried. "Don't you see? The Senator can't be sick now—after your public appearance this noon. Half the people who count in Chicago saw you—him, there—right as a trivet—obviously perfectly well. And we can't keep *you* here, with Crockett and Thompson continually nosing 'round. There's nothing for it but for you to start on that trip. The trip's a godsend. Write your telegram to Riceville!"

Merriam glanced around the circle of faces. Mad as the thing was, they all seemed to agree with Rockwell. Mayor Black and Mr. Wayward and

even Simpson seemed to be asking him, as man to
man, to stand by them. Father Murray was timidly expectant. Dr. Hobart, he noticed, was staring down at the table as if in thought. Aunt Mary,
looking him full in the eyes, gave an affirmative
nod. Alicia's eyes and shoulders registered appeal
as conspicuously as if she had been a movie actress.
And Mollie June seemed to be begging him not to
desert her.

With a gesture of resignation he went over to the
writing table and sat down to compose his third
mendacious telegram to Riceville.

CHAPTER XXVI

THE BUSINESS OF BEING AN IMPOSTOR

THE writing of that telegram occupied Merriam for several minutes. He was distracted by scruples. He did not like lying, and he felt, truly enough, that he was cheating his employers, the Board of Education of Riceville, and the patrons of the school, and his boys and girls, by staying away from the work he was paid to do.

When, after a last momentary hesitation, he wrote his name and looked up, he found Simpson standing by him, ready to take the message. He noticed the man's new air of cheerfulness.

But he had no time to reflect on this phenomenon, for the party was breaking up.

There were four of them left—Merriam and Rockwell, Aunt Mary and Mollie June.

"Well," said Rockwell, with a sigh, "we're off again. You'd better go to your own room—Mr. Wilson's room. I promised the reporters to see them at half past four, and it's nearly that now. You'll need to pack. Take these speeches with you. I'll let you know when the taxi comes."

In a moment Merriam was crossing the Senator's room. Involuntarily he cast a glance at the sick man in the bed. In a small chair by the head of

306

the bed Mollie June was sitting, her eyes on her husband. She looked up as Merriam traversed the room, met his gaze soberly for an instant, and then looked back at Norman.

Merriam passed through the door on the other side into his own room. He closed the door softly behind him, set the portfolio on a chair, and put his hand to his forehead. The tiny connubial tableau of which he had just had a glimpse had brought home to him, as nothing before had done, the fact that Mollie June really was another man's wife. The acute realisation left him blank. He crossed over, sank into a chair by the window, and stared out across the fire escape. Another man's wife! And he loved her. Of course he loved her, just as he had always done. And she loved him, a little at least. That such a thing should happen to him—and her! Because he had been a coward three years ago in Riceville!

How long he sat dully revolving such thoughts as these he had no idea. He was startled by the opening of the door from the Senator's bedroom. He sprang to his feet with the involuntary thought that it might be Mollie June—though of course she would have knocked. It was Simpson.

"Shall I pack your things, sir?"

"Why—yes," said Merriam.

He knew from novels that the valet of the hero always packs his bag. Evidently Simpson had come in this capacity. To Merriam's American self-sufficiency it seemed an absurd practice. Why,

shouldn't any man put his own things into a grip
for himself? But he was glad of company.

"You can help," he added, and took a couple of
steps in the direction of the bureau, with the idea
of taking things out of drawers.

"Oh, don't bother, sir!" said Simpson quickly.
In his tone there was something subtly patronising.
For he who has been a butler and a waiter and a
valet among the real élite feels even himself to be
socially superior to the unbutlered and unvaleted.

"Simpson," said Merriam suddenly, "you've
seen Jennie!"

Simpson stopped absolutely still for a moment
with a couple of folded shirts in his hands. Then
he placed the shirts in the suit case, straightened
up, and looked at Merriam.

"Yes, Mr."—he hesitated and decided to use the
real name—"yes, Mr. Merriam, I have. I went
out there this morning, as you suggested."

"She let you in?"

"Yes, she did. She let me sit down on the sofa
with her, and we had a long talk. I ended by asking her again to marry me—and she said she
would."

"And she kissed you!" Merriam cried gaily.
He had for the moment forgotten his own troubles
in Simpson's happiness, for which he rightly felt
he might claim some credit, and in an appreciative
recollection of Jennie's temperament. Within a
dozen hours she had also kissed Crockett and himself. But Jennie was born to kiss.

Simpson looked quickly at the younger man and returned to his packing. "Yes," he said, "she did."

Merriam regretted his exclamation, which had, in fact, told too much. For several minutes he watched in silence the deft, efficient work of his companion. Then he asked:

"When is it to be?"

"The wedding, sir?"

"Yes."

"As soon as you and Mr. Rockwell can spare me, sir."

Simpson closed the hand bag, closed the suit case and strapped it.

"Is there anything else I can do, sir?"

"I believe not."

The waiter hesitated. Then he decided to speak what was in his heart:

"I am very greatly indebted to you, sir," he said, with an admirable combination of dignity and feeling. "You have made a happy man of a very wretched one and have—saved a young girl who was on a very wrong track. If ever I can render you any service, you can always command me, sir."

Merriam sprang up and advanced, holding out his hand.

"I'm tremendously glad," he said. "I have accomplished one thing anyway with all this miserable imposture."

Simpson shook his hand heartily. Then:

"Shall I leave you now, sir?"

"Why, yes, please," said Merriam. He was loath to be left alone, but there was clearly nothing more to be said between him and Simpson.

In a moment the waiter had withdrawn through the door into the Senator's bedroom. Merriam's thoughts followed him into that room, where Mollie June doubtless still sat by her husband's bed.

But just then a knock sounded at the hall door. He looked up startled. He was not expecting any one to approach from that direction. Who could have any business with "Mr. Wilson"?

Another knock. Merriam hesitated. Should he go to the door, or simply sit tight till the knocker became convinced that there was no one within and went away? He decided upon the latter course. Any one whom he ought to see Rockwell would bring to him.

A third time the knock sounded, discreet but persistent. Then suddenly a key was inserted in the lock and turned, the door opened, and in stepped—Crockett!

Merriam sprang to his feet but did not speak.

"Thank you," said Crockett over his shoulder—to whom Merriam could not see.

He closed the door and advanced:

"Is it Mr. Wilson?" he asked ironically, "or Mr. Merriam—or Senator Norman?"

"Is it Mr. Crockett, the financier, or a housebreaker?" Merriam retorted.

Mr. Crockett laughed, but it was an unpleasant, forced laugh.

" Since you do not answer my question," he said,
" I don't see that I need answer yours. See here,"
he continued, with a change of tone, " how much is
it worth to you to turn over to me those pictures
you took last night—films and all, of course—and
get out of this? "

" You won't accomplish anything by insulting
me! " cried Merriam, a flare of youthful anger
somewhat impairing his dignity.

" Insulting you! " echoed Crockett sneeringly.
" My dear sir, as a complete impostor you can
hardly expect to get away with that pose. I'll admit you're good at it. That impersonation of the
Senator before the Urban Club this noon was a
masterpiece. But what's the game? Does Rockwell really suppose he can swing Senator Norman
over permanently to the so-called Reformers? Let
me tell you that as soon as the real Norman is on
his feet again Thompson and I and the rest of us
will get hold of him and bring him around in no
time. We know too many things about your handsome Boy Senator. He can't shake us now. So
what's the use? Unless," he added suddenly, " the
plan is to kill him off and substitute you permanently! "

" Hardly so desperate as that," said Merriam,
smiling. The other man's long speech had given
him time to recover himself.

" Well, then, why not make a good thing out of it
for yourself and get away while you can? It isn't
as if no one had suspected you. *I* not only suspect

but know. I haven't told any one else yet, but you can hardly expect me to keep your secret indefinitely."

"You forget the pictures," said Merriam, as sweetly as he could.

Crockett obviously mastered a "damn" and chased the expression that rose to accompany it from his face.

"Let's keep to business," he said. "How much is Rockwell paying you for this job?"

"No monetary consideration has been mentioned between us," said Merriam. It was the truth, of course, but perhaps he need not have been so stilted about it.

"You surely don't expect me to believe that. Come! Whatever the amount is, I'll double it. All I ask of you is, first, to hand over to me the pictures, and, second, to pick up your bags, which I see are already packed, and walk out of that door with me. We'll step across the street to my bank, I'll pay you the sum in cash, and you can skidoo. No exposure is involved, you see—of you or your friends. I'm not revengeful. I don't need to be. All I have to do is to wait until I can get hold of Norman. In the meantime you get clear of a situation that otherwise is likely to prove very nasty for you personally and very nasty likewise for your Reformer associates. You will note that I trust to your honour to give me *all* the copies of the pictures and not to sting me on the amount I am to pay you."

"Honour among thieves?" queried Merriam.

"Who's insulting now?" Crockett demanded.

"I am," said Merriam. "At least, I'm trying my best to be. Mr. Crockett, you spoke of walking out of that door. I'll thank you to do that very thing—at once! If you don't, I'll call in Mr. Rockwell, and we'll put you out. I'm tempted to try it by myself, but I don't care to risk any noisy scuffling."

"Prudent young man!" sneered Crockett, retreating nevertheless in the direction of the hall door. "I understand that you reject my offer?"

"I certainly do."

"Very good. I hereby serve notice on you that I shall immediately expose the whole of your atrocious masquerade! It will be the ruin of you and Rockwell and Norman and Mayor Black and every other person who has been mixed up in it. Oh, you'll be a nine days' wonder in the city, but no one of you will ever have a scrap of public credit again!"

"And on the following day," retorted Merriam, "those pretty pictures we know of will be published in *Tidbits*. They'll be running sketches called 'A Financier in a Flat' in every music hall in town."

"You blackmailer!"

"On the contrary you've tried to get me to take blackmail and I've refused it."

With a sound remarkably like the snarling "bah" which regularly accompanies the retreat of the foiled villain of melodrama, Crockett turned towards the door through which he had been invited to depart. But in the course of the three or four steps which he had to take to reach that exit he recovered something of his dignity and finesse.

Having opened the door, he turned and bowed ironically.

" Good evening, Senator," he said. " I'm afraid I shall be prevented from keeping my appointment with you at eight. If you should change your mind within the next half hour, you can reach me by 'phone at the Union League. Otherwise, look out ! "

On this warning note he closed the door behind him.

Merriam found himself with a whirling brain. As a quiet pedagogue he was not accustomed to scenes of battle such as he had just passed through. He walked up and down and mechanically lit a cigarette.

As he did so, his mind seized upon one question. Who had unlocked the door for Crockett? Some chambermaid or bell boy? Or the floor clerk? At any rate it must have been done with her connivance and by her authority, for she was the commanding general of Floor Three. Why had she done or permitted this outrageous thing? Suddenly Merriam recalled her studied ignoring of him on the last two occasions of his passing her desk, and compared it with her whispered " The violets are lovely " when he first asked for

Senator Norman's key. There had been something between her and Norman. He, Merriam, in taking on the Senator's rôle had dropped out that part of it, and she was offended. How seriously he could not tell.

He concluded that he must attempt to reinstate himself—Norman—in the pretty floor clerk's good graces, and rather hastily decided upon a plan. He went to the telephone and asked for the hotel florist. How much were violets? Well, they had some lovely large bunches for five dollars. This figure rather staggered the rural pedagogue, but he promptly asked to have one of those bunches sent up at once to "Mr. Wilson," giving his room number, 325. He would present his peace offering in person. "I am sure these flowers will look lovely on your desk—or if you will wear them at your waist?" he would say, or something of the sort. This was probably not the way Senator Norman would have done—he would have run no such open risk,—but we must make allowances for Merriam's inexperience.

But he never carried out his ill-conceived plan. For he had barely left the telephone when he was arrested by a light knock on the door leading into the Senator's bedroom. This time he was sure it was Mollie June, and he was right.

When he opened the door she stood there with a finger at her lips.

"Aunt Mary has taken my place with George," she said in a low tone. "She says I may give you some tea.   It will be late before you can get your dinner on the train.   Would you like it? "

" Tremendously," said Merriam sincerely.

" Come into the sitting room, then."

She crossed the sick room to the door at the other side which led to the sitting room, and he followed, with a nod to Aunt Mary, who now sat by the sleeping Senator's bed.

Arrived in the sitting room, he was further delighted to find that neither Rockwell nor Simpson was present.   It was to be a genuine tête-à-tête. By one of the windows stood a small table with the tea things upon it, the kettle already singing over an alcohol flame.   Beside the table stood a large armchair and a small rocker.

" The big chair is for you," said Mollie June, seating herself in the rocker and adjusting the flame.

" Thank you," he said and sat.   Then a mingling of pleasure and embarrassment held him awkwardly silent.

Mollie June was apparently quite composed.

" George is ever so much better," she said.   " He was awake a few minutes ago, and he seemed almost well.   He has only a very little fever left."

She smiled brightly at Merriam, who dimly realised that it was to the fact that her mind was now at ease about her husband that he owed this treat.

Mollie June set a brightly flowered cup on a saucer to match and placed a small spoon beside it.

Then she took up the sugar tongs, and her hand hovered over the bowl.

"One lump or two?"

"Two, please," said Merriam, noting the slenderness and whiteness of the fingers that held the tongs and the pinkness of the small nails. (Why else except to display charming fingers and nails were sugar tongs invented?)

"Lemon or cream?"

Merriam was sophisticated enough to know that the right answer was "Lemon," but he preferred cream, and an admirable instinct of honesty led him to say so.

Through the open window came the pleasant air of the spring afternoon. The canyon-like street without, being an east-and-west street, was flooded with sunlight. With the breeze there entered also the stimulating roar of the city's lively traffic. The breeze stirred Mollie June's soft wavy hair. It also caused the alcohol flame under the brass kettle to flutter and sputter, and Mollie June leaned forward to regulate it. The youthful firmness of her cheeks and chin showed like a lovely cameo in the bright light, which would have been unkind to an older face. Having adjusted the flame, she suddenly looked up at Merriam and smiled.

"Mollie June," he cried, "there is nothing lovelier in the world than your eyes when you look up and smile like that!"

He had not meant to say anything of that sort, but it was forced out of him.

Mollie June's smile lingered, and the cameo became faintly, charmingly tinted.   But she evidently felt that some rebuke was needed.

" *Mrs.* Mollie June, you must remember," she said gently.

Then, taking up her cup and leaning back in her small rocker, she asked:

" How did you get along with the speeches? "

" Not very well," said Merriam.   He hesitated in his mind whether to tell her of Crockett's interruption but decided not to.   It would take too long —he could not waste the precious minutes so. " I'll have the dickens of a time with them," he added.

" Oh, no, you won't! " she cried, as if shocked at the idea.   " You were wonderful this noon.   I was so proud of you."

" You had a right to be," said Merriam.   " It was because you were there that I could do well." Which was perhaps partially true.

" Why don't you go into it yourself? " asked Mollie June.

" Public life?   Perhaps I will.   I may go back to the University for a law course and then try to get into politics."

This plan had just occurred to Merriam, but he did not disclose that fact.   In uttering one's inspirations to a pretty woman one usually presents them as though they were the fruit of mature consideration.

" That would be fine," said Mollie June without

much enthusiasm. "But you'll be at Riceville next year?"

"I suppose so. I'll have to save up a bit more."

"I may be at home for Christmas," she said. "I'll see you then."

Merriam considered this painfully.

"No," he said at last slowly. "I shan't be there. I shall be away for the holidays."

"You could stay over," said Mollie June, wonderingly reproachful.

"I suppose I could. But I mustn't. Just to see you—publicly, is too hard on me. And if I see you alone like this,—I say things I oughtn't to—make love to you."

Mollie June sat drooping, with downcast eyes, her cup in her lap.

Suddenly he was on his knees beside her. He put his arms about her, to the great peril of flowered china.

"Mollie June!" he whispered. He softly kissed her cheek.

She raised her eyes and looked deep into his.

"John!" she whispered back, though she seemed to struggle not to do so.

After a moment he smiled sadly and got to his feet.

"I mustn't have any more tea," he said, as if that beverage was too intoxicating, as indeed under the circumstances it was.

Fortunately—since of all things what they needed was a diversion,—Merriam at that moment became conscious of a portentous knocking on a distant door. He realised that it was on the door to " Mr. Wilson's " room and remembered. The flowers—for the floor clerk!

He hurried to the hall and called the boy from the second door down the corridor, where he was about to pound again.

In a moment he reëntered the room, bearing a lovely great bunch of fragrant English violets—and thinking hard. But he was equal to the emergency.

He advanced to Mollie June, who stood now with her back to the window, her slender form outlined against the light, her face in shadow.

" I've never given you anything, Mollie June," he said. " These are for you—and the sick room." He held them for her to smell.

She took them from him, barely touching his hand as she did so, and buried her face in them for a long minute. Then she raised her eyes to him over them.

" Thank you, Mr. John," she said with a sad smile.

And just then Aunt Mary entered from the Senator's bedroom.

" See what Mr. Merriam has ordered for George! " said Mollie June. " Isn't he thoughtful? "

" Very," said Aunt Mary, in her customary dry tone.

CHAPTER XXVII

THE CODE TELEGRAM

ROCKWELL had returned with Alicia. He briskly declared that it was time to start for the train. Mayor Black, it appeared, was below in his car and was going to the station with them.

"I've told Simpson to take your bags down. Except the portfolio. You'd better keep that in your own hands. What progress with the speeches?"

"Not much," said Merriam. "But I shall have the whole evening on the train. I'll get them."

He crossed the sick room, where Dr. Hobart was now bending over the Senator, apparently making an examination. He thrust the pile of manuscripts back into the portfolio. Then, after a glance about the room, reminiscent of his burglarious entry the night before, he caught up his coat and hat and returned to the sitting room again.

"Are we ready?" he asked of Rockwell.

"Waiting for Hobart—for a final report on the Senator's condition."

"Aren't you coming to the station with us, Mollie June?" Alicia was saying.

"No," said Mollie June, her eyes on a large bunch of violets which she was arranging in a bowl. "I must stay with my husband."

321

"But Aunt Mary will be here. I think she owes it to you to come with us, don't you, Mr. Merriam?"

"No," said Merriam, "I think she is right in staying."

Alicia looked from him to Mollie June, then shrugged her shoulders and turned to Rockwell, who was cautioning Aunt Mary—as if Aunt Mary ever needed cautioning!—about maintaining the closest possible guard on the Senator's rooms in their absence.

Merriam moved to Mollie June's side.

"I shan't see you again," he said.

"No," said Mollie June.

For a single moment she looked up from the flowers into his face. Her eyes held tears, and she blushed slightly. In her look he read unwilling love and shame.

He would have moved away, impotently miserable, but her hand, which had dropped to her side between them, suddenly touched his, closed in his for an instant, and was withdrawn, leaving something—something very small, cool, and fragile—a single violet.

He understood, of course, that it was to be his souvenir of her, all he could have of her, through the long years to come while she played out her loathsome rôle as the wife of the dissipated Boy Senator and he taught school at Riceville or—what did it matter what he did?

His hand closed quickly on the violet, and he

turned to face Dr. Hobart, who was just entering from the sick room.

The physician was highly reassuring. The Senator was doing very well indeed.

" He'll be able to meet us in Springfield, then, to-morrow night? " demanded Rockwell.

" I think he'll be well enough to do that," returned Hobart, with a slight evasiveness which Rockwell and Merriam had occasion a few hours later to recall with some vividness. But at the moment they scarcely noticed it.

" Good! " cried Rockwell. " We're off. No! Wait."

He drew a folded paper from his pocket and handed it to Aunt Mary.

" This paper describes a simple form of code telegram. Use it in your messages to us in regard to the Senator's progress and when and where he is to join us. You'll wire at least once a day, of course."

" Yes," said Aunt Mary, accepting the paper.

Merriam shook hands with Aunt Mary.

" I hope," she said, " that some day, after all this is over, we may be able to have you visit us, when George can thank you for the inestimable service you have rendered him."

" I should be delighted," Merriam murmured, though he had no great mind to be thanked by George Norman.

Then he shook hands with Mollie June and met her eyes for a moment, but, under the gaze of Aunt

Mary and Rockwell and Alicia, "Good-bye," was all he could say.

"Good-bye. Thank you for—everything," she replied, and her eyes followed his figure as Rockwell swept him from the room.

The closing of the door of the Senator's sitting room upon Merriam marked the beginning of a period of a dozen hours or more that was utterly phantasmal and unreal to him both at the time and in his recollection afterwards. He seemed to move and speak and act without volition and without any clear realisation of what he was doing or why he was doing it.

After dinner with Rockwell and Mr. Wayward—an excellent meal served in the private car by an amiable gentleman of colour, Merriam read the speech which he was to deliver at Cairo in the morning, and then had to pull himself together and commit that speech, but he did even this mechanically. And finally to bed in his compartment, at first to a long, uneasy dream, in which he appeared to be making an interminable speech to an audience consisting of Mollie June, Jennie, an inattentive floor clerk, Aunt Mary, and Simpson, and then to a heavy slumber, from which he was roused with difficulty the next morning.

In the morning it was the same way with him—everything dully unreal. Breakfast. Going over the speech again. Then it was nine o'clock, and the train was running into Cairo. A crowd at the station. A cheer or two. He was being assisted into an automobile. A sort of procession with a band through several blocks of streets to a small park.

Merriam found himself sitting with Rockwell and Mr. Wayward and several local notables in a band stand, with a considerable concourse of people sitting and standing about on the grass below. Some native orator made a short speech. A number by the band. Then the Mayor of Cairo was effusively introducing Senator Norman. The Mayor sat down amid applause.

Merriam rose, advanced to the rail, and began on his speech. He felt himself to be a sort of animated phonograph. The words which he had learned the night before and reviewed that morning ran trippingly off his tongue. His collegiate training and subsequent experience in public speaking came to the aid of his subconscious self, which seemed to be functioning with practically no direction from his higher centers. He turned pleasantly as he spoke to face now one part of his circle of auditors and now another. He suited his tone to the words in different parts of the speech. He even achieved an occasional appropriate gesture.

At last he came to the end of what he had learned and stopped as the phonograph stops when the end of a record is reached. And for a moment he stood there by the rail, blank, at a loss—as a phonograph would have stood. He had to rouse himself with a jerk of conscious attention before he perceived that

what he had to do next was to step back and sit
down.

The applause was fairly satisfactory. The
Mayor of Cairo leaned across Rockwell to shake
hands and congratulate him, and Mr. Wayward, on
the other side, patted his shoulder and said, "Good
enough!" And the band struck into a patriotic
air.

Merriam awoke. It was as if lights had been
turned on and doors opened. He realised that it
was a bright, sunny morning, that a band was playing, that he, John Merriam, was alive and young,
and that he was having a whimsically glorious
adventure which he could not afford to miss the joy
of even if Mollie June was Senator Norman's wife.

In this rejuvenated mood he joyously descended
with the others from the band stand and climbed
into the automobile and lay back happily, between
Rockwell and the Cairo Mayor, to relish the slow
processional drive—still preceded by the band—
back to the station.

"Feeling better?" asked Rockwell, who had not
failed to note his previous lethargy.

"Feeling fine!" he replied, and gave his attention to the scenery of Cairo's Main Street and the
crowds therein, waiting eagerly for a glimpse of
the remarkable Boy Senator.

As the automobile passed close to the curb on
turning a corner, Merriam caught one remark:

"He *does* look just like a young man!"

The speaker was a decidedly pretty girl in a bold-

ish sort of way. Merriam sensed and seized upon
the privileges of age. He leaned forward:

"Thank you, my dear," he said. "At least I'm
young enough to know a pretty girl when I see
one."

Which incident will serve to show that Merriam
was really awake again. Also, it probably won
more votes for Senator Norman's party at the next
election than the whole of Aunt Mary's able speech
as delivered by the human phonograph a few minutes earlier.

They reached the station and regained the private car. Merriam sank into a wonderful armchair
in the sitting room compartment, glanced about
him at the luxurious appointments, and lit a cigarette with gusto.

"I shouldn't mind this riches-and-fame business
for quite a while," he thought. (Mollie June was
for the time forgotten; thus it is with the fickle
male.)

Rockwell had sat down in the next chair. Merriam made an effort of memory.

"East St. Louis next?" he asked.

"Yes," said Rockwell. "We'll have to get at
the speech as soon as the train starts."

Just then a small but vociferous urchin appeared
in the door of the car. His cap proclaimed him a
telegraph messenger.

"Telegram for Mr. Rockwell!" he shouted, as
though Mr. Rockwell were probably in the next
county.

Rockwell signed the book, and the lad slowly withdrew himself, taking generous eyefuls of Rockwell, "Senator Norman," and the private car. As he lingered with a last backward stare in the doorway, Merriam winked at him, and the boy grinned and generously, democratically winked back.

Turning from that wink to Rockwell, Merriam was startled. The man sat limp with the telegram on his knee and a pencil in his hand. I will not say he was pale, but certainly he was haggard.

He handed the telegram to Merriam.

Merriam tried to read it, but could make no sense at all. It was very long but apparently a mere string of words with little intelligible meaning.

"What ——? " he began.

"It's code," said Rockwell. "I've underlined the words that count."

Picking out the significant words by means of Rockwell's underlining, Merriam read:

George kidnapped from rooms whereabouts unknown doctor disappeared cancel trip return Mary.

CHAPTER XXVIII

A MOMENT later Mr. Wayward, who had stopped at the station cigar stand to replenish his stock of nicotine, rejoined them and was shown the telegram.

His first comment was profane.

"We've got to go back," said Rockwell. "Now that they have Norman in their power—for Crockett is behind this, of course,—they may denounce us—may make Norman himself denounce us—any minute. They have no end of a grip on him, and he has no great love for the rôle of Reformer himself—nor for me. Our only hope is to get back to Chicago and find him and get hold of him again." He jumped to his feet. "I must see the station master at once."

"Yes," said Mr. Wayward, "there's nothing else for it."

Rockwell hastily departed to announce their changed plans to the station master, and Merriam and Mr. Wayward looked at each other. The latter's face had assumed the humorous smile which had been his expression towards the whole affair from the beginning.

"It's been a damn fool business all along," he said.

329

"I suppose it has," said Merriam.

"Good fun for you, though." Mr. Wayward lit a cigar.

"Yes," Merriam assented. But he was thinking of something else. Back to Chicago! The young rascal was realising that that meant he should see Mollie June again.

Mr. Wayward puffed meditatively.

"'Doctor disappeared,'" he quoted from the telegram. "That means Hobart was in it. Prob ably he was the chief agent. Crockett's bribed him."

Merriam suddenly remembered the tableau which Rockwell and he had surprised as they stepped out of the elevator at the Hotel De Soto on the previous afternoon: Dr. Hobart in confidential conference with the floor clerk.

"Probably they bribed the floor clerk, too," he said. "Hobart seemed to be sweet on her."

"So?" said Mr. Wayward. And after a minute's consideration: "Very likely. They could hardly have managed without the floor clerk, in fact."

Presently he added:

"We've got to go back all right. But I don't see what we can do except to surrender."

"We still have my pictures of Crockett at Jennie's."

"Well, I hope so. Unless they've bribed Simpson, too. Those pictures are one of the things that may make them give us a chance to surrender."

The two men smoked in silence for several minutes—until Rockwell returned.

"Well, that's fixed," he announced. "There's a
north-bound express due in half an hour and reported on time that will take us into Chicago by
nine o'clock to-night. You're sick, of course, Senator," he added to Merriam. "Bronchitis again!"

They continued to talk until the north-bound
train arrived and picked up their car, and they
were started on their return trip.

At Carbondale Rockwell sent off telegrams to the
several cities which Merriam was to have visited,
cancelling Senator Norman's speaking tour on account of a renewed attack of bronchitis. He also
sent a message in code to Aunt Mary, giving the
hour when they were due to arrive.

The three men talked, of course, but they had so
few facts to go on that they could only formulate
gloomy speculations, with nothing really in the way
of definite conclusion beyond what Mr. Wayward
and Merriam had reached in their first few minutes
of chat immediately after the arrival of Aunt
Mary's message. How the kidnapping had been
managed or where Norman might be, they simply
could not tell.

They had one practical point to decide, namely,
their first procedure on reaching the city. It was
obviously not safe for "Senator Norman" to go
directly to the Hotel De Soto. They could not tell
what the situation there might be since the kidnapping. It was finally agreed that Rockwell and

Merriam should leave the train at Fifty-Third
Street and take a taxicab to Rockwell's bachelo
apartment on Drexel Boulevard, while Mr. Way
ward should go on to the Twelfth Street Statio
and thence to the hotel to see Aunt Mary. Thei
next step was to depend on what he learned there
Rockwell was afraid even to telephone from hi
apartment, for fear the wire to the Senator's suit
might be tapped. Merriam was not keen on thi
arrangement because it evidently postponed his see
ing Mollie June and might even prevent his doin
so altogether. But this was not an objection whicl
he could raise in the discussion.

At last they were running into the City. Fifty
Third Street was reached, and Rockwell and Mer
riam shook hands with Mr. Wayward and de
scended from the private car.

Rockwell's first act in the station was to buy al
evening paper. He scanned the sheet anxiously
with Merriam looking over his shoulder. The firs
page carried a paragraph reporting the abandon
ment of Senator Norman's down-State speaking
tour "on account of a return of his bronchitis.'
Rockwell had sent no word to this effect to any one
in Chicago, but evidently the news had come ir
from some one or more of the towns to which he
had wired cancellations. There were, however, no
headlines in regard to the kidnapping of a United
States Senator from one of the city's leading hotels
and no exposé of their imposture.

"They're still keeping it dark," said Rockwell,

with a flash of renewed hope on his haggard face. "We're going to have a chance to make terms."

A moment later they were in a taxicab bound for his apartment. They rode in silence. Merriam wondered if he should see Mollie June again— though just what good that would do him or what he should say to her he could not have told.

"I shall see her once—alone," he said to himself, "whatever happens. I've done enough for them to have a right to demand that."

And on that scene of unhappy farewell—for what else could it be?—his thoughts halted. His mind would go no farther.

The taxicab stopped, and they got out, and Merriam found himself in front of a decidedly imposing apartment building. Rockwell hurried him through a sumptuous entry and into an elevator. They shot up three flights. Then in a hallway Rockwell unlocked a door, and they entered the sitting room of his apartment—a large room in quiet tones, furnished somewhat in the taste of a good men's club.

Merriam sank into a chair.

"Played out?" asked Rockwell, standing over him and speaking in his old manner of matter-of-fact good humour, which had deserted him during that trying day.

"Yes," said Merriam. He felt, in fact, quite exhausted, although he had done nothing since ten o'clock that morning except smoke and eat two meals and wait.

"So am I," said Rockwell, "and we must get fit again. We may have a busy night ahead. Suppose we have a shower and then coffee? That'll brace us up."

Three quarters of an hour later, the two men, much refreshed by the shock of cold water and the odd stimulation which always follows re-dressing in fresh clothes, were sitting on opposite sides of Rockwell's writing table, waiting for an electric percolator to "perk," when the doorbell rang.

They looked at each other.

"Curtain up for the last act," said Rockwell as he went to answer it.

It was Mr. Wayward with Aunt Mary and Father Murray and Mayor Black. Mollie June, Merriam saw, was not with them.

"Come in," said Rockwell, oddly formal.

Merriam, as he rose, noticed the change in Aunt Mary. Always before she had seemed a creature of no age at all; now she was obviously a quite elderly woman. The Mayor's plump face was gray and drawn with anxiety. Even Mr. Wayward looked more worried than he had seemed all day.

For a moment the four of them stood together just inside the room, staring at Merriam, accusingly as it were, as if he had been the cause of their trouble.

But Rockwell, having closed the door, turned and after one glance at the group spoke loudly, with exaggerated briskness:

" Sit down, all of you—and tell me. You'll find
this a comfortable chair, Aunt Mary. Over there,
Mayor. You're at home here, Wayward."

Father Murray took Aunt Mary's arm and led
her to the chair Rockwell had indicated. Solemnly
they all sat down.

Rockwell was both daunted and impatient. After
another look at Aunt Mary, he turned to the Mayor:
" When did it happen? "

But before the Mayor could reply, Aunt Mary
spoke up. She was not so far gone as she looked.

" Between five minutes after eight and half past
nine this morning," she said. " Mollie June and I
had gone downstairs for breakfast in the Wedge-
wood Room and then for a short walk—over to
Michigan Avenue and back. Dr. Hobart suggested
both. He said we ought to get out that much before we settled down for the day in the rooms, and
that he would stay with George till we returned.
He said that George was much better, and he looked
better. When we got back—it was exactly half
past nine,—both he and George were gone."

Aunt Mary paused for an instant on this dis-
astrous climax.

" We were terribly upset," she continued. " We
could hardly believe our senses. Mollie June cried,
and at first I could not think what I ought to do.
But presently I had mind enough to telephone for
Mayor Black and Father Murray, and by the time
they came I was calm enough to think quietly and
join them in making plans."

" You were wonderful," said Father Murray.

" We could make no kind of announcement or complaint. George was not supposed to be there. You "—she looked at Merriam—" were probably at that very moment making a speech in his name at Cairo. We could say nothing to anybody. We figured out that you were either still at Cairo or on your way to East St. Louis, and we sent messages to Mr. Rockwell at both places. We had to stop that insane speaking tour and get you both back here as soon as possible. We telephoned to the hotel office for Dr. Hobart, but they said he had resigned as house physician the night before. Then we sent for Simpson. He didn't seem greatly surprised. In fact, he said that Dr. Hobart had offered him money early that morning ' to help in restoring Senator Norman to his real friends.' That seems to have been the way Hobart put it. Simpson refused the money, he said, and didn't learn what the plan was. He said that he had meant to tell me of the offer but hadn't been able to get away from his work. It was still only a couple of hours since Dr. Hobart had talked with him. He said he would try to find Hobart and learn where George was, and then he went away, and we haven't heard from him since. Finally, I went out to see the floor clerk, thinking she must have seen when George was taken out, but there was a new girl. The former one had quit, she said, at nine o'clock— simply telephoned the office that she was leaving and hung up and slipped away."

"Have you tried to see Crockett?" Rockwell asked.

"I have," said the Mayor. "Been trying all day. But both at his office and at his house they say he isn't in and they don't know where he is or when he will be back. And he wasn't at any of his clubs."

"It's a pretty clean get-away," said Rockwell.

Merriam spoke up. "I have some hopes of, Simpson," he said. "His continued absence may mean that he is following some sort of trail."

"Maybe," said Rockwell. "Meanwhile this coffee"—he drew attention to the percolator—"is getting pretty black, and black coffee is what we all need. After that we'll see."

"Where is Mrs. Norman?" Merriam asked timidly while Rockwell was pouring and passing the coffee.

"We left her at the hotel with Alicia," said Mr. Wayward. "We had to leave some one there, in case some message should come from Simpson or from Crockett or from George himself."

The coffee was drunk in a dismal silence. Mr. Wayward attempted one or two semi-cheerful remarks, but they fell flat.

"The first question," said Rockwell when the cups had been emptied, "is: where is George Norman? Crockett may have taken him to his own house. But that is unlikely. Or to some other hotel. Or to one of his clubs. Or, if he is still really sick, to a hospital. I think myself a hotel is the most probable. That could have been managed with a minimum of explanations. In any case we have got to find him. But this is no case for amateurs. I propose to engage a professional private detective and commission him to find George. Also Hobart. It oughtn't to take him more than twenty-four hours. Then we can make further plans. If Norman is still sick, we may have to re-kidnap him. If he is up and himself again, it will be a matter of parleying with him and Crockett and making such terms as we can. Has any one a better suggestion?"

It appeared that no one had, and Rockwell was looking up the detective agency, when the doorbell rang again.

Father Murray sprang to his feet.

"Yes, you answer it," said Rockwell.

Before the priest could reach the door an impatient rat-a-tat-tat sounded on the panel.

He opened to Alicia and Simpson.

"Good heavens, you're slow!" cried Alicia. "And glum as the grave," she added, glancing about the circle of faces. "Simpson has found George."

There were exclamations.

Rockwell put down the telephone book and went to Alicia.

"Dear!" he said.

And Alicia, turning, put her arms about his neck and kissed him. "You poor fellow!" she cried.

Then Rockwell turned to Simpson.

"Sit down here, Simpson," he said. "Have some coffee? You look fagged."

"Thank you, sir. I *am* pretty much all in."

Rockwell drew a cup of coffee and took it to him, and the waiter gulped it down.

"Thank you, sir," he said again. "Now I can tell you. I owe a good deal to that young gentleman"—he indicated Merriam,—"and when I saw the trouble you were all in I decided to do what I could. Of course we knew Mr. Crockett was at the bottom of the thing, and I decided he was the most findable person in it. I figured that he wouldn't appear at his office and wouldn't go home, but that sooner or later he would show up at one of his clubs. You remember I asked you this morning what clubs he belonged to." This to Mayor Black.

The Mayor assented.

"You mentioned five. That was a pretty large order, but I got some of my pals who are taxicab drivers to help me, and between us we kept a pretty close watch on all of them. He didn't come near the one I was watching myself, and I didn't hear anything from the others till five o'clock. Then one of the boys sent word to me that he had entered the Grill Club on Monroe Street. I went right over and hung around there for nearly three hours. It was a quarter to eight when he came out. He took a taxi, and I followed in another. He drove to St. John's Hospital over on the West Side. I was right after him and followed him into the building. He doesn't know me, of course, and paid no attention to me. He spoke to the nurse at the desk and then stepped into a waiting room. The nurse looked hard at me, but I said, 'I'm with him,' and stepped back towards the door. She thought I was his man and took no further notice of me. Pretty soon Dr. Hobart came down. He didn't see me, but I saw him plainly. He looked pretty much worried—scared, I thought. He and Mr. Crockett talked for a while in the waiting room, but I couldn't hear anything they said. Then Mr. Crockett left, and Dr. Hobart went back upstairs. I could have spoken to him after Mr. Crockett had gone out, but I thought I had better not let them know that any one was on their trail—for fear they would move him again. Then I had an idea. I went up to the desk again. I said to the nurse: 'How is Mr. Merriam?' She looked at me. 'He's pretty sick,' she said, and turned away. I didn't see what more I could do, so I took my taxi back to the De Soto and went up to the Senator's suite and found Miss Wayward and Mrs. Norman, and Miss Wayward brought me here."

For a moment Rockwell seemed sunk in thought. Then he roused himself, glanced around the circle of faces, and spoke:

"First of all, Mr. Simpson, I want to say that you have done a very clever bit of work. We were about to engage a private detective to undertake what you have already accomplished. I think I can safely say that we will see that you are suitably rewarded."

"You can," said Mr. Wayward emphatically—

which was satisfactory since he was the person present from whom any substantial monetary reward must come.

"Thank you, sir," said Simpson.

The Mayor broke in:

"It's pretty clear what has happened. They got Norman downstairs while Miss Norman and Mrs. Norman were at breakfast, put him in a taxi, drove to the hospital, and entered him under the name of Merriam. And Dr. Hobart has stayed in attendance."

"And he's still sick—perhaps worse," said Aunt Mary anxiously.

"Why did they enter him as Merriam?" asked Rockwell, thinking aloud. "It must mean that Crockett doesn't dare denounce us or doesn't wish to do so, that he means to make terms with us and preserve the secrecy of the whole affair. As I see it, there will have to be one more substitution"— he addressed the real owner of the name of Merriam,—"of you for Norman—at the hospital. You have reported yourself to your Riceville people as sick. Very well, you have gone to a hospital. From the hospital you return to your work. It will strengthen your alibi. And Norman will be restored to us—on Crockett's conditions, of course. But we shall escape the worst. We shall come off safe yet. But it must happen at once," he continued, with a note of new anxiety. "The whole State knows that Norman's speaking tour has been abandoned, that he came back to Chicago to-day, that he is in the City now. We must get hold of Crockett some way to-night. The final substitution must be made before morning."

Mr. Wayward was looking at his watch. "It's eleven o'clock now," he said. "But you'd better try telephoning. His clubs, I think."

"Yes," said Rockwell. "The Grill Club! That's where you found him, Simpson? He may have gone back there for the night. I'll try that first."

He went quickly to the telephone.

While Rockwell was looking up the number and the rest waiting in painful expectancy, the door-bell for the third time startled them.

"I'll go, sir," said Simpson.

In a moment he had opened the door.

On the threshold stood Crockett—a pale, hesitant, almost seedy Crockett, very different from the serene, confident, well-groomed financier whom Merriam had first encountered forty-eight hours before at Jennie's.

Rockwell dropped the book:

"Come in, Mr. Crockett. I was just going to 'phone to you."

Crockett advanced a couple of steps into the room. Then he stopped. There was something portentous in his air of mournful gravity. His eyes travelled from face to face. For a moment they rested on Merriam. Then they came to a full stop on Aunt Mary.

The whole roomful remained silent, fascinated by his look, which seemed to speak, not of threat, which they might have expected, but of some disaster beyond threat.

At last with an effort he turned his eyes from Aunt Mary to Rockwell.

"I have to tell you," he said, "that George Norman is dead."

CHAPTER XXIX

THE FINAL DILEMMA

I DO not suppose Mr. Crockett desired to be unnecessarily cruel. Doubtless he would have preferred to break his devastating news more gently. But he was himself in a state of nervous exhaustion from fatigue, worry, and perhaps remorse, and the circle of anxious faces had proved too much for his self-control.

Realising too late the brutal bluntness of his announcement, he broke into a hurried flow of words:

"We took him from the hotel this morning to St. John's Hospital. We thought he would be just as well off there—even better off. Dr. Hobart thought he was nearly well anyway. But the ride and the effort of listening to Hobart's explanations apparently fatigued him. By the time they got to the hospital he was very sick again. His bronchitis—if it ever was bronchitis—turned into pneumonia—double acute pneumonia. He got worse and worse all day. Dr. Hobart and the physicians and nurses at the hospital did everything possible for him. But it was no use. He died at nine o'clock."

All eyes turned suddenly to Aunt Mary, who had risen, holding on to the back of her chair.

Father Murray was at her side in an instant, and Alicia hurried to her.

"No," said Aunt Mary, brokenly, " I'm not goi·ig—to faint—or anything. But I want—to be alone."

Rockwell sprang to his feet. " My bedroom," he said, and led the way to the door of his chamber, which opened off the sitting room.

In a moment Aunt Mary, walking between Father Murray and Alicia, had passed into the bedroom.

Mr. Wayward's voice broke the stillness.

" Poor fellow! " he said.

For a minute or two they all paid the tribute of silence to the dead. But it was impossible to be really very sorry for George Norman. He had had an easy, pleasure-filled life—wealth, luxury, fame, and a good time, according to his own conception of a good time, up to the very beginning of his brief illness. That his last few, largely unconscious hours had been passed in a hospital away from his friends had certainly been almost no grief to him. The only sorrow genuinely possible was over the common folly, and the universal final tragedy, of humankind. In a few moments the thoughts of the entire group that remained in Rockwell's sitting room were irresistibly drawn back to the strange and somewhat dangerous situation in which the unexpected death had left them.

Presently Rockwell spoke:

"Technically, Mr. Crockett, I suppose it is not Senator Norman but Mr. Merriam who died at St. John's Hospital."

(Merriam was somewhat startled at this turn of thought; this phase of the matter had not yet occurred to him.)

"You have made no announcement?" Rockwell asked.

"No," said Crockett. "I have done nothing. When Hobart telephoned me that—what had happened, I rushed out to the hospital again—I don't know why. I couldn't believe it. Then I telephoned from the hospital to the De Soto and got Mrs. Norman, and she told me you were all here, so I came here. I have done nothing."

While he was speaking Alicia and Father Murray returned from the bedroom.

"She is all right," said Alicia. "She asked us to leave her alone for a few minutes. Did you tell Mrs. Norman?" she added, addressing Crockett.

"What had happened? Yes," said Crockett.

Merriam's thoughts flew to Mollie June, alone in the vast, heartless hotel with the news of her husband's death.

"Ought not some one to go to her?" he asked.

"Presently," said Rockwell. "We must first consider the situation a little—hers as well as ours."

Mayor Black spoke up:

"It will be pretty awkward for her—aside from natural grief and all that—that her husband should have died in a hospital under another name without her being present, while the man to whom the other name belongs was impersonating him in public. And awkward for Miss Norman. For the rest of us, too. Damned awkward!"

"It is a hard thing to have to close the career of George Norman with such a story," said Mr. Wayward.

"It must never happen!" said a voice behind them.

They all turned. Aunt Mary was standing in the door of the bedroom. She already looked more like herself. She was one of those souls who may sink under passive anxiety and suspense but find themselves again immediately when a call for action comes. She had scarcely been left alone, apparently, when the same thought which the Mayor and Mr. Wayward had expressed had occurred to her—the peril to the name of Norman, which was perhaps even more dear to her than her brother himself had been. And instantly, by some powerful effort of will, she had put grief behind her and turned to face this new danger.

"It must never happen," she repeated, advancing into the room, where Alicia, and the men too, unmindful of the etiquette which should have brought them to their feet, sat staring at her. "The secret must be kept. It is more important now than ever. With George alive, it would not have mattered so much. He would have lived it down triumphantly. Only the rest of us would have suffered—not he, nor the Name. But now— *it must be kept!*"

"But how *can* it be kept?" said Crockett, in a tone of desperation.

For a moment no one spoke.

Then Rockwell, looking from face to face, drew a deep breath.

"There is just one way," he said. "It was John Merriam who died. Senator Norman is alive." He waved his hand at Merriam. "He must go on living!"

"But that is impossible," said Mayor Black and Merriam together.

"Face the alternative first," said Rockwell. "George—the real George—was admitted to the hospital about nine o'clock this morning. At that same hour Senator Norman was making a speech at Cairo before an audience representing the entire county. That is known all over the State. He took the next train back to Chicago. But that train did not reach Chicago until after—after the death."

"We could have the hour of the death changed on the records," proposed Mr. Wayward. "It is already announced all over the State that Senator Norman is ill again. He could be rushed from the train to the hospital and die there during the night."

"Then we should have two deaths on our hands,"

said Rockwell, "and only one body. Unless we
bring Merriam to life again. How are we to do
that? It is pretty hard to get hospital authorities
to falsify their records. And dozens of people
must know the supposed facts—nurses, doctors,
clerks at the hospital. We could never keep them
all from talking. The reporters would get hold
of it within twenty-four hours. No, Senator Norman cannot have died at the hospital. He is alive.
He must go on living!"

"Can't he die at the hotel—to-night or to-morrow?" said Merriam.

"Then what becomes of you?" asked Rockwell.

"Why, I should go back to Riceville."

"You can't. You're dead! And how can Senator Norman die at the hotel when we should not
be able to produce his body there?"

"We could get the body," said Mr. Wayward,
speaking in a lowered tone. "As Mr. Merriam's
friends we would take his body away from the hospital to be buried and bring it to the hotel."

"We shall have to send for the real Merriam's
friends," said Rockwell. "From Riceville and—
wherever your people live." He looked at Merriam. "We should have no body to show them.
We could bury a loaded casket. But why should
we, who must be strangers to him from their point
of view, have been in such a hurry when they could
get here in a few hours? Probably they would
want to take his body elsewhere for burial. Very
likely they would have the coffin we had buried

raised and opened. And how could we get a dead body into the Hotel De Soto? Up a fire escape? "

In the earnestness of his argument Rockwell evidently did not realise the gruesomeness of his language.

Aunt Mary shuddered.

" No! " she said. " I will not have George's body smuggled about the city."

She paused, looking strangely at Merriam. None of the others, not even Rockwell, ventured to speak.

"Alicia told me, I believe, that you have no near relatives? " she said presently.

" None nearer than cousins," Merriam replied.

For a long minute more Aunt Mary stared at him. She closed her eyes, opened them, and looked again. Then her lips shut tight for a moment in an expression of momentous decision. She leaned forward.

" You have the Norman blood in you," she said to Merriam, " on your mother's side. You are fine stuff. We have all seen that. We will make a Norman of you, if you will. You shall take George's place—to save his name! "

" But ——" Merriam began.

But Rockwell cut in:

" It's absolutely the only way," he cried. " The only other alternative is to let the whole story come out."

" Then that's what we have to do," said Mr. Wayward. " Make a clean breast of it."

"No!" said Aunt Mary.

"No!" echoed Rockwell. "Think what that means—to George's memory, first of all. That in his last hours his relatives and friends were conspiring against him, with the help of a stranger double, to force him to abandon the kind of life he was leading and the disreputable interests with which he was associated.—I beg your pardon, Mr. Crockett!"

Crockett waved a feeble hand to indicate forgiveness or indifference.

"And then to Mollie June," Rockwell continued. "That she had connived at the impersonation of her husband during his last illness by another man. How far did that other man take her husband's place, will be the question every man and woman in the State will ask. And all the rest of us. Aunt Mary. And Mr. Merriam, who will lose his job and his professional standing. And the Mayor and myself, who will be ruined politically and every other way. Even you, Mr. Wayward, would find yourself in an exceedingly unpleasant situation. And Mr. Crockett, on the other side, would be no better off. For the story of the kidnapping must come out."

The wilted financier uttered a sort of groan.

"But can the other thing be done?" asked the Mayor, the perspiration of mental anguish showing on his forehead.

"Certainly it can," said Rockwell eagerly. "Senator Norman has come back to Chicago.

Here he is. Presently he will arrive at the hotel. He will be pretty sick. You and I "—he looked at Mr. Wayward—" will support him to the elevator and to his rooms. He will be ill for several days. We must get hold of Hobart again to attend him. Then we will announce that he is threatened with tuberculosis and is to retire from public life. He must resign his seat in the Senate. We daren't go ahead with that. It would be too dangerous—and too serious a fraud besides." (Evidently there was some limit to a Reformer's unscrupulousness.) " He will go to his ranch in Colorado to recuperate. You will actually go." He was addressing Merriam now. " You must live there for a year or so. During that time only a few of Norman's private friends will visit you. We will coach you up on these a few at a time. If any of them notice any slight changes in you, they will lay it to your illness. You will easily take your place in the whole circle of his private life."

" But the property," said Mr. Wayward. " The Norman fortune."

" Reverts to me and Mollie June," said Aunt Mary, who was evidently heart and soul with Rockwell. " If we are satisfied ——"

She stopped. The mention of Mollie June had recalled a phase of the situation which Rockwell and the Mayor and even Mr. Wayward had apparently forgotten—so little are men accustomed to consider their women folk when the real game of business or politics is on. Merriam and Alicia

had not forgotten it, but had not been able so far
to get a word in. As for Aunt Mary I cannot say—
she was so near to being a man herself.

"Mollie June!" repeated Rockwell aghast.

"Exactly," said Merriam, somewhat bitterly.
Him, too, Rockwell had been treating pretty much
as a lifeless pawn in the game.

But Aunt Mary, when roused, was equal to anything.

"We shall manage that," she said. "I will go
to Colorado with Mr. Merriam. Mollie June can
return to her father for a time. We can arrange
a separation—or ——"

Even Aunt Mary hesitated. But Alicia took the
cue.

"Or they can be married—or remarried," she
said, fixing her bright eyes, with a gleam of mis-
chievous understanding in them, on Merriam.

The argument had come to a full stop. The
whole roomful sat looking at Merriam, who tried
to think and found he could not, except that he
realised that all the rest had tacitly accepted Rockwell's plan.

"Come!" said Alicia vivaciously. "It isn't so
bad, is it? The Norman fortune and—Mollie
June!"

Bad! The prospect was so dazzling to Merriam
that he could not take his mind off it in order to
think calmly. To die to his old self—to his poverty
and loneliness, to his teaching with which he had
long been bored,—and to step as if by magic into a

new life with wealth, leisure—and Mollie June! For surely she loved him, and she had not loved George Norman. She would marry him—after an interval, of course.

"I must think," he said, weakly, in response to Alicia's exhortation.

"Of course you must," said Rockwell. "You must accustom your mind to it. But it will all be perfectly easy. You were brought up on a farm, weren't you? You will take to the ranch life like anything. It's mostly stock-raising. You can go in for scientific farming. After a few months it would probably be a good thing for you to travel, perhaps for a year or two—especially if you and Mollie June should marry. Get out of the country, so as to leave Norman's old life entirely behind you for a while. You might take a trip around the world."

Merriam's youthful heart bounded in spite of himself. A trip around the world with Mollie June!

"As to your old self," Rockwell continued, "that's quite simple, too. Norman was entered at the hospital under your name. A death certificate must have been given by now." He looked at Crockett.

"I don't know," said Crockett. "Hobart may have held off on that."

"At any rate it can be. In fact, it will have to be. Hobart shall telegraph to Riceville and to your cousins, wherever they are. He was the house physician at the De Soto where you took sick. That was how he came to be attending you. When you got bad he took you to the hospital. Nothing more natural. The rest of us will not need to appear at all."

"Aunt Mary will have to appear," said Alicia. "She will want to attend the funeral."

"She became acquainted with you at the hotel, then," said Rockwell. "Took an interest in a young man who was alone and ill. When your relatives and friends come Hobart will have the body already laid out in a casket. He can advise immediate burial here in the city. Aunt Mary can offer a lot in the Norman plot at Lakewood. Would your cousins probably consent to that?"

"Very likely," said Merriam, rather in a daze. It was confusing to be discussing the details of one's own interment.

"Then everything will follow in regular course," said Rockwell, speaking as if all difficulties were solved. "George will be buried with his family, and you can start for Colorado."

For a second time the talk came to a full stop. The new plan was outlined in full. It remained only to decide upon it or to reject it and face the alternative of a public confession. All of them except Merriam had already accepted the scheme, apparently, gruesome and bizarre as it was. It was for all the rest so much the easiest way and the most advantageous. But it did not require any of them to die—to die to his own self, his friends, his very name. On the other hand it did not offer them any such positive rewards as were proffered to Merriam—a fortune and love. We can hardly wonder that he was somewhat stupefied by the alternatives that beat upon his mind. The loss of all that up to this point in his life had been his identity versus Mollie June—that was the essence of the struggle within him.

He sat beside Rockwell's table, staring at the now silent percolator, trying to think but able only to feel. The others were looking uneasily at him and at one another. Aunt Mary's eyes and Alicia's demanded of Rockwell, who had always managed everything, that he should manage this too. Once he started to speak, but gave it up and looked appealingly at Alicia instead. Indeed he might justifiably feel that this was Alicia's job. She acknowledged as much in her own mind and was trying to decide what to do or say, when the one person present who had not spoken throughout the entire scene came to the rescue.

Through all their long discussion Simpson had stood unobtrusive and unnoticed in the background, but he had followed every word. For his fortunes too, humble, indeed, but sufficiently important to him, were bound up in this decision. If the deception was to be continued, his assistance, in the matter of silence at least, would be necessary, and he could expect a large—honorarium; if it came to a public confession, he could still expect something, but probably a good deal less; and to win

and hold Jennie he needed a considerable sum of
money.

So now he advanced a step and spoke:

"Shall I call a taxi for you, Mr. Merriam, to
take you to the hotel?"

"Of course!" cried Alicia, jumping up. "You
must go and see Mollie June. It all depends now
upon her."

The others too stirred and expressed more or less
audible acquiescence, and Simpson had his reward
in the shape of approving glances from Rockwell
and Mr. Wayward.

Merriam got to his feet with the other men because Alicia had risen. He was not so obtuse nor
so much dazed that he did not see what they were
doing. They were trying to rush him. They
calculated that though Mollie June in the abstract
might contend indecisively with other abstract con-
siderations, Mollie June in the flesh would decide
him in the twinkling of an eye. He saw that
plainly enough. Nevertheless, for his part it did
now depend altogether upon Mollie June. If he
was to do this thing—to abandon his old self and
enter upon what must be in some degree a lifelong
career of deception,—it would be for her sake—not
only in order to win her sooner, years sooner, than
he could otherwise have the slightest hope of doing,
but to save her from scandal, and because she loved
him and wanted him too at once (comparatively
speaking) as he wanted her.

So his decision was made almost as soon as he

was on his feet.   He looked with some dignity from one waiting face to another about the circle.

"Yes," he said quietly, "it does depend on her. You may call a taxi, Simpson."

CHAPTER XXX

MOLLIE JUNE

ALMOST before Merriam's brief sentence was out of his mouth Simpson had started for the telephone. But Mayor Black spoke up:

"My car and chauffeur are below. We came up from the hotel in it. You can use it."

"You go with him, Aunt Mary," said Rockwell, again taking command. "You see her first," he continued. "Mr. Merriam can wait somewhere— in 'Mr. Wilson's' room. When you have explained the general situation you can call him in and leave them together and—give him his chance."

Even at this moment it was a slight shock to Merriam to realise that the state of feeling between himself and Mollie June, which they had supposed completely hidden, had been clearly perceived by the others—or at least, he thought swiftly, by Rockwell and Aunt Mary and Alicia. He smiled a little cynically to himself as he understood that they had been willing to use this interest of his as a motive in securing his easy acquiescence in their previous schemes. Evidently they were counting on it in Mollie June too. That gave him a thrill of hope which made him forget his cynicism.

Father Murray had put Aunt Mary's wrap about

359

her, and Rockwell had got Merriam's hat and his own.

Merriam found Alicia by his side. She held out her hand, and when he took it she squeezed his fingers in the way she had and said significantly, with all of a woman's interest in a romance:

"Good luck!"

"Thank you," said Merriam, but his answering smile was again a little cynical.

Then he opened the door for Aunt Mary and waved his hand to the others, with some amusement at the anxious looks with which they were regarding him. Even Simpson's countenance was perturbed!

Rockwell and the Mayor went down to the street with them and put them in the limousine. The Mayor directed the chauffeur to drive them to the hotel and then to return for himself and the others. Rockwell spoke to Aunt Mary:

"You put the essential facts before her and then leave them—leave Mr. Merriam to do the rest!"

And again Merriam smiled with an acid amusement that is commonly supposed to belong to the middle-aged and old but is really most characteristic of those who are under thirty.

Rockwell glanced at Merriam as if about to give him too a parting exhortation, but hesitated, checked perhaps by the younger man's expression, and spoke to the driver instead: "All right!"

They had started, and Merriam tried to think. His whole life turned in a very peculiar sense on

the events of the next hour—whether he should continue to be himself or take up the life of another
man. He got that far. But what he should say
to Mollie June—even what it was he wanted to say
to her—he could not get on with it. The mood of
youthful cynicism was by no means the right mood
for the business in hand.

And then—too soon for him now—they were at
the hotel.

So little had he been able to think clearly that it
was not until he was helping Aunt Mary out of the
machine that he realised that in entering the hotel
with her again this way, in the character of the
dead Senator, he was already in effect consenting
to Rockwell's plan and binding its consequences
upon himself and Mollie June.

He had a wild idea of getting back into the
limousine and driving away and later entering the
hotel via the fire escape again. But Aunt Mary
was already on the pavement.

As they entered the lobby Merriam glanced about
to see whether he was noticed and recognised as
the Senator. He was. At least three men whom
he did not know bowed and raised their hats, and
one of them took a step forward as if to approach
them. But Merriam looked away and guided Aunt
Mary as rapidly as possible to the elevators.

When they emerged on Floor Three, Merriam
asked for the key, explaining casually that "Mr.
Wilson" was a friend.

In a couple of minutes he had escorted Aunt

Mary to the door of her sitting room—Senator
Norman's no longer—or was it still to be Senator
Norman's?—and had himself entered "Mr. Wil-
son's" room.

His first act there was to call up the hotel
florist—as he' had done once before on this same
telephone. But this time Merriam's order was for
roses, to be sent up at once.

He hung up the receiver and walked nervously
about the room.

Was it not time for him to go to Mollie June?
Aunt Mary was being terribly long about her explanation. Had Mollie June broken down under
her grief—grief for George Norman?—or merely
from anxiety and conflicting emotions? Was she
refusing to see him? Was she ill?

He jumped up and walked back and forth in his
nervousness, watching the door to the other bedroom, at which he might expect to receive Aunt
Mary's summons.

A knock at last! But it was at the wrong door,
the hall door. In a sort of hesitating amazement
he went to answer it. It was the boy with the
roses. He had forgotten ordering them.

He signed for the flowers and brought them into
the room and took them out of their box and tissue
paper. They were lovely—the most exquisite
colour, between pink and red, that has no name
but that of the flower itself—pink and red harmon-
ised in soft coolness and fragrance—Mollie June's
flowers without a doubt.

But had he done well in ordering them? Was this a time for lover-like gifts? Should he not have got white roses, such as one sends to a funeral?

And then, as he stood in this anxiety, came Aunt Mary's knock at the bedroom door.

He started as if caught in a guilty action and thrust the flowers back into their box before he went to open to her.

"How is she?"

But Aunt Mary herself looked so broken that he led her to a chair.

Then, "How is she?" he repeated. He could not wait.

"She is very quiet."

"You told her the—the plan?"

"Yes."

"She understood it?"

"I think so."

"Am I to go to her?"

"I suppose so," said Aunt Mary with a sigh. "Mr. Rockwell said——" She stopped.

Merriam showed her the roses.

"Should I take these to her?"

Aunt Mary looked at him and at the flowers.

"I think perhaps you might," she said, and then sat staring out across the fire escape.

She looked so very miserable that Merriam impulsively patted her shoulder. She glanced up quickly at that, then turned her eyes to the window again. He could not read her look, but he was not sorry he had betrayed his affectionate sympathy.

If he was to be her brother for the rest of their lives ——

After a moment more of hesitation he picked up the flowers and passed through the former sick room to the sitting room.

Mollie June was sitting in a small straight-backed chair by the window, looking out. But Merriam was sure at the first glance that she saw nothing. She had merely turned automatically towards the light, as all but the old or the self-conscious tend to do. As Aunt Mary had said she was very quiet. Her back was of course towards the room and Merriam.

He waited for a moment just inside the door, looking at her, forgetting the flowers in his hands. He was sorry for her and very uncertain what he ought to do. Then he became a little frightened, because she sat so still. She gave no sign of having heard him.

With conscious effort, because he must do something, he crossed the room till he stood beside her. Still she did not turn her eyes from the window.

He stood looking down at her. She was a pathetic figure as she sat there—the more pathetic, to the eyes of youth at least, because she was so lovely, so young and fresh really, although a little pale and heavy-eyed. He saw dark shadows under her eyes which must have come from tears.

The sight of these unlocked him, drowned all his hesitations in pitying love. He dropped on his

knees beside her chair, laying the long-stemmed
roses regardlessly on the floor and putting one hand
on the back of her chair.

"Mollie June!" he said.

She did not start. Evidently she had known he
was there. She looked first at the flowers on the
floor and then at his face.

"I am so sorry," he cried.

"Are you sorry or glad?" she asked.

"I am terribly sorry for you," he answered.

Her hands lay together in her lap, and he attempted to take one of them.

But she moved them slightly.

"Don't," she said.

"Don't make me strange to you, Mollie June,"
he cried.

"How can I help it?" she answered. "I am
strange to myself too. You see, I am glad! I am
sorry for George," she went on quickly. "It is
terrible to me that he is dead. But I am so glad I
do not have to be his wife any more!"

Once more, as on a former occasion, some dim
notion came to Merriam of what it must mean to a
girl to be connubially in the power of a man she
does not love. He pitied and loved her greatly.
Also he marvelled. How had she come through it
all so fresh and unchanged? The answer, of course,
was youth. But youth could not know the answer.

"I am glad too," he said.

Her eyes, which as she dropped them had rested
on the roses on the floor, came back to his face.

"You are glad I have to marry you."

"But you don't!"

"You know I do."

Instantly he saw that Aunt Mary had not put the thing fairly before her. In Aunt Mary's mind it was settled. The course of action which promised to save the precious Norman name from scandal was the only possible course of action. She had so represented it to Mollie June.

"No, no!" Merriam cried. "You shall not be forced into this. You shall never be forced in anything again if I can help it. I will not be forced myself—even to marry you."

"What else can we do?" asked Mollie June, searching his face.

"It's fairly simple," he said, a little bitterly. "Not easy, but simple. I will write a brief, plain account of the whole affair—the impersonation—from beginning to end, and send for a reporter and give it to him. That will end everything. I will sit down, now at that desk and write it and call for a man and give it to him while Aunt Mary thinks we are still talking—unless you tell me not to."

"Would you do that?"

"Indeed I will!"

He rose to his feet. He meant it, and she saw that he meant it. To be forced in this thing was, in fact, even less to his liking perhaps than to hers.

Standing, he saw the roses at his feet. He

stooped and picked them up and handed them to her.

"You'll let me give you these?" he said, his manner more determined than lover-like. "I saw them from the elevator as I was coming up here with Aunt Mary. They were so like you that I could not help buying them and bringing them to you."

She accepted them passively, looking up at him. Perhaps she liked him determined rather than lover-like.

"I am not giving you up," he went on gravely. "But you will go away somewhere with Aunt Mary, and I will go back to Riceville. I have my contract for the rest of this year at least. And if you will wait a few years—you will want to wait and rest a while,—I will come back and win you in my own right."

She did not answer but looked up at him, still searching his face.

For a moment he stood regarding her. That image of her as she sat there with the flowers in her lap and her uplifted face and questioning eyes, more lovely than ever in their intense gravity in spite of their trace of tears, remained one of the permanent treasures of his memory.

He turned away and walked over to the writing table and sat down. It was a moment or two before he could think why he was there. Then he remembered and drew towards him several sheets of the hotel stationery and took up a pen. He realised that he was in a very poor frame of mind for literary composition, but he mastered his attention and wrote:

Statement by John Merriam regarding His Impersonation of Senator Norman

He underlined those words and resisted an impulse to turn and look at Mollie June. He wanted to know whether she was looking at him or looking out at the window again. He wanted, too, merely to see her. But he would not look. With a heroic effort he brought his mind back to the paper before him. How to begin? Where to begin? It was a long story, he realised. He must make it as brief as possible. He could omit much. But he must introduce himself. The public did not know him from Adam. He seized at this straw.

"My name is John Merriam," he wrote. "I am the principal of the high school at Riceville, Illinois. On my mother's side I am related to ——"

He stopped abruptly. It was the fragrance of roses that interrupted him. Mollie June had risen and come over beside him. His effort of concentration had been so great that he had not heard her. She carried the flowers pressed against the bosom of her dress. The action was probably mechanical; she was too much engrossed to think to put them down. She did not look at him but over his shoulder at his writing. She read it.

Apparently his opening statement caught her

attention. She looked at him and smiled slightly, more with her mouth than her eyes, which were still grave.

" You wouldn't like to change your name, would you? " she said.

" Mollie June! " He was on his feet.

She backed away from him, pressing her flowers tight.

" Would you? " she demanded.

" It's not that," he said, not daring to advance towards her lest she should retreat farther.

"A woman always has to change her name when she marries. Why shouldn't a man do it for once? "

He started forward now and caught her arm and led her back to her chair and dropped on his knees again beside her.

" Dearest Mollie June," he said, " I'll change my name to yours so gladly, if you will let me. So as to have you sooner than I could the other way. But not unless you want me to! " he added fiercely. " For yourself! "

She looked at him, shyly now.

" I would rather have it the other way myself," she said, tears standing in her eyes at last, " and wait and change my name to yours. But I think we ought to do it this way for George."

" For George! "

" Yes, and Aunt Mary. She has been very good to me. George was good to me too in his way. And he was my husband, and he's dead. If we can save his name and save her—this way,—don't you think we ought to? "

Then of course he put his arms about her.

"I won't call you George, though!" she said presently, very emphatically.

"What will you call me, deares ? "

She smiled at him through her tears and with a gesture that ravished him lifted his hand and kissed it.

"Mr. John!" she whispered.

He would have kissed her again, but she hurried on.

"We'll pretend to people that it's a nickname left over from some game or play."

"It *is* left over from a sort of—play," he answered, and then she was ready for another kiss.

THE END